"*Christianity Today* is often—and accurately—dubbed the flagship periodical of the modern American evangelical movement. In these editorials and mercifully concise articles, Timothy Padgett has collected an array of voices addressing virtually every major political question that captured public attention in the United States between the magazine's founding in 1956 and the general election of 2016. The book offers a priceless resource for historians as well as rank-and-file students of contemporary religion. Readers will find that on the whole *CT* writers took a moderately conservative position. Yet they also will find a remarkable range of nuances and not a few contrarian postures, running from the serious right to the serious left. Edited volumes come and go—mostly go. But not this one. It will stand for years as a standard reference for understanding the inner texture of one of the largest and most influential Christian traditions of modern times."

GRANT WACKER, Gilbert T. Rowe Professor Emeritus
of Christian History, Duke Divinity School

"At a time when evangelical Protestant presence in public life has come under significant criticism—including ridicule—this collection of essays from *Christianity Today* will enable insiders and observers to put the religious right in perspective. Instead of using search engines or online archives, in this volume readers have easy access to a plausibly representative sampling of white evangelical voices since 1956. This book could very well confirm biases for and against evangelicals. But it should also shed as much light as it reduces alarm."

D.G. HART, Hillsdale College, author of *American Catholic:
Faith and Politics during the Cold War*

"While so much attention is put on the loudest and most self-aggrandizing evangelical voices, it is *Christianity Today* that actually has the mandate to speak for American evangelicals on issues of import to Christians. *Dual Citizens* collects some of the most cogent writing that *CT* has published over the years. This book is valuable to everyone interested in how evangelicals have thought about public issues and how they have acted in the public square. I also believe Christians will find it edifying as a reminder of the value of a faithful Christian witness, and a God who is working in history for his glory."

MICHAEL WEAR, author of *Reclaiming Hope: Lessons Learned in
the Obama White House About the Future of Faith in America*

★ DUAL ★
CITIZENS

See also these titles in Best of *Christianity Today*

★ **DUAL** ★

CITIZENS

POLITICS *and*
AMERICAN EVANGELICALISM

edited by **Timothy D. Padgett**

LEXHAM PRESS

Dual Citizens: Politics and American Evangelicalism
Best of *Christianity Today*

Lexham Press, 1313 Commercial St., Bellingham, WA 98225
LexhamPress.com

Print ISBN 9781683594079
Digital ISBN 9781683594086
Library of Congress Number 2020938442

Lexham Editorial: Elliot Ritzema, Allisyn Ma, David Bomar
Cover Design: Lydia Dahl
Typesetting: ProjectLuz.com

Lexham Press gratefully acknowledges the support of the **Colson Center for Christian Worldview** in completing this project. The Colson Center equips Christians to live out their faith with clarity, confidence, and courage in this cultural moment.

CONTENTS

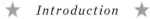

Introduction

THE VISION

In December of 1955, Billy Graham wrote to future editor Carl F. H. Henry about his vision for what was to become *Christianity Today* (*CT*): "Carl, this magazine cannot be another fundamentalist publication, taking hair-splitting views and narrow positions. Instead of attacking [theological] Liberalism altogether from without, with McCarthy tactics, we must use strategy and bore from within, leading these ministers step by step."[1] From the beginning, *CT* was seen by its founders as something quite apart from just another combatant in a culture war. They would speak the truth, and sometimes they would annoy all the right people, but their goal was to convince others to see the wisdom of their position and not just add to the cacophony. This spirit of what we might call *engaged neutrality* was to be a feature of *CT*'s worldview. Different editors and writers have come and gone, different priorities have been emphasized, but the primary goal has remained the same: to keep readers informed about the pressing concerns of the day in light of the eternal truth of God in the Bible.

---

1. Billy Graham, Letter to Carl F. H. Henry, December 22, 1955, Box 1956, File 1956 Correspondence–Graham, Billy, Carl F. H. Henry Collection, Rolfing Library, Trinity International University, Deerfield, Illinois.

GOD AND POLITICS

Achieving this goal is particularly tricky when it comes to politics, especially given the warning to teachers from James 3:1. Rarely is the tension of Christ's call to be in the world but not of it quite so clear as when believers consider their role in public affairs. Are we to remain above the fray, knowing that God's kingdom is not of this world (John 18:36)? Or are we to become involved in the mess of life, loving our neighbors by seeking the welfare of the city (Jer. 29:7)? Do we—like many in the early church, the Anabaptists, or more recent end-times enthusiasts—see ourselves as sojourners and pilgrims who are just passing through toward a greater tomorrow, or do we look to the state's role as minister of God to preserve the peace for today?

These are not easy questions. And, contrary to our earnest hopes, the Bible refuses to give us simple answers. Rather, the Scriptures provide us with a dual answer. To live as faithful Christians in the political world means keeping our heavenly citizenship first in our hearts before any earthly kingdom. At the same time, we are to live in the place of God's calling, fully invested in our families, communities, and nations as citizens of these lesser realms. Our loyalty to our Heavenly Father can never be compromised by our duties to any temporal prince, but neither can our spiritual calling become an excuse for failing to "honor the emperor" in appropriate ways (1 Pet. 2:17). This means living in the already-but-not-yet of a world that is not as it ought to be, and cannot be now what it one day will be, but for which we are still called to work to see it become as good as it can be.

Much of the Christian's path in politics is bound by the tension between Romans and Revelation. In Romans, we see the state as the minister of God, with the same word used in chapter 13 as just two chapters later to describe Paul's office (Rom. 13:6; 15:16). There, the state is entrusted by God with the sword and is given the right to conditional obedience from the faithful. Yet in Revelation 13, the state is cast in a very different light. In this later passage, the state is the epitome of human sin, placing its values at the center of all things. Like the dark spirits in Jude, this state is quick to advance from its proper place of authority, and frail human hearts are apt to follow it with idolatrous loyalty. The Christian's call is to live with this dual citizenship—always subject to proper authorities within contingent limits but never allowing the state to claim itself as final arbiter of truth and morality.

For Americans, this tension is exacerbated by an endemic spirit of chosen-ness. Some citizens of the Land of the Free go so far as to declare the United States to be a covenant nation, a New Israel, in special relationship to God, but even those who deny this in principle cannot easily escape in practice the founding myths of our forebears. Whether we see America as uniquely good or especially evil, Americans are keen to view their nation as being under the unique gaze of God, whitewashing its failures to the point of innocence or highlighting them as viler than the evils of others.

With political parties, this becomes even more exaggerated. We can temper our patriotism in the knowledge that our citizenship is an accident of birth, but the voluntary nature of political parties allows pride to invest our membership with a sense of superiority. It is not our inner selves alone who push us along this way. Whether appealing to the millions of believers in their midst or looking to a quasi-Christian foundation, few partisan announcements can resist the call to connect a given election year's priorities to the eternal will of the God of the Bible. We may claim that Jesus is not a Republican or a Democrat, but we have trouble imagining that he is not whichever one we happen to be.

All this means that any Christian organization, whether local church, national denomination, or parachurch ministry, has an intricate dance to follow. For editors and writers at Christian magazines seeking to impart discernment to their readers about the headlines they witness each day, maintaining an awareness of this tension is paramount. Those at *CT* had to pay special heed to these concerns as their fortunes rose with the rising tide of evangelicalism in the 1960s and 1970s and the decades that followed. Associated as closely as they were with Billy Graham, the most visible member of the evangelical movement, any statement on their part about politics reflected in the minds of many Americans what evangelicalism itself intended.

TAKING STANDS
BUT NOT SIDES

As 2019 drew to a close, *CT* found itself making headlines all around the world. Not only were other evangelicals discussing it, but everyone from left-leaning Israeli papers to the president of the United States took the time to address an editorial from this longstanding flagship evangelical magazine.[2] For a great many, this foray into political disputes came as something of a shock. Even many who were largely familiar with its history were puzzled by this breach of an ostensible neutrality when it came to politics. However, this is to misunderstand the stances it has taken over the years. While moments like this—where an article openly called for the removal of a high official—were uncommon, hardly an issue was published from its founding in 1956 up through the

---

2. Mark Galli, "Trump Should Be Removed from Office," December 19, 2019, https://www.christianitytoday.com/ct/2019/december-web-only/trump-should-be-removed-from-office.html.

present where politics was not addressed, either directly or by discussions of issues with political side effects.

It would be easy to classify the political writings in *CT* as "conservative," and, after a fashion, this is absolutely correct. The now-famous editorial about President Trump notwithstanding, its strong pro-life stance, staunch anti-Communism, and emphasis on the importance of religious liberty make it a reasonable candidate for the right wing of social discourse. At the same time, this would be an oversimplification. After all, one of the things that made the December 2019 op-ed by Mark Galli stand out so very much is that *CT* has long stood for speaking about politics in a nonpartisan manner. Over the course of several decades, the editors and writers have striven to draw out for their readers the implications of their Christian faith for their daily lives, and part of these daily lives included their political lives. At times, this meant noting the affinity for biblical ethics in the political platform of one party, while, at others, it meant pointing out the similar efforts by those in another. There was, however, an evident concern to avoid being overly associated with any one group.

CT has not been somehow indifferent to affairs of state down through the years, nor has it been averse to having government officials offer their insights in its pages, even those with a particular slant. During the 1950s and 1960s, it had on several occasions as a guest contributor the controversial head of the FBI, J. Edgar Hoover. This may be facilely written off by some as the editors bowing to the wishes of the magazine's longtime sponsor and conservative stalwart, J. Howard Pew, but even so, Hoover wrote precious little about the dangers of Communism that was not echoed substantially in the words of the erudite editor Henry, albeit with greater theological acumen. While there have been many times when the analysis of *CT* aligned well with conservatives when it came to anti-Communism, there have also been moments when it fit snugly with liberals on immigration. On the whole, *CT*'s association with either was more a case of correlation than causation. That is, while the principles of the magazine agreed with this or that political faction at this or that time, they were not determined by them.

THE BIG PICTURE

Throughout the sixty years covered in this collection, articles in *CT* discussed a great many topics, and the vast majority of them were not political. This is hardly surprising, given that the magazine has never pretended to be a political news source. Nonetheless, driven as they were by their Christian faith and Reformation heritage, the editors and writers were deeply concerned for the welfare of the *polis* and so often wrote about particular elections and political issues. Not only this, but even their statements about theological and ethical issues carried with them implications that played out in the political world. For example, a long-standing emphasis on the innate dignity of every human being led *CT* to take a firm stance on pro-life matters, even before *Roe v. Wade* made abortion the wedge issue it later became. And while abortion is the most obvious example, the political consequences of theological principles have played out in thousands of other articles over the hundreds of issues published in this sixty-year period.

This being the case, any book attempting to encompass the whole of *CT*'s pieces connected to politics would run into thousands of pages. This is no hyperbole. The original culling of potential articles for this project yielded a total of nearly six thousand pages. What is more, several of the chapters that follow could quite easily have become full books all by themselves. There is simply no way to include over a half-century's worth of political commentary in a single volume. Obviously, this meant that the list of articles had to be quite selective. In practice, this means that a great many interesting things had to be left behind, and often a single article is included to stand in for many others like it.

Rather than trying to include every political issue from every possible angle, this book focuses on a handful of key subjects. These areas can serve as templates for the way *CT*, and the wider evangelical movement it so often spoke for, interacted with political concerns across the board during this dynamic period of history. Each of these issues presents a different aspect of the problem of Christianity and politics. With chapter 1, on presidents, comes the concerns over cults of personality, the limits of power, and the way different issues animated articles in different eras. With chapter 2, on the Religious Right and Evangelical Left, we see questions about the way Christians interact with other believers who see things differently while maintaining a core faith. With chapter 3, on foreign affairs, we catch a glimpse of the often lethal consequences of our philosophical ideals and the way Christian principles of human dignity applied to others. With chapter 4, on domestic concerns, we can see the pragmatics of working out a moral theory in the real world, specifically in the contexts of the civil rights and pro-life movements. And finally, with chapter 5, on the question of God and country, we are forced to distinguish the contingent good of the nation from the ultimate good that comes from God.

THE CONTEXT

CT once ran a story about Canadian Prime Minister Trudeau. Noting his rock star-like following of adoring fans and consistent support for abortion and homosexual rights, the writer contrasted him with the more staid demeanor of his Conservative opponent. As much as this might seem ripped from recent headlines, the article in question was about *Pierre* Trudeau in 1968 and not his son Justin in 2020.[3] Knowing the historical context of articles enables those of us coming along later to better understand what is meant and also create a space of grace for any oversights they may include. This is true for any medium, but magazine articles, unlike books or other long-term projects, are very much a product of their times—with often only a few weeks of preparation beforehand and perhaps even less shelf life afterward.

We must bear in mind that many of the articles that follow were written in very different times than our own. President Eisenhower was an august figure who was barely a decade removed from having rid Western Europe of Nazi oppression. Communism was no historical abstraction but a real and menacing threat sitting atop an ever-expanding cut of the world. The civil rights movement was a hotly debated domestic concern for Christians, and conservative evangelicals were far more likely to oppose the presidential aspirations of then-Senator Kennedy on account of his Roman Catholicism than for being a Democrat. Over the decades that followed, nearly all of this would change. Roman Catholics and other non-evangelicals would write regularly for *CT*. Abortion would overtake race relations in its contentiousness. The Soviet Union would collapse with a whimper, and the promise of peace would last only a decade before the rise of Islamism. The various reactions to the ups and downs of the White House and its occupants would make the most stable mind dizzy.

But these differences and fluctuations do not mean that there is nothing we can or should learn from the past. The fundamental characteristics of human nature and the eternal decrees of God are as true now as they were a half-century or two thousand years

---

3. Aubrey Wice, "Canada's Trudeaumania," *Christianity Today* 12, No. 21 (July 19, 1968): 48–49.

ago. Questions over the role of the state, the Christian's responsibility in society, conflicts both domestic and foreign, and the moral crises facing the church—all of these remain as central to our political lives today as they did at the height of the Cold War. We would do well to listen to our older siblings as they wrestled with them in their time, if we are to be wise in our own.

Timothy D. Padgett
Managing Editor, BreakPoint
The Colson Center for Christian Worldview

Chapter 1

U.S. PRESIDENTS

*C*T's treatment of presidents in the years 1956–2016 varied greatly, and not always in the ways that we might expect. Eisenhower was the sort of figure whose military career had already earned him a place in the history books even before he ascended to the presidency. He was also the first chief executive to associate himself with the emerging neo-evangelicalism of Billy Graham and Carl F. H. Henry. Some have suggested that this was nothing but a ploy, but evangelicals at the time tended to take him at his word.

Kennedy presented evangelical commentators with something of a conundrum. Before he came to power, they were less concerned with his policies than his faith. Writers at *CT* were genuinely concerned that he would use the powers of his office to impose Roman rule on America's churches. Johnson, on the other hand, was treated in largely sympathetic terms, with some articles verging on pity. His place at the heart of the 1960s, with its assassinations, civil unrest, and an increasingly unpopular war, allowed for few easy roads to glory.

Nixon's time in office was complicated, to put it mildly. He was staunchly anti-Communist, was able to talk with China and bring North Vietnam to the negotiating table, and was on famously good terms with Billy Graham. And yet his role in Watergate could not be, and was not, ignored. Because of the unique challenges of squaring the president's professed Christianity with this scandal, the section on Nixon in this chapter is longer than the others. Ford's administration was so brief that, aside from some interest in his faith and life, his treatment was closer to a study of an interregnum than a stand-alone presidency.

Contrary to what we might expect, the first American president to capture the hearts of evangelical writers was not Reagan but Carter. There were clear statements of regret in *CT* articles over his support of abortion, but there were also rosy portrayals of his evangelical faith and active church life.

Reagan's role in these articles evolved over the years. There was a great sense of opportunity at his election, but there were also concerns about seeking political solutions in all things. More than anything else, it was the way he brought the abortion debate to center stage that earned him plaudits. In contrast, with the exception of his wartime leadership, of which *CT* writers largely approved, George H. W. Bush earned little praise, but this was less for what he did than for the ways he failed their expectations.

George W. Bush came the closest to the popular opinion of an evangelical president. He was not bashful about his faith, nor were *CT*'s writers shy about showering him with praise. Certainly, he was not a perfect man or leader, but his steadfastness during 9/11 and willingness to pursue a broad pro-life agenda gave him grace enough to last through his presidency.

Clinton and Obama, though separated by eight years, were alike in the way they came across in *CT* articles. In many very clear ways, their policies were a genuine threat to several dearly held beliefs of evangelicalism—around such things as abortion, homosexuality, and freedom of religion in particular—and many wrote accordingly. And yet, other editorials and articles attempted to build bridges and calm fears in their readers' hearts.

While Trump had not yet taken office at the close of 2016, it was clear he presented a unique challenge to evangelicals. His planned policies aligned well with many of the hopes and frustrations highlighted in *CT* over the years, but other things like his statements on immigration and his often uncouth persona led many to wonder how voting for him comported with their evangelical faith. His then-future administration made incarnate the tensions implicit in the Christian's dual citizenship.

DWIGHT D. EISENHOWER

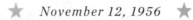

November 12, 1956

WHERE DO WE GO
FROM HERE?

THE EDITORS

Protestant ministers of all denominations throughout the United States responded with candor and directness to *Christianity Today*'s inquiry: "What change for the better in American affairs do you desire for your candidate if elected?" More than 2,000 clergymen, participating in this representative sampling of personal conviction, mirrored their long-range concern for a brighter America.

Their answers hold a significant interest not simply for the victors at the polls, but for the large and influential Christian community in American life.

In its pre-election news section (Oct. 29 issue), *Christianity Today* reported that its random sampling of ministers from all states indicated favor for President Eisenhower over Governor Stevenson by eight-to-one. These percentages were more than confirmed by many hundreds of additional replies received after press time. Yet the manses, parsonages and rectories of America left no doubt that, whichever party would be triumphant at the polls, the national scene calls urgently for specific improvements during the next four years.

The wide disparity between the eight-to-one ministerial vote and the public vote generally sounds a warning against

13

regarding ministerial conviction as an automatic index to the public mind. Less disparity exists between the Protestant clergy and Protestant church members, doubtless, than between the clergy and the citizenry as a whole. Yet the clergy are often motivated more intensely (dare we say, always more highly?) and their statistics provide a specialized index of opinion.

Ministers expressed deep conviction that the future of America depends more upon the application of spiritual concepts in national and international life and less upon a specific political party or candidate. The pulpit popularity of President Eisenhower in his re-election campaign sprang from his identification with an attitude of faith in God and in objective moral norms more than sheer party considerations, although policy issues bore conspicuous weight.

FACING THE RIGHT WAY

Ministerial anxiety for the enhancement of national life is not confined simply to one party or shade of political conviction. It included, however, an underlying confidence in the direction given to political life by the Eisenhower administration. This accounts, no doubt, for the relative absence of any radical indictment of prevailing American outlook. Almost one in eighteen of the ministers who voted for Eisenhower in both 1952 and 1956 in effect wrote: "No change; he is doing O.K." Endorsement of policy ran considerably higher among pro-Eisenhower clergy who had no vote in 1952. Better than one in three in this category urged simply that he "keep up the good work."

Although no sense of panic prevails about the temper of national life, the ministerial hope for the future nonetheless incorporated the hope of dramatic change. Appreciative of the fact that America in the last four years had been put somewhat more conspicuously "under God" than in recent decades, they shared no illusion that "God's in the White House (or hovers very near)," as a writer in *The Manchester Guardian* recently opined. The significant proposals came from clergy of Republican and Democratic vision alike, as well as from those identified with neither party. They came from ministers who supported the same candidate both in 1952 and 1956 as insistently as from switch-voters.

FOREIGN POLICY A CONCERN

Christianity Today returns were tabulated as pro-Eisenhower, pro-Stevenson, and Others (Undecided), with special alertness to switch-voting. In almost every block of clergy votes, an improved foreign policy during the next four years was marked the greatest imperative. Ministers who switched from Stevenson in 1952 to Eisenhower in 1956 provided the lone exception, for they assigned greater urgency to the pursuit of an aggressive and realistic program of racial desegregation.

Dissatisfactions over foreign policy ran deeper than agreement on a satisfactory alternative. Many recommendations were vague and general, favoring a program more vigorous, stable and progressive. The goal of "continuing maturity" and of "less sporadic moves" in foreign policy was vigorously pressed.

Specific suggestions for implementing a program of strong world leadership were not lacking, however, and ministers sought to outline elements of "a more decidedly Christian foreign policy."

Clergymen voting for Stevenson both in 1952 and 1956 suggested that a realistic grasp of international affairs would involve less reliance on military measures and more active support of international cooperation.

Clergymen twice supporting Eisenhower also worked their creative concern for continued progress and integrity in world affairs into specific suggestions for the easing of international tension. Only occasionally was there a protest against "many blunders" and a demand for "changes in the State Department," for example, "get rid of Dulles." Most expressions reflected a more moderate pursuit of "wise and planned foreign policy."

Specific recommendations divided almost equally along four lines: world peace, the United Nations, foreign aid, and long-term moral perspective.

INTERNATIONAL MORALITY

An aggressive spiritual-moral international policy was a recurring plea. Ministers asked for "foreign relations from idealistic principles and not from opportunistic motivation," for "world security built on a trusting spiritual level, and less on military spending," for "more consistent emphasis on spiritual values," for "continued stress on moral and spiritual uplift." "Russia is ahead of us in propaganda," wrote one minister, adding a plea for good will. Virtually all who touched the subject asked for a tougher policy with Russia: "less bending before Russian bluff," "a firmer stand toward Russia ... whose pledged word cannot be trusted. Oh, for a Teddy Roosevelt!"; "more drastic stand against Russia and the Communist party," "no dealings with Russia, no recognition of Red China," "firmer policy with regard to Red Countries, and passage of the Bricker amendment." On the positive side were suggestions like: "stand up more firmly for freedom all over the world," "help the colonial states obtain independence."

The subject of future relations to the United Nations was as frequently raised. Some clergymen, without any reference to the U.N., urged greater appreciation of world responsibility: "internationally-minded government," "improved relations with Far East and India as well as Near East," "more interest in under-dog nations," "less nationalism, more world vision." But nationalistic emphasis was not lacking. Comment on U.N. participation was sharply divided, with a seven to five edge for those favoring greater activity. Opposition to U.N. participation was often strongly worded: "take U.S. out of the U.N. and U.N. out of the U.S."

PURSUIT OF PEACE

Yet Protestant ministers reflected the need for greater determination in the pursuit of world peace. Only one minister, however, went so far as to urge "peace at any cost." But others stressed the need for "creative world-peace pursuits." One in five of the ministers who stipulated world peace as the major concern of the future called for a lessening of preparation for war: "cut spending for war efforts," "less emphasis on bombs and materials of war," "more effort on international disarmament." On the positive side, ministers urged a stronger peace program "by a firmer stand on equity," "work diligently for international friendships," "work in the interests of world peace through the U.N."

FOREIGN AID

The controversial subject of foreign aid drew wide suggestion of future overhauling. The conviction that foreign aid should be reduced outweighed that emphasis that it be increased three and one-half to one. For increased spending came such sentiment as: "more Point IV aid to backward foreign peoples," "more liberal policy of aid to needy peoples or nations," "use of U.S. power, food, natural resources for world-wide peaceful progress," "more foreign aid—in the form of raising their standard of living." On the negative side, ministers urged curtailment, but only one called for "cancellation of foreign aid." The prevailing tenor was for "foreign aid—but less," "re-evaluation of our foreign give away," "a gradual weaning from federal giveaway." Suggested principles of limitation were: "stop aid to Yugoslavia," "support freedom and justice only in foreign policy," "foreign aid reduced and the money used to improve America," "quit trying to buy friendship from other nations," "less military, more economical and technical assistance."

CHANGES FROM EISENHOWER

Foreign policy aside, the main areas of hoped for improvement revealed in *Christianity Today*'s poll, by those who had supported the Eisenhower candidacy twice, were ranged in the following order of priority: readjustment of the economic outlook (10%); intensification of the spiritual-moral emphasis (10%); decentralization of government, with stress on state rights (7.5%); implementing of desegration (3.5%); anti-liquor legislation (2%); more vigorous policy of church-state separation (1.25%); more vigorous anti-communist program (1.25%); federal aid to schools (1%). The only conspicuous counter-trend was in the priority assigned by almost 4% to "care for the little man," mostly in the interest of the farmer. The antisocialist sentiment (3%), included in the figures for decentralization of government, was frequently linked to a plea for curbing labor unions. The top priority was given foreign policy by just under 11% of the clergy twice supporting Eisenhower.

The issues just indicated accounted for half of the returns in this category. They do not reflect, however, vigorous pleas (although in lesser number) for curtailing military spending, special interest legislation, and for increasing old age benefits, strengthening social security laws, improved solution of the Palestine refugee problems, and scores of other problems assigned first importance by individual clergymen.

THE UNDECIDED VOTE

The "undecided" vote included almost twice as many ministers who had voted for Eisenhower in 1952 as for Stevenson, and as many who had not voted in 1952. Some reflected dissatisfaction with both major parties and candidates. "We need a new party, or a candidate who will dare to commit himself to constitutional government," wrote a New York City pastor. One Indiana minister wrote that he would vote for "nobody," and another, "either the third party or none at all." A Florida minister said he is still looking for a candidate "who will balance well all interests in American life—labor, financial interests, segregation." The bulk of the disappointment over President Eisenhower's first term concerned the failure to reverse the trend to socialism, and the failure to curtail the huge foreign aid program and to reduce taxes at home. The plea for a stronger anti-communist foreign policy, for an end of creeping socialism ("get government out of business"), for drastic reduction of expenditures and taxes, represented more than half the replies in this category. The defection from Governor Stevenson reflected greater confidence in the current Republican foreign policy, despite criticisms, than with the Democratic alternative. A number of "undecided" ministers called for a firmer stand on church-state separation, asking, for example, for "a positive stand on freedom of religion wherever American money and troops are sent abroad" and for a cessation of federal aid "to any church-sponsored institutions at home and abroad." Undecided ministers voting for the first time showed, proportionately, the greatest concern over the liquor traffic in America, coupled with a marked determination to vote the Prohibition ticket. Ministers in at least five states called insistently for outlawing the liquor traffic.

RISKS IN A LOBBY

Christianity Today's poll of Protestant ministers dramatizes the risk of attempting to express "the position" of a denomination—either the views of its clergy or of the church members—on political and economic issues.

Among Protestant clergymen, remarkable diversity of conviction prevails on the direction in which spiritual priorities are to be applied, and hence on social issues of the day. Protestant ministers do not receive socio-economic directives from a church hierarchy, which imposes upon them an official ecclesiastical "party line." The turmoil of conflicting Protestant opinion on far-reaching social issues may provide little comfort for those who feel that the church should vote and act with one mind on the political scene. But the unanimity which the church should have is the proclamation of the gospel of personal salvation, which in turn shapes a new social order by shaping new men. The fact of conflict in assessing politico-social options is not wholly disastrous, although in some respects it grows out of a departure from the principles of biblical social ethics—as when Christianity is identified, as it has been by liberal thinkers, with pacifism, Communism, or some other "ism." For biblical principles applied even to secondary options will have a way of inspiriting them and lessening their lameness.

But the stark fact of disagreement on leading social issues is a reminder that official church agencies only at great risk constitute themselves pressure lobbies for specific politico-economic objectives. Seldom do they actually have a mandate from the ministers of their churches, let alone the laity, to absolutize such objectives in the name of their denominational constituencies. In doing so, they run the peril of violating democratic rights within their churches, in the presumed course of contributing stability to democracy in the nation.

Protestantism obviously lacks an authoritative view on social issues in a generation plagued by social ills. The division on social strategy runs as deep today as the theological cleavage in Protestantism, although the two factions do not correspond absolutely. More liberal churchmen, whose theology has not undergone a full conservative revision, today acknowledge the fallacy of socialism, and appear ready to combine the theological left with the economic right. In the welter of confusion, it is understandable that men with a concern for the Protestant witness to a culture near chaos should promote the idea of unity in social reconstruction. But to compensate for a disunity which grows out of a basic departure from biblical norms by a unity which is manmade is to jump out of confusion into caprice.

THE PRESENT IMPERATIVE

The great need today, as American Protestantism recoils from the invasion of its theology and social ethics by speculative evolutionary principles during the century of Liberalism, is to find its way back to the centrality of the gospel, and to the recognition that hope for a new society is best mediated to any nation through the spiritual regeneration of its masses. In the long run, it is the decision made at this level which will answer the question of where America goes from here.

The Editors, "Where Do We Go From Here?" *Christianity Today* 1, No. 3 (November 12, 1956): 16–18.

TRANSITION IN WASHINGTON AND THE NEED OF PRAYER

THE EDITORS

The retirement of one United States president and the inauguration of another seem in our time to carry more the mood of destiny than in the past. While the flow of events witnesses to the fact that we are still crowded by historical options, rather than faced by the necessities of eternity, an atmosphere of awe today hangs over national and international affairs. It was therefore fitting that Mr. Eisenhower should end his political service to the nation, even as he started it, with a prayer.

In these days the power struggle can easily erase man's sense of the power of prayer and of true faith, even in the lives of the good and godly. President Eisenhower needed the prayers of the people. He himself prayed, though he seldom talked publicly about prayer or about his religious beliefs. When Secretary of the Interior Fred A. Seaton early one day in 1955 slipped unannounced into the president's office, he found him on his knees in prayer. Waving aside Seaton's profuse apology, Mr. Eisenhower said he was praying for divine guidance in a decision that could mean war or peace in the Far East. Mr. Eisenhower invited prayer at the opening of Cabinet meetings. At National Presbyterian

Church, after his instruction thrice in the meaning of the Cross and his coming into membership, he was respected as a devout believer. When running the risks of personal diplomacy with Khrushchev at St. David's, he matter-of-factly said: "It is my custom to attend church on Sunday mornings; I'd be glad to have you accompany me." Many an American churchgoer has done less with his neighbors. Mr. Khrushchev demurred, on the ground that in Russia (where atheism is the official line) his action would be misunderstood. Had he attended the church service, he might have found a greater than Marx.

Many churchmen will note that Mr. Eisenhower's farewell prayer, alongside its virtues of simplicity and sincerity, was theologically flaccid by Christian standards. In some respects it was perhaps as nebulous as certain exhortations to faith which simmer down to little more than "faith in faith." But it also brings into view a problem not yet resolved in American political life. In view of the principle of separation of church and state, even some churchmen insist that a leader whose private convictions are Christological should formulate only theistic pronouncements in his public life. The danger is that of gliding into a vague theism, and beyond that, into humanism. On the other hand, some quarters today increasingly stress the Christian history of the nation. America can doubtless profit from a sharpening of theological perspectives, even in political affairs. Such a recovery must not, however, involve us in a philosophy of church and state which our forefathers hoped they had left far behind on European shores.

One order has changed, and another begun. But the season for prayer remains. We join Mr. Eisenhower in bidding President Kennedy "Godspeed." The perils of misplaced trust in earthly power—the power of weapons of destruction, the power of intellectual or scientific genius, the power (even if shrinking) of American dollars—remain with us. What we need now, as never before, is new vision of the power of God and of regenerate morality in the lives of men. Without it, one nation after the other spends its last days as a heap of rubble.

In such an hour, some were dismayed to observe a symbol like Sinatra and the Hollywood assortment of characters around him looming upon the capital scene, making use of inauguration celebrations, national in intent, for partisan fund-raising purposes. Certain unsavory aspects of American life are amplified quite enough already. Kindred ties are no excuse for blurring the image of the White House, or making it a suburb of Beverly Hills. Let the Sinatras return to Hollywood and, if they must, its manners, mores, and foibles.

But let us stay with the Book. There is more light in any of the versions than all the radiant neon of Hollywood Boulevard.

The Editors, "Transition in Washington and the Need of Prayer," *Christianity Today* 5, No. 9 (January 30, 1961): 24.

JOHN F. KENNEDY

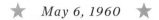 *May 6, 1960*

THE BIG DEBATE: A CATHOLIC PRESIDENT?

THE EDITORS

The advent of the West Virginia primary May 10 saw the religious issue take on wholesome new meaning within the U.S. political scene.

Whatever the outcome, this much was clear: Candid debate about the political ramifications of Senator John F. Kennedy's Catholicism marked a significant step forward in American church-state understanding.

"Some very calm and respected national voices are saying that the open discussion of the religious issue is a sign of progress," reported *The Christian Science Monitor*, "far better than the whispers which accompanied the 1928 presidential campaign."

The spontaneous origin of the 1960 debate at grass roots may indicate that there has developed a fuller sensitivity to the role of religion in politics.

Some observers even dare to hope that discussions may permanently lay to rest the notorious notion that only bigots raise the religious issue.

As the Catholic hierarchy watched quietly, Kennedy began to speak freely of the religious issue even while discrediting its importance (as did other presidential contenders: Nixon, "inexcusable"; Stevenson, "irrelevant"; and Humphrey, "divisive").

Pivotal point in the Kennedy strategy was his April 21 address to the American Society of Newspaper Editors. It marked the first time he had gone out of his way to discuss religion. He scolded the press so severely that not a single editor of the 400 present took up his offer to answer questions.

"The great bulk of West Virginians paid very little attention to my religion—until they read repeatedly in the nation's press that this was the decisive issue in West Virginia," Kennedy said. "I do not think that religion is the decisive issue in any state."

"I do not speak for the Catholic church on issues of public policy," he added, "and no one in that church speaks for me. My record on aid to education, aid to Tito, the Conant nomination and other issues has displeased some prominent Catholic clergymen and organizations; and it has been approved by others."

"The fact is," he asserted, "that the Catholic church is not a monolith—it is committed in this country to the principles of individual liberty—and it has no claim over my conduct as a public officer sworn to do the public interest."

Senator Kennedy became less convincing when he endeavored to cast doubt on the existence of Catholic bloc voting. Columnist Doris Fleeson promptly dug out a 3,000-word memorandum prepared for the 1956 Democratic National Convention under the direction of Theodore C. Sorensen, a Unitarian who was and still is Kennedy's chief of staff. The memo spelled out in detail the "Catholic vote" which was drifting to the Republicans but which could be lured back by a Catholic vice presidential nominee.

Questioned privately of how he would define his primary allegiance, Kennedy initially described it to a *Christianity Today* reporter in terms of the "public interest," then indicated that it would be better expressed as a "composite" which includes "conscience."

Did he feel that only a bigot would cite religious grounds for opposing a presidential candidate? No, but he said he found it hard to understand what intellectual anxiety there would be when one has answered in the negative (as Kennedy has) the all-important question: Would you be responsive to ecclesiastical pressures or obligations that might influence you in conducting the affairs of office in the national interest?

The Editors, "The Big Debate: A Catholic President?" *Christianity Today* 4, No. 16 (May 6, 1960): 33.

THE ASSASSINATION OF THE PRESIDENT

THE EDITORS

A shot came out of nowhere and changed a thousand things around the world. An unknown assassin brought sudden and tragic end to the life of a world-renowned figure; John F. Kennedy was dead by the hand of an evil man whom nobody knew, and who will be known only as long as his infamy is remembered. Three months before a father laid his infant son to rest; he now lies down to rest beside him.

In one tragic moment, an unexpected event changed the plans and hopes of many people and of a nation. Strategies devised with an eye to next year's presidential elections were suddenly obsolete. The whole civil rights issue at once took on new but unknown dimensions.

Lyndon B. Johnson, who had hoped for the office of president and had seen his hopes vanish like a bubble in the rough conflicts of politics, was by unforeseen tragedy and no plans of his own the president of the United States. So little, one shot, by one unknown man, changed so much. The president's death was not only a national tragedy but an event of great international significance. The fragile fabric of personal diplomacy patiently built up by Kennedy and Khrushchev was broken by the same evil that broke his life.

While the news that President Kennedy had been shot was flashed around the world, the White House paradoxically appeared as quiet as the eye of a storm. The usual traffic moved slowly on Pennsylvania Avenue and the usual number of people walked the broad sidewalks in front of the White House. During the 35 minutes that the fallen president lay dying in a Dallas hospital, three men gathered dead leaves and leisurely loaded them into a truck that stood on the circular drive that fronts the White House. The whirring blades of a helicopter could be seen above the grass in the back of what was the Kennedy home. Here of all places everything looked normal on this warm, gray, November day. But suddenly a flag was quietly lowered to half mast above the white mansion. Others on surrounding public buildings were similarly lowered, and the eye received the message that the mind found impossible to believe. The president was dead.

America lost a man of great intellectual gifts, a president of strong courage and of great political imagination. Kennedy had kept his promise to the nation and had held the line on the church-state issue. And whatever one may feel about his civil rights stand, he held it with integrity and undeviating moral conviction, even when it threatened to be politically disadvantageous. Men of goodwill long will pay him tribute and the nation long will sorrow for such a man, cut down in the strength of his years and the height of his service.

As night fell on the Capital, the shriek of a traffic officer's whistle arose from the now snarled traffic, and the White House loomed in the deepening night, all dark within, the only lights those illuminating the portico outside. A similar darkness fell over the hearts of a nation. For the moment there is no light

within, only sadness at such tragedy, and a dumb perplexity at
so absurd and ugly an evil.

One of the eye-witnesses to the assassination was a 25-year-
old senior at Dallas Theological Seminary, Malcom Couch, a television cameraman who was riding in one of the cars following the
president's. Couch saw the president slump as a rifle was pulled
in from a window overlooking the street. The president's car then
sped to a hospital.

Concerned Christians sympathize not only with Mrs. Kennedy
and the two youngsters, but with the late president's father and
mother, his brothers and sisters. The Joseph P. Kennedy family,
known to be so closely knit, has through the years experienced
many deep sorrows, including the World War II deaths of Joseph
P. Kennedy, Jr., and a son-in-law, the Marquess of Hartington, and
only last summer the death of the infant Patrick Bouvier Kennedy.

Seven blocks away from the White House is old Ford's Theater,
now a Lincoln museum, which yet stands as mute testimony to
the hazards of public service—particularly in times of national
division and strife. Lincoln, Garfield, McKinley ... and now John
Kennedy. Believers in man's upward progress could be tempted
to point to the lessening frequency of U.S. presidential assassinations as symbolic of their dreams, for the last instance was the
1901 shooting of William McKinley. But before one could relegate such phenomena to the shadows of the nineteenth century—
giving way to the "glorious light" of the twentieth—he would
have to ponder the attempts on the lives of Franklin Roosevelt
in Miami and Harry Truman at Blair House.

The assassin represents the temporary breakdown of the
democratic process. With a single move of his index finger he
annuls the decision of millions of voters. A dark spot in his brain
vetoes carefully thought out decisions of national leaders.

But the democratic process makes allowances for the exigency. We now have a new president. We are grateful for belated progress in our system which has resulted in more careful thought being given to the qualities of vice-presidential candidates. A recent example is the warning that President Eisenhower's illnesses carried for the 1960 conventions of both major political parties, who nominated eminent and politically-experienced candidates for the vice-presidency.

Thus an illness has left us a legacy. Such a turn of events could also well leave us a reminder of the providence of which our forefathers so often spoke. We sing of a God who is both sovereign and loving, a God who brings good from evil, a God who moves in a mysterious way, a God who rides upon the storm:

Behind a frowning providence
He hides a smiling face.

Let Christians pray for the bereaved; let them pray for the recovery of Governor Connally; let them hold up the arms of President Lyndon B. Johnson in prayer, that the nation may experience a new unity in time of crisis. There are cruel foes without; there are agonizing problems within. God grant that the Psalmist's affirmation become our own: "Some trust in chariots, and some in horses: But we will remember the name of the Lord our God."

The Editors, "The Assassination of the President," *Christianity Today* 8, No. 5 (December 6, 1963): 24–25.

December 20, 1963

PRAYER AND PROTEST

THE EDITORS

In his first address to the nation, President Lyndon B. Johnson expressed his dependence on Almighty God and requested the people of America to beseech God to help him in the execution of his new and high office. In so doing the president echoed what was to be the closing remark of the late President Kennedy's speech that he did not live to make in Dallas: "Except the Lord keep the city, the watchman waketh but in vain."

Christians were impressed by the humility of their new president and by his expressed need of their prayers and the help of Almighty God. When the occupant of the most powerful office in the world publicly acknowledges such reliance upon the One who is higher than he, the Christian heart is touched. Yet how often, when the sincere emotion of the moment is past, Christians forget in daily life to invoke the blessings of God upon those who rule over them. Too many churches rarely remember their government in congregational prayer. It is not only reassuring for Christians to hear the president of the United States ask their prayers; it is their duty to pray for him. Paul enjoins that "supplications, prayers, intercessions, thanksgivings, be made for all men," and he singles out and specifically mentions "kings and all that are in high place" (1 Tim. 2:1, 2, ARV). The purpose of such prayer is "that we may lead a tranquil and quiet life in all godliness and gravity," a state devoutly to be desired in our troublous times, when the patterns of our national and social life are threatened almost daily. Paul adds the reason such prayer should be offered: "This is good and acceptable in the sight of God our Saviour, who would have all men to be saved, and come to the knowledge of the truth."

Christians who find it difficult to pray and even to make "thanksgivings" for presidents and administrations that they dislike or that are of another political party, should remember that when Paul thus exhorted Timothy, both lived under the tyranny of Nero.

American churches often pray little for their government because they lack a sense of solidarity with the nation, a sense of being America. Doubtless, immigrant origins help to account for this. But we do well to remember that such men as John Huss, Martin Luther, and Ulrich Zwingli were not only great churchmen but also great patriots. Many evangelical churches need to gain or to regain a sense of belonging to the country. Such a sense of identification will make praying for their presidents and congressmen, their governors and mayors an easier and more natural thing.

Not a little embittered criticism and hateful denunciation of the federal government has come from Christian sources. To protest and express critical evaluations of government is the right of every citizen. If, however, it is to be done responsibly, it must be done not out of a spirit of detachment but out of a sense of solidarity, a deep feeling that this is my government.

Christians too may exercise their right to criticize their president, his leadership and policies, their congressmen and courts; but they must do it in a mood that does not exclude the possibility of praying for what they criticize. Unless they can make "supplications, prayers, intercessions, thanksgivings" for the president, the Congress, the Supreme Court, they cannot render such criticisms as are "good and acceptable in the sight of God our Saviour." He who "will have all men to be saved" will not tolerate critics who self-righteously detach themselves from the institutions and political personages they denounce. It is a shame of America, and a greater one of the church, that some Christians criticize in a spirit that cannot intercede and that has no will to save. Unless Christians learn to pray for what they protest, they will not protest in a manner that becomes their high calling and promotes the country's good. Like the ancient prophets, they must learn to denounce with tears in their eyes.

Let Christians of every political and religious affiliation respond to Paul's exhortation and to President Johnson's request.

The Editors, "Prayer and Protest," *Christianity Today* 8, No. 6 (December 20, 1963): 24.

THE POLITICAL TIGHTROPE

THE EDITORS

L yndon B. Johnson is now feeling strong vibrations on the tightrope of American politics he nimbly treads as president of the United States. Cautiously seeking to maintain his balance— to follow high principles as he leads the nation and yet retain the broad-based popular appeal necessary for continuing in public office—he finds himself in peril of falling on either side. Critics are vociferously accusing him of forsaking the policy of peace in his conduct of the Viet Nam war. Others are claiming he has thrown economy and efficiency to the winds in waging his war on poverty. Now his plight is complicated by reports in last month's Gallup Poll that his popularity among voters has been eclipsed by that of the junior senator from New York via Massachusetts. Small wonder that the president has recently increased the frequency of his visits and the forthrightness of his speeches to people in various parts of the country.

Past presidents of recent years have said that no one who has not been president can fully comprehend the burden of the Presidency. As Lyndon B. Johnson seeks to carry this enormous burden with sureness of foot and with head held high, we repledge our prayerful support of him, not out of political partisanship but because he is president of all the people and needs assurance that the electorate will support a leader who abides by righteousness and justice. Let him not be influenced by the fickle responses of impressionable people attracted by the charisma of other political figures. Let him not become defensive and turn a deaf ear to his critics. Let him not be concerned about how this generation or those to come will rank him as a president. But let him be true to the motto that West Point men swear to uphold: duty, honor, country.

The American people have shown they will support a president whose foreign policy is based on freedom for all men, opposition to all tyranny, and peace with justice. They will follow a leader whose domestic policies endorse equal opportunity for all, fiscal responsibility, freedom in the marketplace of ideas and goods, and tender-hearted concern for people. If a president devotes himself, before God and his fellow countrymen, to policies that accord with these principles, he should not tremble as he contemplates his own political destiny.

America long remembers, loves, and respects not those leaders who quaver at the blasts of critics or at the growing popularity of political opponents, but those who would rather be right than be president. Lyndon B. Johnson's political tightrope may feel shakier these days. But let us hope it will not send a shiver up his spine. Only a president with courage, wisdom, and perseverance can provide the leadership the nation needs in these critical days.

The Editors, "The Political Tightrope," *Christianity Today* 10, No. 25 (September 30, 1966): 34.

September 11, 1970

A PETITION FOR THE PRESIDENT

THE EDITORS

I n all the years of history few empires have displayed the might of ancient Babylon. And few men have wielded the power of the Babylonian kings, Nebuchadnezzar and Belshazzar. Yet in a period of an hour Nebuchadnezzar became a madman and was driven from his throne to keep company with the beasts of the field. And Belshazzar and the Babylonian empire suddenly and surprisingly met their doom only hours after Daniel's interpretation of the handwriting on the wall warned that both the king and his kingdom were finished.

Why did these things happen? Daniel gives the answer: "Thereby the living will know that the most high is sovereign in the kingdom of men: he gives the kingdom to whom he will and he may set over it the humblest of mankind" (Daniel 4:17 NEB). Isaiah expresses God's sovereignty over the nations of earth in these words: "Why, to him nations are but drops from a bucket ... all nations dwindle to nothing before him. ..." (Isaiah 40:15, 17 NEB).

No nation has ever become so great or powerful that God cannot bring it down; no nation is so small that God cannot raise it to a place of power if he chooses. God has promised to bless and exalt the nation that honors and obeys him (Psalm 33:12,

Proverbs 14:34). He also promises to judge the nations that forget him (Psalm 9:17).

By the grace of God, America is a powerful and prosperous nation. But many things about America reflect a lack of gratitude to God or concern to obey him. Certainly this is an hour in which the people of America need to gather together to pray for their nation—to thank God for his goodness, to repent of the evils that exist, to affirm allegiance to the will of God, and to seek the wisdom and strength to know and do his will.

We call upon President Nixon to exercise the privilege given him by Congress to set aside an annual day of prayer. And we respectfully request that it be announced long enough in advance of the date so that there might be ample publicity and preparation for it. Only with the help of God can America be a nation worthy of honor, and only as America genuinely honors and obeys God can we expect his continued blessings. The alternatives are frightening.

The Editors, "A Petition for the President," *Christianity Today* 14, No. 24 (September 11, 1970): 35.

ON BEFRIENDING PRESIDENTS

THE EDITORS

Billy Graham's friendship with Richard Nixon and other American presidents has subjected the evangelist to considerable criticism. Often the accusations revolve around the idea that this liaison demeans evangelical Christianity by identifying the leading Bible preacher of our time with a particular political outlook.

We grant that there is risk involved when a clergyman becomes a confidant of powerful figures in the secular world. But is not the risk far outweighed by the opportunity? Have not many evangelicals long prayed for an entrée without compromise into the affairs of state?

Our view on this point coincides with that expressed last month by Editor Louis Benes of the *Church Herald*, official weekly organ of the Reformed Church in America. "We ought to thank God," wrote Benes, "that four presidents have recognized the integrity of this man of God and sought the friendship and counsel of a man of his character and faith in God. Who else would we want there? What if our presidents instead sought the counsel and advice of a member of the Mafia, or a 'God is dead' theologian, or someone dedicated to the 'playboy' philosophy?"

Benes expressed the hope that Graham "and other Christian leaders, both Roman Catholic and Protestant, who have contacts with responsible men at all levels of government, will use such contacts for good, and thus make their influence count for truth and righteousness."

In the case of Graham, there is no evidence that he has watered down his convictions to gain access to the White House. Those who make such charges aren't listening to him. Hardly a week goes by that Graham does not warn America of coming judgment unless there is repentance.

Some critics seem to be saying that Graham must keep his distance from government leaders lest he be identified as a "court preacher." Indeed, there are numerous examples from the Bible and in church history of false prophets who said what rulers wanted to hear instead of God's Word. Surely Graham would welcome our prayers that he will be faithful as he tries to avoid the separatistic "holier-than-thou" mentality that would minimize contact with the affairs of this world for fear of contamination. There are ample biblical precedents for what he is doing: Esther and Mordecai, Joseph, and Daniel show that one can make his influence for God felt through private relationships with heads of state. "Who can say but that God has brought you into the palace for just such a time as this?" (Esther 4:14b, Living Bible).

The Editors, "On Befriending Presidents," *Christianity Today* 16, No. 12 (March 17, 1972): 26.

THE WATERGATE WRANGLE

THE EDITORS

Every administration is plagued by the misdeeds of some of its appointees to public office. Harry Truman felt the lash of scandal in the case of the deep freezes; Eisenhower was caught up in the scandal that sent Sherman Adams home in disgrace; Lyndon Johnson had the shadow of the Bobby Baker case hanging over his head. Now President Nixon is squeezed in the middle of the Watergate debacle. And debacle it is.

At stake are moral and ethical issues that cannot be overlooked. Citizens have a right to expect their government to act uprightly. When public figures breach the common canons of conduct, every citizen should be morally outraged. No stone should be left unturned to bring the culprits to justice.

We will accept at face value the claim of the president that he was not personally involved in the sordid Watergate affair. But now that he knows of its existence and is aware of the names of those who have already been tried and found guilty, and probably of others who have not yet been brought to justice, his duty is clear. It is Mr. Nixon's solemn responsibility as president and as a Christian to see that the matter is thoroughly and fully investigated, that executive privilege is waived so that the facts can be uncovered, and that the full weight of the judicial processes is employed to guarantee that justice is done.

Mr. Nixon has one other responsibility. He should purge his administration of all who have been involved in this squalid affair. In this way people everywhere will know that his administration will not put up with this sort of thing, and even more, that he himself has taken a stand for ethical and moral principles that have suffered so greatly because of Watergate.

Any failure by Mr. Nixon to act and to act promptly can only lead to the conclusion that there is something he wishes to keep hidden, and justify the caustic comments of his severest critics. He owes it to his friends and supporters to clean the slate. As Shakespeare said, "Lilies that fester smell far worse than weeds."

The Editors, "The Watergate Wrangle," *Christianity Today* 17, No. 14 (April 13, 1973): 31.

★ *September 28, 1973* ★

PERSONAL PIETISM AND WATERGATE

HAROLD B. KUHN

I t was to be expected that segments of the press, both secular and religious, would seek to identify religious events and trends that contributed to the tragedy of Watergate. This falls within the function of a free press. To the surprise of no one, some journalists took the way of the easy answer. Typical of this was the assigning of major responsibility to what is variously called Personal Pietism, the American Style of Religion, and White House Religion.

At first the liberal religious press traced the scandals to individual pietistic conditioning. This is, of course, shorthand for personal and public evangelism that presses for personal conversions, personal commitments to Christ. The assertion is made that this emphasis leads inevitably to privatistic understandings of religious faith, and to blindness to corporate or systemic evil.

Lying behind much of this allegation is the implication, frequently left unexpressed, that the East Wing religious services, and President Nixon's personal acquaintance with conservative-evangelical ministers, actually led to Watergate. What is lacking, to date at least, is any clear evidence that such men as Messrs. Dean,

Ehrlichman, Haldeman, or Magruder were regular attenders at such services. More difficult to establish would be any contention that such men were interested in what was said there.

It is easy to allege that the East Room services produced a "climate" in which illegal and unprincipled conduct followed as a matter of course. The challenge lies in trying to produce any solid supporting evidence.

Then the testimony of Jeb Stuart Magruder before the Senate Watergate Committee compelled a shift of emphasis, particularly upon the part of the established religious press. Mr. Magruder suggested that he drew inspiration for some of his conduct from the behavior of his former professor of ethics at Williams College, the Reverend William Sloane Coffin, Jr.

This brought into prominence the sacred motif of "situation" ethics and drew immediate fire from editorialists of the more liberal religious organs. This is not the place to decide whether Magruder was justified in what he said about Dr. Coffin. What is worthy of note is that the line of attack now shifted to become as follows: Those accused of wrongdoing in the Watergate affair had, because of their pietistic conditioning, developed "a new kind of situation ethics."

Presumably this new brand of situationism was a deterioration or betrayal of the (good) older form articulated by Joseph Fletcher, Bishop Robinson, and others. We are not told precisely what new factors have been introduced. We may surmise that the reply would be that the older situationism was socially sensitive and group-welfare controlled, while the newer form is privatistic.

The lead editorial in the May 30 *Christian Century* declared that the "new situation ethic rests its decisions upon such questions as: Was anyone killed? Was anyone robbed? Was anyone hurt?" The so-called love ethic appeals to the same sort of pragmatic considerations. On these bases, the theft and publication of the Pentagon Papers could no doubt be justified.

It helps little to say that the results at Watergate differed from those issuing from the older situational criteria. Loving objectives were sought and obtained—the reelection of the president, the protection of his peace of mind. A greater good was secured by the defeat of a candidate felt to possess inferior qualifications for the office. The point is that the apparent principals in the Watergate case and its aftermath applied the same old criteria that have marked situationism in its long history, and have in recent years been popularized as a rationale for the more articulated form of this consequence-ethic.

It was to be expected that Magruder's former teacher, now chaplain of Yale University, would proclaim a total disjunction between his own breaking of laws as part of resistance to the Viet Nam war and the alleged breaking of laws in the current Watergate affair. Because I have not seen Coffin's complete reply, it is perhaps unfair to comment upon it. There does seem to be in his response, as quoted in the newspapers, a certain self-righteousness, or at least a lack of recognition of the ambiguities inherent in his own position. He and other war resisters seem to have reached rather easily the conclusion that the means they used were the best available for the achievement of their objectives, or at least necessary to gain the desired end.

It may be shown to be true that their motives and ends were pure and their means in harmony with the best tradition of nonviolent resistance. One is tempted, however, to wonder why these resisters uniformly employed attorneys equipped with knowledge of every legal loophole by which they could secure acquittal for their clients upon technicalities. If they were willing to go to prison for conscience's sake, they were seldom willing to remain there.

The secular press quotes a Texas pastor as inquiring: "What were all those preachers doing in the White House on Sunday mornings? What were they preaching?" The implication is that if liberal clergymen (who are by definition "prophetic") had been invited to preach on these occasions, they would have thundered forth effectively against the conditions that produced Watergate. This represents fine hindsight. Actually, most of them were so preoccupied with Southeast Asia that they would probably have done little more than denounce U.S. policies in Viet Nam. It is open to doubt whether any would have been able to rise above this sufficiently to deal in the major moral principles greatly needing emphasis.

The fact remains that those who have lined up behind the pipers who for a decade now have trumpeted the "New Morality" have little grounds for placing the responsibility for Watergate upon the preaching of personal pietism. Certainly the empirical elements in ethics have been no more in evidence here than in the case of the Harrisburg group or the dealers in the Pentagon Papers.

I believe it can be shown that evangelicals have generally stood up reasonably well at the point of manifesting a principial rather than a situational or contextual ethic. And in those cases in which they have felt it necessary, in the name of a higher law, to challenge existing conditions, they have done so with no larger an admixture of empirical elements than that displayed by theological liberals.

Possibly those who in the name of a "new morality" have disavowed the application of principles as doing violence to people should take another look at their own posture. It is likely that they, no less than the apparent principals in Watergate, should enter the behavioral situation armed with some clear-cut rules concerning right and wrong.

Harold B. Kuhn, "Personal Pietism and Watergate," *Christianity Today* 17, No. 25 (September 28, 1973): 61–62.

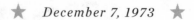

★ *December 7, 1973* ★

THE FORD IN OUR FUTURE

BARRIE DOYLE

Vice President-designate Gerald R. Ford is a man "very committed to God," says his son Michael, 23, a seminary student. "He's not outspoken or vocal about his commitment—he's not that kind of a man," he said in an interview. "Dad is more a man of action who incorporates his faith into his work."

The quiet faith is what makes Ford a "real man" to his old friend and constituent, evangelist Billy Zeoli. Zeoli, president of Gospel Films in Grand Rapids, Michigan, and also noted for evangelistic work among professional football teams, says Ford has taken a definite Christian stand. "I can say he has accepted Christ as his Savior and that he is a growing Christian." Zeoli says he has spent time praying and studying the Bible with Ford for years.

Ford, a football star at the University of Michigan (he was voted outstanding player in 1934, when his team won only one game), and still a fan, accepted Christ at a Washington Redskins–Dallas Cowboys pre-game chapel service Zeoli conducted two years ago, according to the evangelist. Since then, Zeoli has met often with Ford, who as House Minority Leader invited the evangelist to lead Congress in prayer on October 11—as it turned out, the day following former vice president Spiro Agnew's resignation. Ford and Zeoli also jointly sponsored an athletes' luncheon the day of the Presidential Prayer Breakfast last winter.

Ford, 60, a lifelong Episcopalian, attends Immanuel (Episcopal) Church-on-the-Hill in Alexandria, Virginia. His home church is Grace Episcopal in Grand Rapids, where parishioners remember him as a Sunday-school teacher "who believed in what he said," according to a *Detroit Free Press* story by reporter Hiley Ward.

While awaiting confirmation, Ford's closely knit family was apparently finding growing unity through prayer. Said his son Michael: "It's been an uplifting experience. We've all been drawn closer together and we're giving each other spiritual support through prayer. ... [The prospects] are so crucial, so demanding, that I know he's getting deeper into the faith."

Michael Ford, a first-year student at Gordon-Conwell Seminary in Wenham, Massachusetts, said he plans a career in full-time Christian service as a youth minister. The decision to drop out of a political science–law program (the course his father followed) and opt for the ministry came after he made a commitment to Christ at Wake Forest University last year. It caused some surprise at home, Michael said, "but Dad knew my Christian faith was playing a strong part in my decision." He said his father helped him investigate seminaries, warning him away from "liberal" schools and suggesting instead a seminary that held a "strong orthodox view of Christianity."

With all eyes on the vice-presidential post, the Ford family is hesitant about discussing the possibility of his becoming president (the family believes President Nixon will see his term through), Michael said. "Dad takes one step at a time."

Ford, a leader of the congressional prayer groups, spends time in prayer meetings with presidential assistant Melvin Laird, says Zeoli. "He [Ford] has a real evangelical involvement." To help him along, Zeoli sends him a weekly letter containing a Bible verse and a prayer.

The Ford family's lifestyle has changed from the moment he was picked as Agnew's successor, said Michael. "But I think it's brought about a real revival of our dependence and trust in God. I think all of these events show that God is going to work his will for the glory of his Kingdom."

Barrie Doyle, "The Ford in Our Future," *Christianity Today* 18, No. 5 (December 7, 1973): 50.

FIFTEEN TURBULENT YEARS

THE EDITORS

T he last fifteen years probably have been the most turbulent in the history of the United States since the adoption of the Constitution and the inauguration of President George Washington.

During the last decade and a half John F. Kennedy was assassinated; the armed forces fought in Viet Nam and finally came home; Lyndon B. Johnson was eliminated from the 1968 presidential campaign by the pressures of an unpopular war despite his election in 1964 by a great landslide; Robert Kennedy was assassinated at a time when his candidacy for the office of president was reaching a high tide; Richard Nixon won the election in 1968 with the promise to end the war in Viet Nam and bring peace to the world. The end of Nixon's first term was marred by the Watergate charges, but his reelection was an overwhelming victory against Senator George McGovern, whose campaign never got off the ground.

Early in his second term Nixon succeeded in bringing U.S. participation in the Viet Nam war to a conclusion. Not long thereafter came the exposure and finally the resignation from the vice-presidency of Spiro Agnew, whose "law and order" mentality was grossly at variance with his personal practices. Meanwhile the Watergate situation was moving slowly but inexorably to a climax, which finally came on the evening of August 8, when President Nixon announced to the nation that he would resign the following day.

During the time that the Watergate break-in was being investigated Mr. Nixon was changing the face of the global struggle with Communism by his rapprochement with Red China and the Soviet Union. This new direction in American foreign policy and the political realignments wrought more profound changes than have yet been realized by the citizenry; the effects are still to be fully understood.

The resignation of Richard M. Nixon meant that for the first time in almost two hundred years the White House would be occupied by a man selected not by the people but by his predecessor, with the approval of Congress. And he would then propose his own successor for the vacant office of vice president, for confirmation by Congress. This meant that the two chief offices of the United States would be filled by men not chosen by popular ballot. Truly the United States has come through a radical series of events, the meaning of which the historians will try hard to grasp and interpret for years to come.

In the confusion surrounding Mr. Nixon's resignation some things stand out clearly. On August 5 he released a statement in connection with the surrender of three tapes of conversations with H. R. Haldeman. Mr. Nixon admitted that the tapes were at variance with earlier statements he had made and that he had ordered a halt to the investigation of the Watergate break-in for political reasons as well as for national security reasons. He acknowledged that he had kept this damaging information from his attorneys and that he had failed to notify the House Judiciary Committee of the variance. It became apparent immediately that the House would vote to impeach him, and there was little doubt that the Senate would then remove him from office. His guilt was established beyond reasonable doubt; his claim that the cover-up was done in the interest of the nation revealed his commitment to situation ethics. His most loyal defenders were left helpless by his announcement of this deception, and his cause was lost.

Many unresolved problems remain. Will the full truth of Watergate be made known to the American people? Will Mr. Nixon be prosecuted, or has his resignation from office been sufficient punishment? Will it be considered just for those who aided and abetted the commission of these crimes to serve prison sentences if their leader himself remains free? And if he is not to be sentenced, should not the lesser luminaries be pardoned, too? Until these questions have been answered satisfactorily the unsavory odor of Watergate will linger.

America's new president, Gerald Ford, seems to have grasped the central demand of the nation from the ethical standpoint: the need for truth, honesty, and integrity in the White House and throughout the government. He has promised to make these principles the pole-stars of his administration. No government can long stand when these virtues have disappeared. We hope that Mr. Ford will clearly exemplify them, that in his conduct of the government there will be an openness and honesty and an obvious commitment to righteousness.

President Ford would be well advised to choose men and women of Christian faith and prayer to work with him—not just career bureaucrats, businessmen, and financiers. He should appoint to high office people who have shown their spiritual colors and their commitment to the same standards of morality he himself has professed. He should be prepared to espouse the cause of persecuted Christians even as men like Senator Jackson have that of persecuted Jews. He should not kowtow to either Red

China or the Soviet Union—friendship, yes; blind collaboration with injustice, no!

One of his chief priorities should be the battle against inflation, and at the heart of this struggle is the need for a return to honest fiscal policies in which the nation spends no more than it takes in in taxes from its people.

Mr. Ford assumes the presidency after a decade and a half in which the nation has suffered one tragic event after another. We wish him well and assure him of our prayers and, we hope, of the prayers of the nation. With them the going will still be rough; without them he stands little chance of solving the grave problems that beset the American people.

The Editors, "Fifteen Turbulent Years," *Christianity Today* 18, No. 23 (August 30, 1974): 24–25.

★ *August 30, 1974* ★

THE NEW PRESIDENT: PRAYER AND A QUIET FAITH

BARRIE DOYLE AND JAMES C. HEFLEY

W hen he assumed the vice-presidency ten months ago, Gerald R. Ford told newspaper reporters that his faith "is a personal thing. It's not something one shouts from the house-tops or wears on his sleeve. For me, my religious feeling is a deep personal faith I rely on for guidance from my God." Now that he is president, Ford is still reluctant to publicize his faith—but he's not about to hide it, either.

Faced with uncertainties and conflicting reports about his status in the week preceding Richard Nixon's resignation, Ford continued his regular routine, which included a prayer meeting with two of his close friends in the House of Representatives—Albert Quie, a Minnesota Republican, and John Rhodes, House Republican leader, who is from Arizona (the fourth member of the group, former defense secretary Melvin Laird, was not present). Questioned by reporters who were convinced it was a political strategy session, Ford said the prayer meeting was "a very quiet, much off-the-record group." He reportedly assured his three friends that if he were to become president, the meetings—which have been held at 11 a.m. every Wednesday for several months—would continue.

There were other signs of Ford's quiet faith. At the swearing-in ceremony his left hand rested on a family Bible open at Proverbs 3:5, 6, one of the new president's favorite Scripture passages and one that he reportedly repeats nightly as a prayer. On his first Sunday as president, Ford attended Immanuel Church-on-the-Hill (Episcopal), the Fords' family church in the Washington area. (Ford is the nation's tenth Episcopal president). The Ford family arrived at the Alexandria, Virginia, church shortly before the service started and slipped quietly into a back pew. There they heard prayers for the new president—something he'd asked for at his swearing-in ceremony—and a sermon urging parishioners not to "gloat and glower and grimace" over the events of the week.

Ford's request that he be confirmed as president "by your prayers" was typical of the man, say his congressional colleagues. It was, said his closest friend, Congressman Quie (who was listed by some as a vice-presidential possibility), "the real Jerry Ford." The swearing-in speech plus Ford's address to Congress also impressed Oregon Republican John Dellenback, chairman of the House Prayer Breakfast Committee. "There were such easy references to God," said Dellenback. "They weren't strained or laborious speechwriters' references." In the Senate, Iowa's Harold Hughes, who is leaving the Senate this year for full-time Christian work, said of Ford, "There's no doubt he's with it. He's really committed to God." Senator Jennings Randolph, a West Virginia Democrat, added that Ford brings to the presidency "strength of character, belief in God, and a record of family devotion, regular church attendance, and a reliance on our common Creator." Nebraska's Senator Carl Curtis noted that the intensive investigation of Ford after his nomination to the vice-presidency gave him a clean bill of health for honesty, integrity, and ability.

Ford's words, Curtis added, indicate that his thinking "is based on sound Christian doctrine."

But while they are pleased with the new president, many evangelicals in congress are also cautious. Few are willing to go out on a limb regarding Ford's faith; they'd rather he speak for himself. "Let's not make the same mistake we made with President Nixon," said one congressman, who preferred not to be named. "That is, present him as a born-again Christian without really knowing his true commitment." The congressman said that in several speeches to religiously oriented bodies (Ford spoke to the National Religious Broadcasters in January and the Southern Baptist Convention in June) the president had not mentioned "the name of Christ." Arizona Republican John Conlan agreed that evangelicals should tread lightly on the spiritual side of the president's life. "We should let him speak out for himself about his spiritual commitment and relationship rather than others speaking for him. It's wise for a man to give his own testimony."

But if evangelicals expect President Ford to declare himself on national television, say his supporters, they may have a wait. There are dangers that a president closely identified with one group or another might use his association with that group to garner votes, or else be accused of doing so, said Quie. There is also the danger that religious groups would use that association to further their own ends, he added. Ford, he said, is aware that many people are suspicious of such declarations while others want to turn people "into something they're not." For Quie, it is enough that the president "is a man who believes in prayer and doesn't wear his religion on his sleeve."

While some evangelicals in Washington are reluctant to name Ford as a fellow believer—even though they welcome the signs—*Newsweek* magazine and the *New York Times* showed no such hesitancy. In a post-resignation cover story *Newsweek* flatly declared that "like a growing number of Washington figures, Ford is an evangelical Christian." Said the *Times*: "It is widely assumed that [Ford's religious beliefs] embrace the evangelical Christian faith." Similar thoughts were expressed by friends and supporters when Ford became vice president (see December 7, 1973, issue, page 50).[1] At that time also, his son Michael, a 24-year-old student at Gordon-Conwell Seminary in South Hamilton, Massachusetts, described his father as "a man very committed to God" who preferred to show his faith through deeds rather than words.

And the son's faith has been an influence on the father. At a House prayer breakfast earlier this year Ford told his colleagues that he had been strengthened in faith himself by seeing the impact of a strong faith on Mike's life. Said Dellenback: "Normally, influence flows from parent to child. In this case it flowed the other way. [Ford and his wife Betty] were impressed by the way the Lord took a grip on Mike's life." At a prayer meeting in Congress shortly before his father became president, Michael prayed: "Protect him and keep him strong in spirit. ... Grant him the courage to trust in you always and not in the things of this world. Work in his heart ... to seek your guidance and direction in all things."

Meanwhile evangelist Billy Graham called for thankfulness that "the trauma of the past months is passing" and that "a man of the moral caliber of Gerald Ford was waiting in the wings to take over." Graham, along with others, also called for prayer for the former president and his family.

But there were also some backward glimpses. Presbyterian minister John Huffman, formerly pastor of the Presbyterian church that the Nixon family sometimes attended in Key Biscayne, Florida, told newspapers that the Nixon resignation

---

1. "The Ford in Our Future," pages 48–50 in this volume.

was "the very best thing for the nation." He added that Nixon had "lied to the American people and to me personally." Huffman, now pastor of First Presbyterian Church in Pittsburgh, Pennsylvania, said that he was assured by Nixon in personal conversations that the president was "doing everything in his power" to get to the bottom of Watergate. The resignation and disgrace were a tragedy for the family, Huffman declared, "but justice must be served."

At the Southern Baptist Convention's Home Missions Week in Glorieta, New Mexico, some 2,200 heard Nixon's resignation speech and then knelt in prayer for Nixon, Ford, and the nation.

The troubles facing Ford as he assumed office were many. High on the list were inflation, lingering bitterness over Watergate, a shaky Mideast peace, and the crisis in Cyprus. But his congressional prayer colleagues are convinced that President Ford will meet those problems as he has met many others—in prayer and with a quiet faith.

Barrie Doyle and James C. Hefley, "The New President: Prayer and a Quiet Faith," *Christianity Today* 18, No. 23 (August 30, 1974): 33–34.

★ *November 19, 1976* ★

THE MAN FROM PLAINS

DAVID KUCHARSKY

President-elect Jimmy Carter has supplied historians and political analysts with a question they can debate for a long time: Was his narrow victory aided by his outspokenness about his Christian faith, or was he chosen in spite of it?

Not since President Kennedy became the first Roman Catholic to be elected chief executive (1960) has there been a comparable religious issue in an American political campaign. Many voters said they were put off by Carter's references to his personal Christian beliefs and experiences. These complaints were countered by the argument that political office ought not to be denied to anyone on those grounds any more than it is denied to someone because of Catholic ties.

Some evangelicals cheered Carter on, while other evangelicals harbored suspicions that he regarded their terminology as a political asset. Actually, he seldom talked about religion on his own initiative during the campaign. However, he readily answered questions about his faith. In one such exchange, the now famous *Playboy* interview, Carter tried to deal with the charge of self-righteousness and wound up using a couple of vulgar terms that were generally believed to have cost him many votes.

Carter also lost both evangelical and Catholic votes because, although he says he personally opposes abortion and does not want government to support it, he opposes a constitutional amendment to ban abortions.

Carter will be the third Baptist to become president in American history (the others were Truman and Harding). He has been a member of the Southern Baptist church in his home town, Plains, Georgia, since he was eleven years old. His mother says he was baptized on a Sunday evening after he had responded to an invitation during revival services conducted at the church by a visiting evangelist the previous week. *Christian Life* magazine has quoted him as saying, "I recited the necessary steps of acknowledging my sinfulness, of repentance and asking Jesus to enter into my heart and life as Lord and Saviour."

Carter grew up in a small community just outside Plains. He and his wife have lived in Plains since he got out of the Navy in the mid-fifties. The town is just south of a now abandoned settlement that appears on historical maps as the Plains of Dura. That name appears in the third chapter of Daniel as the place where Nebuchadnezzar set up his image of gold (which Shadrach, Meshach, and Abednego refused to worship and so were cast into a furnace). A Georgia historian who recently compiled a book on place names says his research failed to turn up any reason why that name was chosen.

Carter has always been a faithful church-goer and has served as a deacon. While attending the Naval Academy at Annapolis he taught a class of junior girls in a local Baptist church. Later he conducted services on a submarine at sea. He has also taught the men's class in the Plains church many times.

Carter has said much about a spiritual experience he had a decade or so ago. At that time he confessed a number of personal shortcomings and began to read the Bible and pray much more regularly. The experience also left him with a desire to engage in Christian witnessing, and he made trips north to help establish new churches under the aegis of the Southern Baptist Home Missions Board. Carter has credited his sister, Ruth Stapleton, with helping him to come to grips with spiritual realities. Mrs. Stapleton travels widely in a spiritual counseling ministry.

David Kucharsky, "The Man from Plains," *Christianity Today* 21, No. 4 (November 19, 1976): 49.

FAITH, VIRTUE, AND HONOR ARE NOT ENOUGH: JIMMY CARTER IS NO HARRY TRUMAN

The world is too complicated to substitute good intentions for experience.

JOHN B. ANDERSON

D espite the appealing image that President Jimmy Carter has tried to cultivate—of being open and candid and honest—doubt lingers as to how well he lives up to his own standards. Maybe they are impossibly high, but by proclaiming them so strongly, Carter should have expected to be judged harshly. The question is: How hard does he try?

Perhaps Jimmy Carter has not been president long enough, but it might be useful to try to put him in historical perspective. Let's look first at the campaign of 1976.

As a candidate, Jimmy Carter was criticized—roundly and rightly, I believe—for being vague on the issues. It may be that he was not sufficiently well-informed or even sufficiently concerned to take strong positions. More charitably, you might speculate that he deliberately side-stepped controversy in the interests of continuing the post-Watergate healing process that Gerald Ford had nobly begun.

Whatever the motivation, the result was that Carter soft-pedaled ideology and instead appealed for support on the basis of that more amorphous quality he liked to call "character." He consciously tried to subordinate substance to style. It is hard to remember, looking back, what major philosophical positions he took, what clear programmatic commitments he made—or even where, in general, he seemed to place himself on the political spectrum. On the other hand, it is easy to recall the personal image he projected: the soft-spoken Georgian outsider tilting with the Washington Goliath; a leader "as good as the American people"; our own latter-day George Washington who would never tell a lie.

If his purpose were simply to emerge as the least objectionable candidate and paper over party divisions, he could not have devised a better strategy. Avoiding specifics, he avoided giving offense. The constituency he cultivated was oriented to Jimmy Carter the man, rather than to any set of ideas, plans, and goals that he represented.

Now, I have no objection to a candidate selling himself on the basis of his innate virtue and honor; indeed, I wish there were more to go around. But although virtue and honor have their place and constitute a necessary consideration in electing a president, they are, in and of themselves, hardly sufficient.

The world is too complicated and precarious to be led by those who think good intentions are a reasonable substitute for knowledge and experience. The patience of our citizens is tried enough as it is to be governed by leaders who require on-the-job training in the massive and mysterious ways of the federal government. I'm all for fresh faces and new blood, but, really: The task is so challenging, you have to get off to a running start if you intend to have any impact.

Yet I can understand the public mood that propelled the one-term Georgia governor to the highest office in our land. It was a mood that had soured on politicians who seem to know and promise too much. Issue-oriented campaigns like those of Goldwater and McGovern held unpleasant memories of ideological wrangling. Too specific and aggressive in their platforms, they antagonized as many voters as they attracted. As for the Hubert Humphreys and Gerald Fords, they were perceived, however unfairly, to be shop-worn apologists for any despised thing a voter associated with Washington.

Moreover, the credibility gap that had plagued administrations of both parties during the previous decade cheapened the very value of platforms and promises: They didn't seem to be kept very often. In 1964, candidate Lyndon Johnson affected to be practically a peace-nik compared to his opponent. But shortly into his new term he plunged this nation into its most disastrous episode of war. Richard Nixon some years later campaigned on his unimpeachable record of anticommunism, and then, safely elected, announced to the world one night that he had decided to go to Peking and propose toasts to Chairman Mao.

Given the rapid pace of events in the third quarter of the twentieth century, it is possible voters found themselves hoping that false promises would not be made, that the president would preserve for himself the flexibility to examine each situation anew and adapt to changing circumstances. Finally, Americans had developed such a mainstream of values and policies that, to many, the critical concern about a candidate was not his stand on particular issues but more intangible things, such as his leadership ability or his trustworthiness. All in all, the electorate was left by

1976 not a little susceptible to candidates who were "fuzzy" on the issues, yet righteous in their rhetoric.

Jimmy Carter sensed this mood and exploited it well. In fact, he even went to the trouble of developing two quite different images to suit the new public mood. One conveyed competence, the ability to run the government efficiently and decisively; the other conveyed character, the ability to run it honestly and morally. He struck at times the pose of the competent manager: the Annapolis graduate who understood discipline, the nuclear engineer conversant in the detail and complexity of policy problems, the successful businessman who knew how to make decisions and meet a payroll. At other times Jimmy Carter could have been mistaken for a Baptist preacher: sprung up from the red clay of Georgia, heir to the homespun wisdom of a small-time farmer, just regular straight-and-narrow plain folk, making speeches from the stump that sounded like sermons from the pulpit.

If the public wasn't sure what specifics Carter stood for, one or another of those general images was apparently enough to convince it he could be president. After an era of worldly and sophisticated types at the White House who still managed to go so wrong, the romantic notion of the American presidency had again become appealing: that all it takes to run the country is common sense and hard work. That, of course, is why Truman has enjoyed such a revival. Lest Jimmy Carter lose a chance to bathe in reflected glory, you may remember that one of our new president's first official acts was to recall from the Truman Library in Independence, Missouri, that famous desk plate that says, "The Buck Stops Here." It is reminiscent of the none-too-subtle way Richard Nixon once compared himself to a famous predecessor: When Watergate was at its height, and Nixon was coming under unceasing attack, he volunteered the analysis that

Abraham Lincoln had been maligned in his day, too. Regrettably, this did not in truth make Nixon a Lincoln, nor is Jimmy Carter necessarily a Harry Truman.

Nonetheless, from the outset of his presidency, Carter behaved boldly, as though the comparison and confidence were deserved. It was the preacher and political activist in him coming out. He had not run for two long years to be president only to arrive at the White House and sit on the Truman balcony.

For all his previous fuzziness on the issues, it turned out Carter had a huge agenda tucked away in his coat pocket. He took it out, turned to Congress, and demanded immediate action. Among other things he wanted: national health insurance, welfare reform, an energy package that even Santa Claus couldn't deliver, civil service reform, extensive reorganization of the Executive Branch, wholesale reforms of the tax code he had called a "disgrace to the human race," hospital cost-containment, and a streamlining of Pentagon operations that would save the country a promised $8 billion.

Never mind if these proposals were only half-developed or still in the conception stage, or if they were delivered to Congress with amazing naïveté about what it takes to get something passed in that complex, independent body. It should have surprised no one that the president found himself stalled on major fronts. And for having raised expectations so unrealistically high, respect for his performance plummeted all the more. He only slowly learned the need for compromise—let alone the art of it—and his relations with the Congress have often been in disrepair. His standing in the polls has been at times an embarrassment to the country as well as to the president himself.

It is one thing when the president acts this way on the domestic front; the damage can be limited because the Congress acts as a check and balance. In foreign affairs, however, where the president serves as our one spokesman, the damage can be much more severe and less reversible.

The litany of missteps is long and familiar: the confused and indelicate handling of Mideast matters, which has been overcome at strategic points largely because the countries involved are strong and independent enough to make progress on their own; the costly battles with the Senate over Panama and the F-15 sale to Saudi Arabia, which might have been averted by more adroit Congressional relations; the abortive Anglo-American initiatives in Rhodesia; the fiasco of our nonpolicy toward Ethiopia and Somalia in the Horn of Africa; the quarrels with Japan over trade and with Pakistan over nuclear reprocessing; the blunt announcement of a timetable for Korean withdrawal, unnerving allies who hadn't been consulted; and our dangerously unstable relations with the Soviet Union—and, in their trail, uncertain prospects for a timely, fair, and meaningful agreement on strategic arms limitations. Even the much-touted administration success in lifting the Turkish arms embargo was achieved more in spite of, than because of, the president's efforts, considering that on this issue Republicans were his mainstay, and fellow Democrats his leading antagonists.

The pattern in these cases is distressingly similar: Carter, the moralist, receives a revelation, hands it down uncompromisingly, and is startled when it is rebuffed. He then starts over at square one, having lost valuable time, as well as the advantage.

Perhaps the classic example of this modus operandi in foreign affairs was his early lecturing on human rights, which, admirable as its motivation, turned out to have been conducted in such a public and sanctimonious way as to provoke the pride of the offenders, cause hardening of positions, and in the end proved counterproductive. Carter's actions, more ideological than

practical, confirmed the age-old paradox that the best is sometimes the enemy of the good. Our black-and-white perceptions
of right and wrong are not always shared universally, and to try
to impose American standards on countries of widely varying
circumstances itself raises moral questions. It's true that much
of the American public seemed in the last election to have soured
on too much Kissinger-like realpolitik. Americans yearned for
more undiluted morality in our foreign policy. This showed up
in the responsive chord that both Carter and Reagan struck in
seeming to take strong ideological stands on such issues as human
rights and the Panama Canal. People do like to stand for something, and it is much more exciting to talk boldly than in a wishy-
washy, though practical, way. And it is much more satisfying to
the conscience.

But look at it another way. If we're really determined to be
so perfectly moral, why is there no greater public outcry raised
against continued deployment of tens of thousands of troops in
Korea serving to defend the repressive regime of President Park?
Why do we prop up Mobutu in Zaire with economic and military
aid, or Baby Doc in Haiti, or Somoza in Nicaragua? For that matter,
if we want to make an unambiguous moral statement, why not
just unilaterally disarm this very moment?

Of course, the reason in all these cases is that foreign policy
issues, like most situations, are complex and have to be judged in
context rather than in isolation. America has many interests, and
they all have to be assigned a certain importance and weighed one
against the other. Opinions may differ on what policy is proper
in those particular cases, but reasonable people should be of one
mind that the decisions at the bottom line should be balanced.
They cannot be dictated by any absolute standard. I believe
that President Carter has come around to this viewpoint. I will
credit him with this: He's a good learner. It is unfortunate that

the Administration has had to learn its lessons at the expense of the leadership our nation has urgently needed for two years.

Indeed, Carter's greatest success on the foreign affairs front, the Camp David agreements, is testimony to how far the president has come around in terms of his diplomatic style and perspective, and a vindication of the approach favored by his predecessors. It is hard to remember at this point how severely he once criticized the quiet and personalistic diplomacy of Henry Kissinger, so much does he seem now to have emulated it, certainly in the instances of his success. With respect to Mideast peace, the discovery should not have been unexpected: Having first tried to impose grand American designs and exert public pressure on the sensitive parties, he finally realized that the most effective way to resolve problems is simply to let the parties negotiate for themselves, though the president can still perform a key role in getting them together and, in a low-key way, offering them options.

Jimmy Carter is a good man; I respect him. But the problem is that he is too conscious of his image, and, unfortunately, hasn't decided what kind of image to project. The unhappy result for both him and his country is that he sometimes exemplifies two very different personalities, alternating between one of excessive moralism, and one that represents politics-as-usual, when he seems to suspend his proudest virtues. We are left to wonder: Why not choose a more down-to-earth middle ground? Say what you mean, and mean what you say. For a decent man, morality at that point will only come naturally.

John B. Anderson is Republican Congressman
from Rockford, Illinois.

John B. Anderson, "Faith, Virtue, and Honor Are Not Enough," *Christianity Today* 23, No. 3 (November 3, 1978): 14–15.

RONALD W. REAGAN

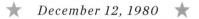 *December 12, 1980*

JUST BECAUSE
REAGAN HAS WON ...

The battle for righteous and sane government is not over.

THE EDITORS

Who won the November 4 election? We hope the American people did, and that the entire world will benefit. Ronald Reagan is president-elect of all Americans, not just of evangelicals. He gained that office by the votes of a majority of American people, not just of evangelicals. And not all evangelicals voted for Mr. Reagan. Many opted for Mr. Carter or Mr. Anderson. But the people have spoken; for better or worse, Ronald Reagan is the next president—of us all. What is the significance of a Reagan presidency for evangelicals? No doubt that question can be answered better four years hence. But we can take stock now, and begin to prepare for the coming days.

We must acknowledge an important role played by Jerry Falwell, Pat Robertson, James Robison, and other representatives of organizations representing politically conservative segments of evangelicalism. We commend them for getting Christians to register and vote; these are clear Christian duties. For the first time in half a century, evangelicals generally became involved in a national election. They registered, took sides, worked actively to select candidates they preferred, and voted their choice. And the politically conservative evangelical vote was significant. Particularly in the South and in contests below the level of presidency their votes sometimes proved decisive.

Having said this, however, we must caution politically conservative evangelicals against taking too much credit for the outcome of the election. American evangelicals are a minority in a pluralistic society. Certainly conservatives among them could not alone have elected Mr. Reagan. He had to draw on other groups as well. He came to power partly because he increasingly took a moderate stand, allaying fear that he was an extremist.

One segment of a small minority cannot win and hold the people. Conservative evangelicals must take this fact into account as they plan their future strategies. They must neither expect nor encourage Mr. Reagan to adopt a dogmatic, uncompromising stand on all positions of deep concern to them. While we may hope and pray that he will serve as a committed evangelical, we must remember that to prove effective, he must work as president of the entire nation.

Mr. Reagan himself must seek to move people by persuasion and not by force. He must seek as broad a consensus as possible. If he cannot do this, he will only generate a backlash. And evangelicals will be discredited along with him.

In our pluralistic society, the key to evangelical power lies in its careful use. Evangelicals must be wary of the temptation to abuse it. If they try to do more than they can or ought, they will soon lose their credibility and whatever momentum they now possess.

But we commend them in this political involvement. They functioned as responsible citizens seeking to further the cause of public morality in a pluralistic democracy. Leaders within the National Council of Churches and other politically liberal religious groups were unjustified in charging that conservative evangelicals were wrong to mix religion and politics.

Whatever separation of church and state means, it clearly does not mean that all people with religious and moral convictions are disqualified from participating in the political process. Certainly evangelicals have the right, even the duty, to speak out on moral issues; and some moral issues also become political issues. Setting aside for the moment whether Moral Majority and other religious groups may at times have overstepped the legitimate sphere of church and Christian ministry, we support their recognition that some moral and religious issues must be fought for in the political arena.

At the same time, we must caution politically conservative evangelicals against any taint of triumphalism. The battle for righteous and sane government has not been finally won. On the contrary, right-wing evangelicals must prepare themselves for a let-down as evil forces continue to show their clout in government; scandals are not all in the past—nor are imprudent, unstatesman-like decisions. It is important to guard against disillusionment leading to a cynicism that could once again deprive society of evangelical moral influence. The doctrine of separation of church and state does not support the theory that politics is so evil that biblical Christians should withdraw from it altogether. If evangelicals expect too much too soon, they may once again become disenchanted and withdraw; that would be a disastrous step backward.

We live in a sinful society that includes many who freely reject Christ, but whose views still must be heard because they are citizens. God is not going to work miracles just because of Christian influence in or on the White House. Conservative evangelicals must not place their hope in a "quick fix." Mr. Reagan will not bring the millennium to America, nor will he restore an imaginary golden age of an earlier day. We should neither expect nor demand this. The wheels of state grind very slowly. It is not humanly possible to change a social structure overnight. Immense pressures will be placed on Ronald Reagan, and on occasion he will yield. Some compromises are necessary and wise; evangelical Christians should prepare to accept them. Other compromises are harmful. The wisdom of American evangelicals will become evident as they learn when to work with and support a president who makes compromises for the common good, and when to stand up and be counted in opposition because that boundary of the common good has been crossed.

Further, it is clear that one grand splurge on a presidential race every four years is useless. Evangelicals must set themselves to a rigorous agenda for the next ten years. First, they must seek to win people to Christ and to the moral and spiritual values essential for right judgments in matters relating to the good of human kind. They may be at the cutting edge of a great reversal of moral trends in America, but for the better part of a century they have not provided political leadership in the United States. Once again they are moving back into the mainstream of the political life of America. But today they are novices. They need to learn how to apply their high moral values honestly and intelligently to the world scene.

In God's providence, evangelicals are a growing body. If they were small they could shrug off responsibility for the direction of the ship of state, for there would be no possibility of effecting change. With their steady growth over the last several decades their opportunity—and responsibility—for the destiny of this nation became correspondingly greater. If they choose unintelligent, uninformed, misguided leaders, they will have to answer to God. If the American government makes unwise laws, evangelicals will have had a decisive voice in making them and must be held responsible.

Clearly, the growing political and social responsibility requires of evangelicals a corresponding political and social education so they can function as mature citizens. They must develop a basic Christian world-and-life view out of which will stem a consistent political and social philosophy of life. No doubt they will make many mistakes. They must, for example, avoid being drawn into "single issue" voting. The folly of this became evident in the unfortunate support of officeholders whose voting record fit the litmus test of a few select items, but who proved themselves unworthy for office by their dishonesty and disgusting sexual offenses. Evangelicals need far greater sophistication in their political action. Certainly they need to make plain they are not seeking a theocratic kingdom or a return to the Massachusetts Bay Colony of three centuries ago. Fortunately, even the most extreme right among conservative evangelicals have stressed their commitment to basic freedoms.

Again, evangelicals cannot allow themselves to be used as the tool of any particular party or candidate—whether from right, left, or middle. They must maintain their own integrity so they may be free to provide a moral and spiritual critique of all parties and all candidates.

And if the church as church and its ministers as ministers limit their emphasis to those political issues that involve moral and spiritual values, they can expect their voices to be heard and to be received with far greater effect. They must avoid pronouncing on every issue, particularly where they have no special expertise.

Evangelicals must also be careful not to neglect key issues they have stood for in the past. If they display an indifference to the rights of minority groups, to freedoms of speech and press and religion, to civil rights, and to just treatment of the poor, their moral hypocrisy will be evident. The Bible addresses itself to such issues, and so binds the evangelical conscience to serve God here. Moreover, if they fail to emphasize these broader requirements for just government, aligning themselves instead with only a few select issues, their very failure will draw just criticism to their position, and drive away many who see this inconsistency.

But if evangelicals seek the whole counsel of the God of Abraham, Isaac, and Jacob—and of our Lord Jesus Christ—they stand on the threshold of great opportunities that may never again open up in our generation.

The Editors, "Just Because Reagan Has Won ..." *Christianity Today* 24, No. 21 (December 12, 1980): 14–15.

★ *February 20, 1987* ★

TOO GOOD TO TRUST

RODNEY CLAPP

The Iran-*contra* scandal has demonstrated once again the strength of one aspect of America's constitutional government that is perhaps most congruent with biblical revelation: The Constitution's careful system of checks and balances indicates its profound suspicion of the accumulation of power by fallible human beings, however decent they may be.

Similarly, biblical narrative is unflinching in its depiction of power's potential to mislead even the best of leaders—consider Kings Saul, David, and Solomon, all shown in their shame as well as in their glory. Biblically understood, sin is pervasive, and all persons are subject to self-deception. Jesus said men prefer darkness to the light. And Paul, in Romans 1, called attention to the human inertia toward proud illusion rather than humble reality.

In a democracy, popularity and power are synonymous, and Ronald Reagan has been nothing if not popular. The "Reagan magic" and "Teflon presidency" are results of Mr. Reagan's popularity. Polls showed nearly 70 percent of the population has approved of his presidency.

And even in late December, when journalists and politicos inside Washington's Beltway were very near hysteria over the Iran-*contra* debacle, a majority of Americans continued to regard Ronald Reagan as a basically decent and trustworthy man.

Ironically, there is evidence that the Iran-*contra* affair unfolded largely due to the power that popularity afforded members of the Reagan administration. Lt. Col. Oliver North's activism on behalf of the *contras* was raising eyebrows as early as 1984 (he was then soliciting funds from private American sources). But congressional investigation of North ended when it garnered no public support and was stonewalled by the administration.

Rep. Michael D. Barnes (D. Md.) suggests that failure made North and his colleagues believe "they were immune," facilitating the development of the Iran-*contra* connection. Stansfield Turner, former director of the Central Intelligence Agency, agrees: "It was the popularity of the president that deterred the oversight committees and the press from pursuing the issue."

In short, some people in the Reagan administration were reckless and emboldened because Mr. Reagan has such a solid reputation and political base. Colloquially speaking, their power went to their heads. The Iran-*contra* scandal is a painful but valuable reminder that:

- We all have mixed motives, however noble our causes.

- We tend to overestimate our innate goodness, and with it the rightness of whatever we undertake.

- We cannot really trust ourselves, and need a check on our abilities to rationalize our abuse of power.

In the end, the Reagan administration is learning an out-and-out theological lesson: we must be saved even from ourselves.

Rodney Clapp, "Too Good to Trust," *Christianity Today* 31, No. 3 (February 20, 1987): 15–17.

February 17, 1989

WHITE HOUSE RELIGION

Is there more to George Bush's faith than
public prayers and church attendance?

KIM A. LAWTON

"Heavenly Father, we bow our heads and thank you for your
love. Accept our thanks for the peace that yields this day
and the shared faith that makes its continuance likely.
Make us strong to do your work, willing to heed and hear
your will, and write on our hearts these words: Use power
to help people. For we are given power not to advance our
own purposes, nor to make a great show in the world, nor a
name. There is but one just use of power, and it is to serve
people. Help us remember, Lord. Amen."

—A prayer offered by George Bush at the beginning of
his inaugural speech, January 20, 1989

M any evangelicals who once thought President George
Bush's proclamations of faith may have been politically
motivated are now warming to the notion of a genuinely Christian
president. And as the Bush administration takes shape, many
Christians will be watching closely to see how—or if—Bush's religious beliefs will affect his policy making.

"NEVER ANY DOUBT"

Bush never used to talk openly or easily about his religious beliefs. In an interview with *Christianity Today* last fall, Bush said his faith "has been very personal." Yet, in the same interview, he asserted that "there was never any doubt that Jesus Christ was my Savior and Lord" (*CT*, Sept. 16, 1988, p. 40).

While many politicians stop talking about their religion after they are elected, Bush has seemed to increase his public discussion of religious matters. On the day following his election, he told reporters he and his wife had gone to church that morning because "God's help is absolutely essential."

Similarly, during last month's inaugural events, the Bushes scheduled both private and public worship services, and Bush proclaimed the Sunday following his inauguration a national day of prayer. During his inaugural speech, Bush said that his first act as president would be a prayer (see above).

The Bushes have followed through with their stated intention to attend church every Sunday. The family, lifelong Episcopalians, generally rotate worship at several Episcopal churches in the Washington area, but they have also visited other churches, including a black Baptist church. The Bushes have said they will not allow security precautions to hamper their worship pattern, and, indeed, Barbara Bush told one television interviewer that she believes one of her duties as First Lady is to "get my husband to church."

Billy Graham, who has been a close personal friend of the president and his family for more than 25 years, believes Bush's faith is "strong and genuine." Graham told *Christianity Today*, "I've had prayer with him many times and discussed spiritual things with his whole family on a number of occasions."

Bush has included other Christians in the leadership of his administration. Vice President Dan Quayle and his wife have regularly attended McLean Presbyterian Church in northern Virginia and are considered evangelicals. Mrs. Quayle has been part of a Bible study along with Joanne Kemp, wife of Secretary of Housing and Urban Development Jack Kemp, and Susan Baker, wife of Secretary of State James Baker. In addition to the Quayles, two Cabinet members, Kemp and Labor Secretary Elizabeth Hanford Dole, have been outspoken about their evangelical beliefs.

FAITH AND PUBLIC POLICY

While many Americans might concede that faith is a good thing for the nation's highest leader, determining how that faith is worked out may be more complicated. Robert Maddox, speech writer and religious liaison for President Jimmy Carter—a president who was very open about his born-again Christian faith—said a deep personal faith has many benefits for a president. "The personal strength that he can gain from his faith—from his own study of the Scripture, from his prayer life, from his own walk with the Lord—can bring great strength and a sense that he is not walking alone," Maddox said.

Maddox noted how the Bible can "push the president to think about human problems in biblical terms. Mr. Carter did that, and it came out in a public way in his commitment to human rights, and in other quiet ways that frequently affected domestic and foreign policy."

However, Maddox said deep faith can also pose difficulties for political leaders. "Presidents can wear their religion on their sleeve too much ... and polarize people," he said. "Politicians always have the subtle temptation to use their religion to make it look like God is on their side."

James Skillen, executive director of the Association for Public Justice, also cautions that a Christian president could end up pushing a "civil religion" where "God is the nationalistic god of the American republic."

Skillen said Christian citizens need to take more care in distinguishing between how a person performs the duties of office and how he confesses his faith in office. "Christians should be far more astute in looking at how George Bush is going to set his priorities, how he's going to work on them, and at his agenda, regardless of what he says about his faith," Skillen said. "Judge him on those deeds and not so much on how he wraps [religious] language around it."

Bob Dugan, director of the National Association of Evangelicals' Washington Office on Public Affairs, said his concern is "that people may read too much by way of assumption into a statement of personal faith. A personal faith in Christ does not necessarily imply any particular political position, or, as in the case of Jimmy Carter and abortion, that he would be willing to translate personal conviction into political conviction." In the case of George Bush, Dugan said, "We're still going to have to look at his individual policies and see how he translates the personal faith into his political convictions."

In making such translations, Maddox advises Bush to go to Scripture. "I would like some sense that Mr. Bush struggles with the biblical mandates about the poor and the hungry and the widow and the orphan, that he struggles with the concepts of war and peace," Maddox said.

Skillen urges the president to "learn to call on others with whom he could pray, with whom he could get encouragement." Dugan suggests that Bush place an evangelical at the top level of his staff in the White House. In addition, Dugan advises Bush to continue with regular church worship. He said he was "always disappointed" that Reagan did not attend church.

Some evangelicals remain skeptical about how Bush's faith will be worked out, but evangelist Graham said he is confident "it will have a great influence." Said Graham, "[Bush] desperately wants to see the moral values of this country restored and implemented, and when he says he wants to see a kinder, gentler nation, it means he wants to reach out to the people who feel discriminated against and the homeless and the poor."

Kim A. Lawton, "White House Religion," *Christianity Today* 33, No. 3 (February 17, 1989): 36–37.

September 24, 1990

AM-BUSHED?

Where is the president who campaigned on
traditional values when we need him most?

LYN CRYDERMAN

T he George Bush we have seen lately looks a lot different from
the one we saw in 1988. *That* George Bush campaigned heavily on traditional moral values, the family, and a "kinder, gentler"
America—stuff most Americans love to hear. For evangelicals,
that kind of talk worked: 80 percent of us voted for him. Now
we are not so sure where Mr. Bush stands on the issues he at one
time thought were important to us.

Exhibit A. On the issue of abortion, the president has gone from
being a vocal opponent to a timid observer. He seems satisfied
with the views of Vice President Quayle and Republican National
Committee Chairman Lee Atwater that the Republican tent is big
enough to include strong prochoicers. As Fred Barnes observes in
the *New Republic*, Mr. Bush says his views haven't changed, but
cannot bring himself to say what those views are. True, he vetoed
legislation that would have expanded federal funding for abortions, but as acting RNC spokesman Charlie Black admitted on
"Face the Nation," "The prolife plank of Mr. Bush's party is merely
a gesture toward the prolife position." The brave, moral leadership we were told to expect on this issue just hasn't been there.

Exhibit B. To help celebrate the signing of the Hate Crimes Bill, our president made history by inviting prominent gay-rights activists to participate. With the White House doors finally opened to those who would like to see all restrictions to a homosexual lifestyle eliminated, it was not surprising that gay-rights activists attended yet another high-level White House function last month. From a president who courted evangelicals with warm words about the family, this landmark invitation is both puzzling and alarming.

Exhibit C. Okay, we shouldn't beat up on the president for finally admitting he will have to raise taxes. A Democratic-controlled Congress would never have given him the budget cuts he wanted. But his flip-flop on this issue makes us wonder if we misread his lips about other things—like Exhibit D.

Exhibit D. We really wonder just how kind and gentle this land will be if Mr. Bush gets his way at the budget summit. One of the proposals is to seriously scale back (or even eliminate) the tax deduction for charitable giving. Much of that charitable giving helps pay for many of the "thousand points of light" he held up as an inspiration during his campaign.

In fairness, Mr. Bush has shown occasional flashes of his old campaign self. His appointments to the FCC and the Department of Health and Human Services, his vow to veto a forthcoming child-care bill if it threatens religious day care, and his accessibility to evangelical leaders all give us reason to hope. But the momentum seems to be in the other direction.

Mr. Bush apparently learned our language to ensure our vote. Although that is disappointing, our yearning for a president who would stand up to attacks on the family, the unborn, and the church made us ripe for the picking.

The lesson to learn from all this is that in the world of hardball politics, pragmatic pressures are fierce, and idealism and principle sometimes get left behind. We can no longer afford to be naive.

At the same time, we must remember that the game Mr. Bush is playing is not the only one in town. The church is still best at lighting the way where darkness prevails. No president or platform can do it for us, and we would do well to remember this whenever we are tempted to let George do it.

Lyn Cryderman, "Am-Bushed?" *Christianity Today* 34, No. 13 (September 24, 1990): 16–17.

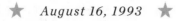 *August 16, 1993*

WHY CLINTON IS NOT ANTICHRIST

PHILIP YANCEY

I've not yet heard anyone call Bill Clinton the Antichrist, but it wouldn't surprise me. Not since John Kennedy has a president caused such alarm in evangelical churches. (Remember the scary bestseller, *If America Elects a Catholic President*?)

Ironically, Bill Clinton is a lifelong Southern Baptist who can knowledgeably discuss the doctrines of original sin and justification by faith. He attends church, speaks warmly of his long friendship with Billy Graham, and points to the Graham crusade in Little Rock as a life-changing event for him as a teenager. Even so, evangelicals opposed his candidacy by a wide margin and have raised strident voices against his policies.

"I just have the feeling the country's headed in the wrong direction," said one friend of mine. Many share her uneasiness, for reasons that go far beyond Bill Clinton. The crime rate in 1960 was about 15 percent of the current rate. Promiscuity—in sex, drugs, violence, materialism—has become the spirit of the age. The United States can be considered a "Christian nation" only in the loosest sense. "God will turn his back on America," said my friend, shaking her head sadly.

All this concern about "the decline of America" got me wondering how much attention God pays to national boundaries.

Does God really judge the United States or any other country *as a national entity*? I have often heard this verse quoted as a formula for national revival: "If my people, who are called by my name, will humble themselves and pray and seek my face and turn from their wicked ways, then will I hear from heaven and will forgive their sin and will heal their land" (2 Chron. 7:14, NIV). Yet that promise was given as part of God's covenantal relationship with the ancient Hebrews; its occasion was the dedication of Solomon's temple, God's dwelling place. Have we any reason to assume God has a similar covenant with the U.S.A.?

Certainly the Old Testament shows God dealing with national entities: the prophets called down judgment on Israel and Judah, as well as Philistia and Babylon. But the New Testament seems to introduce a major shift. Jesus stressed "the kingdom of heaven" as the central focus of God's activity, a kingdom that transcends national boundaries and permeates society so as to affect the whole gradually, like salt sprinkled on meat.

Pentecost got the new kingdom off to a rousing international start, an Ethiopian eunuch soon spread it into Africa, and before long a man named Paul declared himself "apostle to the Gentiles." Paul cared deeply about individual churches in Galatia, Ephesus, Corinth, and Rome, but I find no indication that he gave any thought to a "Christianized" Roman Empire. The Revelation of John continues the pattern: that book records specific messages to seven churches but dismisses the political entity of what many conclude was Rome as "Babylon the great, the mother of prostitutes and of the abominations of the earth" (17:5, NIV).

A WORLD OF FUGITIVES

Some historians argue that the church loses sight of its mission as it moves closer to the seat of power. Witness the era of Constantine or Europe just before the Reformation. We may be seeing history repeat itself. In 1991, as communism fell in Poland, 70 percent of Poles approved of the Catholic church as a moral and spiritual force. Now only 40 percent approve, mainly because of the church's "interference" in politics. Modern Poland does not practice church/state separation: a new law says radio and TV broadcasts must "respect the Christian system of values," and the state funds the teaching of Catholicism in public schools. Yet the coziness between church and government has led to a loss of respect for the church.

At various points in U.S. history (the 1850s, the time of Prohibition, and most recently the Moral Majority movement of the 1980s), the Christian church has marked an ascendancy into politics. Now, it appears, the church and politics may be heading in different directions. I, for one, feel no great sense of alarm over that fact. Our real challenge, the focus of our energy, should not be to Christianize the United States (always a losing battle) but rather to strive to be Christ's church in an increasingly hostile world. As Karl Barth said, "[The church] exists ... to set up in the world a new sign which is radically dissimilar to [the world's] own manner and which contradicts it in a way which is full of promise."

If indeed the United States is sliding down a slippery moral slope, that may better allow the church to set up "a new sign ... which is full of promise." Already I see evidence of that trend. Last spring a cover story in *The Atlantic Monthly* concluded that "Dan Quayle Was Right" about the grievously harmful effects of single-parent families. Meanwhile, sociologist Robert Bellah, after interviewing hundreds of married couples, identified evangelical Christians as the only group who could articulate a reason for marriage commitments that went beyond selfish interests.

"In a world of fugitives," said T. S. Eliot, "the person taking the opposite direction will appear to run away." It would be pleasant, I must admit, to live in a country where the majority of people followed the Ten Commandments, acted with civility toward one another, and bowed heads once a day for a nonpartisan prayer. There is much to be said for the social atmosphere of the 1950s. But if that environment does not return, I won't lose any sleep. As America slides, I will work and pray for the kingdom of God. If the gates of hell cannot prevail against the church, the current political scene has little chance of impeding its advance.

Philip Yancey, "Why Clinton Is Not Antichrist," *Christianity Today* 37, No. 9 (August 16, 1993): 72.

★ *April 25, 1994* ★

HOW TO CONFRONT A PRESIDENT

CHARLES COLSON

A t this year's National Religious Broadcasters convention, the most talked-about topic was what evangelicals' attitude should be toward President Clinton. Through the centuries, no question has been more vexing for Christians than how to confront the state—whether in the first century, when believers paid with their lives for refusing to bow to Caesar, or in the Middle Ages, when the church shamelessly married the state. The question is being debated anew by evangelicals today in a simmering controversy that threatens to divide our ranks.

In one corner are politically moderate evangelicals who charge conservatives with leveling nothing but harsh criticism against President Clinton—even stooping to personal attacks on him and his family. Conservatives fire back that moderates, enjoying unaccustomed access, are a bit too cozy with the White House and are forsaking their prophetic role, especially regarding homosexuality and abortion. Some evangelicals have pronounced a plague on both houses; they call us to forsake the political arena and stick to our spiritual knitting.

Clearly, evangelicals need to step back and regroup around basic biblical principles. What are those principles?

First and most obviously for Christians: there is never an excuse for disrespect. The Bible commands us to "fear God, honor the king," to pray for "all those in authority." The reason we pray, Paul tells Timothy, is so that they may rule well and we may live peaceably. It has nothing to do with whether they are Democrats or Republicans, or whether we voted for them. How can Christians encourage fellow citizens to respect authority if we ourselves do not show the utmost civility?

Admittedly, on the evangelical fringes some have fallen short of this high standard and should repent. None of us should be above examining our own conscience. I confess to my own private indiscretions—jokes and jabs.

But does civility mean silence—or even withdrawal from politics? No. As Augustine taught, Christians should be "the best of citizens." What does it mean to be model citizens in our day, when many of the administration's policies run contrary to our deepest beliefs?

In the 1980s, the duties of citizenship seemed easy since much of our agenda was embraced by national leaders. But no longer. Take the abortion issue. President Clinton's policies have been consistently pro-choice. On the twentieth anniversary of *Roe v. Wade*, he rescinded all executive orders restricting abortion access. Recently his administration announced that all abortions resulting from rape and incest would henceforth be defined as "medically necessary," to be covered by Medicaid. With a stroke of the pen, the federal government overrode the laws of all the states that prohibit or limit taxpayer funding of abortion. So how can we resist "the king" while still honoring him?

Consider the teaching of Samuel Rutherford, a seventeenth-century Scottish cleric. Rutherford wrote a passionate treatise entitled *Lex, Rex* challenging the divine right of kings, contending that the law stands above the king. Rutherford's analysis rested on the crucial distinction between the office of the magistrate and the person of the magistrate. Christians are commanded to respect the office, he wrote; but if the person acts contrary to God's law, Christians have a duty to challenge him.

In modern times, theologian Reinhold Niebuhr drew a similar distinction. On one hand, Niebuhr says, Christians are called to honor the ruling authority as a reflection of divine authority. On the other hand, the Bible is replete with prophetic judgments on particular rulers for oppressing the poor and defying divine law. A genuinely biblical understanding of government must retain both these elements in tension: what Niebuhr called "priestly sanctification" of the principle of government coupled with "prophetic criticism" of any particular government.

Ironically, the very week evangelicals were debating these issues at the NRB convention, a nonevangelical arrived in Washington and provided a vivid model: Mother Teresa, keynote speaker at the National Prayer Breakfast. Barely visible over the podium, the tiny nun started her address not with customary niceties but with a verse from Matthew 25. Then she stunned the assembled dignitaries, including the president and vice president, by saying, "The greatest destroyer of peace today is abortion. ... [For] if we accept that a mother can kill even her own child, how can we tell other people not to kill each other?"

In her simple, white habit, reading from a hand-typed manuscript, Mother Teresa was invariably polite and respectful. Yet she did not flinch in speaking the truth. She demonstrated civility wedded to bold conviction, confronting world leaders with a message of biblical righteousness.

It was also a message of help and hope. To anyone considering abortion, Mother Teresa pleaded, "Please don't kill the child. I want the child. Please give me the child." With a small smile that broke her somber expression, she spoke of the young women she had cared for through their pregnancies, of the infertile couples who had eagerly adopted babies into loving homes.

Regardless of political persuasion, evangelicals must strive to be of one mind. We ought to show unfailing civility to government officials. But being civil does not mean being silent or forsaking politics. "Priestly sanctification" must always be balanced with "prophetic criticism." To fall short of either responsibility is to betray our richest heritage and deny our biblical calling.

Charles Colson, "How to Confront a President," *Christianity Today* 38, No. 5 (April 25, 1994): 64.

November 12, 2001

BUSH'S DEFINING MOMENT

The president, facing a grief-stricken nation under attack, finds his voice and his mission.

TONY CARNES

President Bush, from the day of the attacks on the World Trade Center, has led the nation with a deft spiritual presence that radiates solidarity with people of all faiths. "Bush's stature as a leader rose right before your very eyes," says Richard Cizik, vice president of the National Association of Evangelicals. The nation seemed to agree. A *Newsweek* poll taken a week after the WTC catastrophe found that 83 percent of Americans thought that the president appeared to be a strong leader. Bush administration aide Timothy Goeglein said he agrees with the widespread view that the terrorist catastrophe is "absolutely a spiritually defining moment for the country and its leader."

After the September 11 attack, Bush displayed great skill at expressing his spiritual and moral convictions. His development as a political leader took enormous strides forward as he spoke at the National Cathedral, at Ground Zero of the collapsed World Trade Center, at the White House, at a joint session of Congress, and on national television.

As revealing as those public moments were, the president has been more open about his Christian convictions in private. *Christianity Today* interviewed several religious leaders who have visited with Bush since September 11.

A few hours before his address to Congress on September 20, President Bush met at the White House with a broad spectrum of religion leaders. Bush had asked Goeglein, deputy director of White House public liaison, to organize a meeting of religious leaders before the speech. Goeglein and his staff started calling.

Twenty-seven leaders, including 13 evangelicals, attended. The group included evangelists Luis Palau and Franklin Graham, pastors Max Lucado, Bill Hybels, T. D. Jakes, and Charles Blake, and Edward Cardinal Egan of New York. Buddhist, Hindu, Sikh, and Mormon leaders also attended the meeting.

These leaders were scattered across the nation at the time of the terrorist attacks. Lucado had just flown back to his home in San Antonio, Texas, when the White House called. He changed shirts and hopped back on a plane.

Palau, based in Portland, Oregon, was conducting an evangelistic festival in Santa Cruz, California. He took the first flight to Washington on a nearly empty Boeing 757. Arriving at his hotel, he noticed that "the only people roaming around were the military," he recalls. "The security people all had gas masks." The contrast of the beaches of Santa Cruz and the armed camp that was Washington couldn't have been starker for him.

Once inside the White House, the leaders were ushered into the Roosevelt Room. A circle of chairs was set up. Bush's chair was vacant and no one took chairs nearby. When the president entered and sat down, he looked around and said, "Hey, I feel lonely, somebody come and sit next to me!" Cardinal Bernard Law of Boston and Greek Orthodox Archbishop Demetrios Trakatellis of New York scooted over.

Bush crossed his legs, putting himself at ease. "I am not Pollyannaish, imagining things are great," the president declared. "I feel at peace, but a lot of that is due to the prayers of the American people. This is a major wake-up call for America. ... Now, I need your help as spiritual leaders to be truthful with the American people without creating panic."

Bush then outlined what his speech to Congress and the nation would cover. He told the group that only religious leaders could give the comfort and handle the spiritual questions.

"Government will do some things, but you need to be praying and be prepared for questions," Bush told them.

Palau, who took notes at the meeting, said Bush drew a comparison between himself and the country. Bush told the gathering, "I was a sinner in a need of redemption and I found it." The president was referring to the difficult time earlier in life when he was a heavy drinker and lacked a sense of purpose. But the gospel became clear to him through a conversation with evangelist Billy Graham.

Bush told the group that the nation was staggering and needed to get back on its feet. He said the devastation in New York challenged the nation to look deep into its heart. "I think this is part of a spiritual awakening in America," the president said.

Others who have talked with Bush recently and asked not to be named said Bush's disciplines of Bible reading and prayer sustain him.

Bush's faith is a vital part of his politics. "I don't think the president would consider himself an evangelical leader," says a prominent evangelical who knows Bush well. "He sees himself as a political leader and a man of faith."

Says another friend of Bush's, "He sees himself as the president of a nation made up of Jews, Muslims, evangelicals, Roman Catholics."

At the White House prayer session, Bush referred to his Christian faith indirectly. It was "a candid, natural way of talking about the Lord and his faith," one participant said. "He was very cautious and respectful in talking with the Muslims present, and he let them talk."

One purpose of the September 20 meeting was to "get Christian leaders around non-Christian ones so that [non-Christians] would feel welcomed," says Pastor Tim Keller of Redeemer Presbyterian Church in New York City.

The embrace was welcomed. Bush managed to be true to his personal evangelical testimony, while also creating a tolerant and inclusive meeting.

Gerald Kieschnick, president of the Lutheran Church—Missouri Synod, said Bush has a divine calling in this crisis, and he read aloud from Romans 13.

"Mr. President, I have just come from the World Trade Center site in lower Manhattan. I stood where you stood. I saw what you saw. I smelled what you smelled," Kieschnick said. "You not only have a civil calling, but a divine calling. ... You are not just a civil servant; you are a servant of God called for such a time like this."

"I accept the responsibility," Bush said, nodding.

The president came close to tears only when he described his first thoughts after hearing that the fourth hijacked airliner may have been headed for the White House. "The White House is an old building made of plaster and brick," Bush said. "If it had been struck, it would have collapsed and many people would have been killed, including my wife."

The president paused for a long moment, squinching the side of his face as he does when he wants to hold back his emotions. One observer said the president reminded him of a baseball pitcher before throwing—tension, restraint, and then the delivery.

"Those fellows who gave their lives—they gave their lives for freedom," Bush said.

After squinching a bit more, the president said, "We need to keep people praying."

Franklin Graham and four other religious leaders were invited into the Oval Office to pray with the president. Bush pointed out a portrait of Abraham Lincoln and said it was a reminder of his own calling to extend freedom and bring the nation together.

The fusion of personal piety and civic responsibility comes from Bush's deep sense of vocation. Bush says he sensed a higher call during his second inauguration as governor of Texas. He called a friend in Fort Worth, telling him, "I believe God wants me to run for president." The president now tells friends he understands God's call with greater clarity.

"Bush believes that the Lord prepares you for whatever he gives us," says one friend who visits the White House regularly. "The president really feels that this is his mission."

By meeting with top religious leaders and addressing Congress in the span of a few hours on September 20, Bush sharply focused the nation's attention against global terrorism as the country's greatest threat. "In our grief and anger," the president told the nation, "we have found our mission and our moment." ✦

"GOD IS BACK"

Since the terrorist attacks and the subsequent military action in Afghanistan, the change in national mood is unmistakable.

Relativism seems obsolete, or at least on the decline. A culture columnist at the *Chicago Tribune* recently declared that postmodernism, which rejects objective truth and traditional morality, has expired. "What lies in the mess in lower Manhattan and in the black gash in the Pentagon and in a field in southern

Pennsylvania may be this," Julia Keller wrote, "the end of post-modernism and its chokehold on the late twentieth century cultural imagination." Praying and going to a religious service seems a natural, normal thing to do. As *Wall Street Journal* columnist Peggy Noonan put it, "God is back."

But for many American Christians, pulling faith and politics together poses grave risks. If one political perspective is identified as divinely guided, opposition may be branded as godless and immoral. Some fear that the fusion of the Stars and Stripes and the cross may again make civil religion a threat to biblical Christianity. American civil religion usually has downplayed denominational differences in order to exploit citizens' patriotism, essentially putting faith in the service of the nation. That, critics say, is idolatry.

But most analysts don't think this is a current danger.

"[Bush] simply didn't establish a new civil religion," Peter Berger, a sociologist of religion at Boston University, told *CT*. "But the scope of religions that are recognized—that range was widened to include Islam, and to some extent the religions of South and East Asia."

Berger added, "I think Bush has been remarkable in promoting pluralism, especially when you compare this to what happened after Pearl Harbor with Japanese Americans. It went from the president on down. They all said that it is absolutely unacceptable to hold all Arabs or Muslims accountable."

The U.S. response in Afghanistan is not immoral, Berger said. "Unless you are a complete pacifist, the U.S. is responding to an attack of horrendous dimensions and that fits any category of just war."

Bush's example of coping has been a powerful tonic to the national mood. Political observers say the president seems genuine, not calculated or manipulative. Ari Fleischer, press spokesman for Bush, watched the president interact with grieving families of the missing New York firefighters and police officers three days after the attack.

"He spent time listening and talking with everybody, just one on one, hearing their individual stories of their family members. It was gut-wrenching," Fleischer says. "Just having watched the president throughout all of this, there was a real transformation. It was almost cathartic. I just watched him change in the course of that meeting."

At the National Cathedral service, the president revealed how carefully he selected his words to fit the nation's mood. "We are here in the middle hour of our grief," he began. "We come before God to pray for the missing and the dead, and for those who loved them."

Bush said the providence of God may not be what we expect, but we can count on the grace of God. "God's signs are not always the ones we look for," he told the congregation. "We learn in tragedy that his purposes are not always our own."

From Berger's perspective, the president has every right to speak more openly of religious matters while attending a church service (as opposed to addressing Congress). "If I had to put myself in that role, and I am a practicing Christian, if I am asked to make a speech at my own church, I would use different language than if I was speaking to my class."

Since September 11, Bush's speeches have married his informal, choppy syntax with his newly forceful vision for the country. Presidential historian Wayne Fields points out that Michael Gerson, Bush's chief speechwriter and a graduate of Wheaton College, shares similar religious convictions with Bush.

Gerson crafted this elegant sentence in Bush's September 20 national address: "Freedom and fear, justice and cruelty, have always been at war, and we know that God is not neutral between them."

The Bush speech was widely praised. One political columnist wrote a favorable comparison of Bush and President Lincoln. "The yardstick on how to judge a president will always be Lincoln," says Allen Guelzo, a Lincoln scholar at Eastern College near Philadelphia.

Bush has "projected an image as a determined, farsighted leader," Guelzo says, but his pieties "are still bland and conventional" compared to those of Lincoln, who was tried by the fires of the American Civil War. "Whether Bush's growth and impact lasts will depend on his resolve" as he meets further tragedies.

Guelzo says Bush's "gift for malapropisms stimulated contempt in the communication classes. But when he has really had to do so, he has shown a real capacity to communicate to the American people at large. He will not ever be the Great Communicator, but he has surprised many." Like Lincoln, Bush seems to have a "third ear" for public opinion, Guelzo says, meaning Bush knows how to pick his words to fit the national occasion.

As Bush has spoken about his faith, he has expanded his role as a national spiritual leader, especially for evangelicals who have been his strongest political supporters. For some Americans, Bush is refreshingly different from Bill Clinton. "Clinton's religious gestures were such that people were immediately skeptical of them," Guelzo says. "He shows up at Foundry Methodist with a pulpit Bible under his arm. [He] thinks he can mimic the gesture and do the trick."

Bush used the power of the presidential bully pulpit when the nation's mood of grief and unity was disrupted by Jerry Falwell. Speaking as a guest on Pat Robertson's *700 Club*, the religious broadcaster and chancellor of Liberty University said the terrorist attack was the fault of the ACLU, abortionists, feminists, homosexuals, and: others, who provoked God's wrath. A Bush representative immediately contacted Falwell and Robertson to express his displeasure, and both withdrew their remarks.

Now that the U.S. military is engaged in Afghanistan, the American campaign against terrorism enters its next lethal chapter. In the coming months, the content of the president's and the nation's character will be tested in part by the Bush administration's progress in the war against terrorism.

During White House meetings, Bush frequently shows visitors a painting inspired by the hymn "A Charge to Keep." His autobiography, released during the 2000 campaign, bears the same title as the hymn. "I still have a charge to keep," Bush tells his visitors.

Indeed, a verse from the hymn seems to fit Bush's convictions: "To serve the present age, my calling to fulfill. / Oh may it all my powers engage, to do my Master's will."

Tony Carnes, "Bush's Defining Moment," *Christianity Today* 45, No. 14 (November 12, 2001): 38–42.

THE BUSH DOCTRINE: THE MORAL VISION THAT LAUNCHED THE IRAQ WAR

TONY CARNES

T he Bush administration hasn't used a distinctive shorthand phrase to signal its foreign policy goals. *The Weekly Standard* has described it as "morality-based," and *Newsweek*'s Howard Fineman has called it "faith-based" foreign policy. Commerce Secretary Don Evans, Bush's closest friend, told *CT*, "It's love your neighbor like yourself. The neighbors happen to be everyone on the planet."

Whatever one calls it, it represents a distinctive change. In the past three years, President Bush has traveled a long way from the cautious foreign policies he spoke about as a presidential candidate. During the October 2000 debate, Bush said the United States was attempting too much abroad. "If we are an arrogant nation, they will resent us," he said. "If we're a humble nation but strong, they'll welcome us."

On March 19, as Bush added the words "God bless our troops" to the order launching Operation Iraqi Freedom to disarm

Saddam Hussein, he was not just dressing up policy with pious language—he was summing up more than a year's intensive thinking about the relation of his Christian faith and American foreign affairs. And for some influential conservative Catholics, Jews, and evangelicals, the president's faith-based foreign policy brings to fruition a decade-long effort to link their vision for international human rights, religious freedom, democracy, free trade, and public health directly with the executive branch of the federal government.

Bush's new approach has roots in the 1980s, when a handful of President Ronald Reagan's supporters began to focus on international religious persecution. The movement did not spread far beyond Washington think tanks until 1995. Then Michael Horowitz, former general counsel in Reagan's Office of Management and Budget, published an essay in *The Wall Street Journal* titled "New Intolerance Between the Crescent and the Cross." Horowitz was a catalyst for alliances of Prison Fellowship's Chuck Colson, Rep. Frank Wolf (R-Va.), and conservative Jews. In January 1996, another key link formed when the National Association of Evangelicals (NAE) and Freedom House, a religious-freedom advocacy group, hosted a "Global Persecution of Christians" conference in Washington.

In the meantime, then-Governor Bush was testing the waters with his domestically oriented compassionate conservatism. Bush has never been a globetrotter—before he became president, he had traveled abroad three times in his adult life. As governor, Bush's foreign policy amounted mostly to advocating freer trade with Mexico.

At his inauguration, Bush laid down themes that would blossom later. America, Bush said, is "the story of a power that went into the world to protect but not possess." He also reached back to the Declaration of Independence to talk about "our democratic faith" that "is the inborn hope of our humanity, an ideal we carry but do not own."

Richard Cizik, the NAE's vice president for governmental affairs, talked at length with two sympathetic Bush speechwriters about religious persecution in Sudan and China. Horowitz, Colson, and others lobbied Bush's political guru Karl Rove on the same issue. That spring, at the christening of the USS Ronald Reagan, Bush declared his concern for religious freedom abroad, but also declared his reluctance to criticize religious persecutors; he thought it immodest to "lecture the world."

White House staffers admit that both Bush's foreign policy initiatives and domestic agenda were stalling in early September 2001, before the devastating terrorist attacks of September 11. In response to 9/11, Bush's vision became coherent and deeply linked to his Christian convictions. He declared during the Washington National Cathedral's 9/11 memorial service, "Our responsibility to history is already clear: to answer these attacks and rid the world of evil." Bush no longer sounded like a balance-of-power realist, but like an abolitionist intent on ridding the world of vice. The service ended with a powerful rendition of the abolitionist war song, "The Battle Hymn of the Republic."

A few days later Bush told the nation that terrorists were trying to remake the world so that they could impose their beliefs on others. "They hate our freedoms: our freedom of religion, our freedom of speech, our freedom to vote and assemble and disagree with each other." Bush said God is not neutral in this conflict between "freedom and fear, justice and cruelty."

In the war against terrorism, Bush said in his 2002 State of the Union address, "History has called America and our allies to action."

According to former White House speechwriter David Frum, at the time Bush felt betrayed by Palestinian leader Yasser Arafat, who had blatantly lied to Bush when he denied smuggling terrorist weapons on the freighter Karine-A. Bush began to see that the webs of terror had compromised some nations. He called terror-supporting nations an "axis of evil." He enunciated a policy of "extending American compassion throughout the world."

ABOLISH EVIL, PROMOTE FREEDOM

After the relatively quick and dramatic war in Afghanistan, Bush and his advisers worked out their international strategy, which has been outlined in presidential speeches during the past 16 months.

In his 2002 graduation speech at West Point, Bush announced a new policy of pre-emptive attacks against terrorists and "unbalanced dictators." The president declared, "Moral truth is the same in every culture, in every time, and in every place. America will call evil by its name."

Bush proposed that a democratic model based "on nonnegotiable demands of human dignity," including religious tolerance, be adopted by other societies. Yet, he warned, "America cannot impose this vision," so it would reward pro-democracy governments with developmental and educational aid and protection against enemies of freedom.

In September the Bush administration issued the National Security Strategy of the United States. Bush summarized his broad global vision and America's preeminent role: "People everywhere want to be able to speak freely; choose who will govern them; worship as they please; educate their children—male and female; own property; and enjoy the benefits of their labor. These values of freedom are right and true for every person, in every society."

The strategy statement addressed a wide spectrum of international concerns, from fighting the HIV/AIDS pandemic and religious persecution to promoting economic freedom and democracy. The president emphasized that his national security strategy would include "special efforts to promote freedom of religion and conscience and defend it from encroachment by repressive regimes." This is the first time that a president's national security statement has so explicitly mentioned defending religious liberty. Bush called his strategy "a distinctly American internationalism that reflects the union of our values and our national interests."

In January's State of the Union address and February's speech to the National Religious Broadcasters convention, Bush outlined the key "doctrines" underpinning his foreign policy:

- America has a special responsibility to the world. "We must also remember our calling as a blessed country to make this world better," Bush declared in his State of the Union address, and the U.S. is being led "into the world to help the afflicted, and defend the peace, and confound the designs of evil men." He weighed in against moral relativism, saying of torture chambers in Iraq, "if this is not evil, then evil has no meaning."

- U.S. foreign policy is to extend and protect freedom to choose one's government and to "worship the Almighty God the way we see fit." Freedom, Bush told the religious broadcasters, is rooted in "people born to freedom in the image of God." America's advocacy of freedom is not just a special interest of America, he told the nation, because freedom is not "America's gift to the world. It is God's gift to humanity."

- Foreign policy is to be based on a belief in God-given human dignity. Bush told the broadcasters, "Faith teaches that every person is equal in God's sight, and must be treated with equal dignity here on earth."

- Compassion is a key motive of foreign policy. "The qualities of ... compassion that we strive for in America also determine our conduct abroad," he reminded the nation.

- Peacemaking remains an overarching priority, even if it means taking up arms from time to time. Bush told the religious broadcasters, "We are called ... to lead the world to peace."

Bush told Japanese prime minister Junichiro Koizumi, "I will seize the opportunity to achieve big goals. There is nothing bigger than to achieve world peace."

CAN AMERICA BE HUMBLE AND RIGHT?

Many foreign-policy experts question this new approach, including Carol Hamrin, a recently retired State Department expert on China and a senior associate of the Institute for Global Engagement, a Christian think tank. "I agree that there is evil," Hamrin said. "But my point is practical: if we operate on the mindset that we are right and they are wrong, we lose the complexities. People need to sense you are willing to accept them if they don't accept your values or ideas. Have we communicated that to the Muslims?"

European critics are aghast at the very idea of any religious motivations in foreign policy. Some question how far the president has departed from his spirit of humility that he said would characterize his foreign policy. They wonder how one can humbly use the power of the Army's Third Infantry Division or attack helicopters.

Elliott Abrams, a key staff member of the National Security Council in the White House, told *CT* that humility is "a decent and God-fearing value; [it] will be shown when we give back Iraqis their freedom."

Various Christians, like Jim Wallis of *Sojourners* magazine and Greg Smith of Britain, have sharply criticized the war with Iraq.

"I fear above all that the religion that is burgeoning in the U.S.A. in the context of the current crisis is not true Christianity," Smith said, "but a nationalistic heresy, a mirror image of some of the extreme forms of politicized Islam."

Some critics on the Right are isolationists. Patrick Buchanan in his *American Conservative* magazine decries Bush's pro-war "cabal" that is "colluding with Israel."

Doug Bandow of the libertarian Cato Institute worries that Bush's sense of calling to better the whole world will lead to widespread conflict. "This 'our calling' statement is extremely dangerous. There are 40 wars we can intervene in," Bandow said. "Americans don't have patience for imperialism."

Some worry that Bush is confusing genuine faith with nationalist ideology. A Methodist pastor wrote to *The Washington Post* to charge that Bush had committed blasphemy in his State of the Union address when he changed a hymn's lyric from "There is power, power, wonder-working power in the blood of the lamb" to "in the goodness and idealism and faith of the American people."

Because President Bush and American evangelicals share many of the same values, some evangelicals sense a stronger burden to address the president's willingness to use might for right. Regarding Bush's foreign policy, "I waver over whether this is good or bad," said Hamrin, who recently received a Center for Public Justice award for promoting religious freedom in China.

"My culture and education tells me this is bad. Hubris that 'God is on our side' is wrong." But Hamrin says that morality requires action, too. "I read in Isaiah about God using his people in foreign affairs to do justice. We have to be careful. If we don't listen to criticism, we could easily get the worst of both realism and idealism in foreign policy."

There is no answer to most of these concerns—yet. How Bush prosecutes the current war, and maintains the subsequent peace, is only part of what is clearly a larger vision for America's role in the world. Jay Lefkowitz, deputy assistant to the president, says Bush starts every policy discussion on action by asking, "What is the right thing to do?"—meaning, Lefkowitz says, "What is the morally correct thing to do?" Whether this question can guide U.S. foreign policy in the 21st century, only time will tell.

Tony Carnes, "The Bush Doctrine: The Moral Vision That Launched the Iraq War," *Christianity Today* 47, No. 5 (May 2003): 38–42.

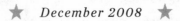

★ *December 2008* ★

ELECTION HONEYMOON

Will evangelicals learn to work with
an Obama administration?

SARAH PULLIAM

Despite Barack Obama's heavy religious outreach, exit-poll results suggested that white evangelicals voted for John McCain 74 to 25 percent, similar to 2004 results. Now evangelicals must decide how they will work with the new administration.

"Typically in America, we give our leaders a honeymoon," said John Green, senior fellow at the Pew Forum on Religion and Public Life. "It will be interesting to see if conservative evangelicals give Obama breathing room, and give him a chance to perform before they start criticizing him."

On election night, social conservatives claimed victories with amendments in California, Arizona, and Florida that would ban same-sex marriage. However, anti-abortion measures in Colorado and South Dakota failed to pass, and at least four social conservatives in Congress were ousted: Elizabeth Dole (N.C.), Steve Chabot (Ohio), Marilyn Musgrave (Colo.), and Bill Sali (Idaho).

Obama chose a different path from John Kerry's when he built a religious outreach team and attended forums at Saddleback Church and Messiah College. Just before his acceptance speech, Obama prayed with Joel Hunter, an evangelical pastor in Florida.

Michael Cromartie, vice president at the Ethics and Public Policy Center, is interested to see if Obama continues his outreach to evangelicals.

"In one sense, everyone can have good feelings about an African American being elected president," he said. "But is President-elect Obama an ultraliberal dressed up in moderate, soothing garb?"

In 2007, Obama promised Planned Parenthood that he would sign an act removing all restrictions on abortion at state and federal levels. He has also said he would appoint justices that would uphold *Roe v. Wade*.

Obama appealed to evangelicals by emphasizing his desire to reduce the number of abortions by providing more resources for women to carry pregnancies to term. Today the number of abortions—1.2 million in 2005—is nearly the same as in 1976, according to the Guttmacher Institute.

"Barack Obama will be held accountable on a serious commitment to abortion reduction," said Jim Wallis, founder of *Sojourners*. "He called for that, his campaign platform said that, and he should be held accountable to that. He needs prayer and accountability, support and pushing, both at the same time."

In July, Obama pledged to increase funding for faith-based initiatives but said recipients could not discriminate based on religion.

If this happens, "there won't be too many takers among evangelicals," said Richard Land, president of the Southern Baptist Convention's Ethics and Religious Liberty Commission. "You have taken away the thing that makes faith-based initiatives successful and attractive in the first place."

Richard Cizik, vice president of the National Association of Evangelicals, said evangelicals have serious disagreements with Obama on certain issues, but thinks the president-elect understands evangelicals better than any Democrat since Jimmy Carter.

"I have a strong confidence that evangelicals will find a willing ear [from] this new president," Cizik said. "We need to respond."

Sarah Pulliam, "Election Honeymoon," *Christianity Today* 52, No. 12 (December 2008): 15.

CIVIL RELIGION'S SHARPER TEETH

MOLLIE ZIEGLER HEMINGWAY

Shortly after he was asked to deliver a prayer at President Barack Obama's inaugural festivities, Episcopal Bishop Gene Robinson proudly announced it wouldn't be a Christian one. He had been "horrified" at how "specifically and aggressively Christian" previous inaugural prayers were. Robinson, whose elevation as his church's first gay bishop has been a major factor in bringing the Anglican Communion to the brink of schism, ended up addressing his prayer to the "God of our many understandings."

The day after Obama became president, the Episcopal Church's National Cathedral hosted an interfaith worship service featuring Muslims, Jews, and Hindus. The service's liturgical framework was Christian while the content was strictly nonsectarian. The sermon cited Hindu, Jewish, Muslim, and Cherokee sources, avoided exclusive truth claims, and shied away from particular names for deities. Cathedral staff even rewrote the Book of Common Prayer's responsive prayers to avoid any overt Christian witness. The only way the service could have been more inclusive was if they had replaced the altar with a kitchen sink.

While many Christians might be alarmed by civil religion in the Obama era, the Bush era wasn't terribly different. In his second inaugural address, for instance, Bush praised the "truths of Sinai, the Sermon on the Mount, the words of the Koran." And he told Arab news channel Al Arabiya, "I believe in an almighty God, and I believe that all the world, whether they be Muslim, Christian, or any other religion, prays to the same God."

Still, the Obama era of religious inclusivity has new—and very exclusive—teeth that may leave some Christians wondering if they are welcome. Take Obama's proposal for changing the faith-based initiative rules. "If you get a federal grant, you can't use that grant money to proselytize to the people you help and you can't discriminate against them—or against the people you hire—on the basis of their religion," he said during the campaign.

In his 2000 campaign, President Bush promised, "We will never ask an organization to compromise its core values and spiritual mission to get the help it needs." If it sounded too good to be true, it was. Soon, religious groups had to wipe doctrine out of their charity programs and had to teach morality without the basis for morality. They couldn't witness to or discriminate against those they were trying to help. Still, at least Baptists could staff Baptist charities with Baptists.

But now that right may be threatened. Officially, Bush's policy still stands. But the new head of faith-based initiatives said the hiring issue would be handled on a "case-by-case basis," and both of the church-state experts on Obama's new religious advisory council oppose the right of religious groups who receive federal funds to use religion as a hiring criterion. (Other members of the council disagree.)

What do policymakers think is so special about these faith-based groups in the first place? Everyone acknowledges that the nation's congregations and religious charities have an unparalleled track record of helping feed, clothe, and comfort the needy, especially compared with federal programs. Regulations that force religious charities to obscure or ignore their doctrine not only decrease their life-changing capabilities but also diminish enthusiasm among their staff, volunteers, and donors.

British atheist Matthew Parris used to laud the practical work of mission churches in Africa while lamenting their evangelism. Now, he recently wrote, he can't deny the fact that faith motivates not just the missionaries but also those they are helping. Providing the material means and know-how for economic development doesn't produce change. Providing Christianity does, he said. We can safely say that the teachings of Richard Dawkins have never inspired anybody to move their family to sub-Saharan Africa to dig wells.

Soon, charities might not be able to ensure that faith motivates their employees. No word yet on whether the program will be renamed Somebody-Here-Used-to-Have-a-Faith-Based Initiative.

The late Yale church historian Jaroslav Pelikan said it was an American conviction to believe that morality can be stripped of doctrine, that it is possible to summarize the best that men everywhere have discovered about the good life.

"Biblical morality is inseparable from biblical doctrine and biblical doctrine is inseparable from the community of believers," he said.

If the previous pressure to secularize didn't give pause to religious charities seeking federal funds, it should terrify them now. Being forced into silence about one's faith and being told you can't hire fellow believers is too high a price to pay.

Mollie Ziegler Hemingway, "Civil Religion's Sharper Teeth," *Christianity Today* 53, No. 4 (April 2009): 56.

★ *October 2016* ★

"WHY I'M VOTING FOR HILLARY CLINTON"

This year there are only two meaningful
choices. Why one is the far wiser choice.

RON SIDER

I have not publicly endorsed a presidential candidate in 44 years. But this year—the most important presidential election in my lifetime—I feel compelled to do so.

For decades I have advocated a completely pro-life agenda: pro-life and pro-poor; pro-family and pro-racial justice; pro-sexual integrity and pro-peacemaking and pro-creation care. This agenda is expressed in the National Association of Evangelicals' public policy document "For the Health of the Nation." For decades, as I applied this agenda, I regularly concluded that Republican presidential candidates were better on issues like abortion, marriage and family, and religious freedom, while Democratic candidates were better on racial justice, economic justice, and the environment. So I have voted for both Republicans (George W. Bush) and Democrats (Barack Obama).

But 2016 is astonishingly different from other election years. Hillary Clinton is bad and good in the usual ways. But Donald Trump is not only bad in many of the usual ways—he is also bad in the ways in which I have usually preferred Republicans.

Trump's recent pro-life stand is not credible. Historically he has supported abortion access, even to partial-birth abortion, and still supports Planned Parenthood, the country's largest supplier of abortions.

Trump's personal marriage record is horrendous. He humiliated his first wife by publicly flaunting an affair. He is now in his third marriage, while Clinton has remained with her husband in spite of his despicable behavior.

Trump's call to ban all Muslims from immigrating to the United States was a fundamental violation of the constitutional protection of religious freedom.

SO WHAT ABOUT CLINTON?

I have major disagreements with her. She and the Democratic platform are wrong on abortion—period. And I disagree with Clinton on gay marriage.

Further, I fear that Clinton will not retain the longstanding right (protected by Presidents Clinton, Bush, and Obama) of faith-based organizations that receive government funding to hire on the basis of their beliefs. She is too close to Wall Street billionaires and made a serious mistake using private email servers as Secretary of State.

But there is also much to like about Clinton. She has a decades-long history of working hard for racial and economic justice. One of her earliest jobs was working as a lawyer at the black-led Children's Defense Fund to improve the lives of poor children. At a time when racial injustice and mistrust threaten to tear the nation apart, her experience and trust in minority communities is invaluable.

Clinton realizes that lower-income Americans have lost ground in the past 30 years, and has advocated concrete policies to alleviate the growing divide between rich and poor. Her $350 billion college affordability program would help lower-income students afford higher education. Raising the minimum wage to $12 and tax cuts (15%) for companies that share profits with workers would help. Her proposed expansion of health insurance to cover all Americans is surely pro-life.

Clinton has a realistic and just way to pay for these programs. The middle class would get a modest tax cut, while those with annual incomes over $5 million would have a 4-percent tax increase. She has promised to close tax loopholes that allow corporations to avoid their fair share of taxes. Warren Buffett supports Clinton, saying she would help poor working Americans. The independent, bipartisan Committee for a Responsible Federal Budget says Clinton's plan would not add significantly to the national debt.

Clinton also endorses serious proposals to protect the environment. And in foreign affairs, the former senator and Secretary of State is probably the most knowledgeable and experienced presidential candidate in decades. Global peace urgently requires a U.S. president who is thoroughly familiar with geopolitics and has a judicious track record.

How does Trump compare? Since the only meaningful choice this fall is Clinton or Trump, my evaluation of Trump is an appropriate part of my decision.

UNJUST AND DESTRUCTIVE

Major parts of Trump's economic agenda are both morally unjust and economically destructive. Trump proposed lowering the top income tax rate from 39.6 percent to 25 percent—an annual tax cut of $275,000 for the richest 1 percent, including Trump. That is blatant injustice since today, more than 90 percent of all the increase in income in the total U.S. economy goes to the richest 1 percent.

Trump's economic plans would also be *economically* disastrous, adding $9.5 trillion to the national debt over ten years. More recent modifications would still add trillions to the national debt. The pro-business U.S. Chamber of Commerce has predicted a recession "within the first year" of a Trump presidency.

Trump promised to expel the approximately 11.3 million undocumented immigrants, millions of whom have children born in this country—who are therefore U.S. citizens. This plan would tear apart millions of families and defies the biblical command to love and care for the "sojourner" (i.e., non-citizen). Deporting 11 million people would cost $400 billion to $600 billion. And because there are not enough workers here to replace the roughly 6.8 million employed undocumented workers, the economy would decline by an estimated $1 trillion.

Trump grossly distorts facts and makes ridiculous promises. He said the United States is "the highest taxed nation in the world." Economists show the United States is nearly the least-taxed (32nd out of 34th) of all industrialized nations. His repeated promise to make Mexico pay for his border wall is flatly absurd.

Trump said the judge in charge of the legal case against Trump University should be disqualified because he is "Mexican"—a "textbook" case of racism, said Republican Speaker of the House Paul Ryan. Trump has called Mexican immigrants "rapists" and "criminals." Russell Moore, president of the Southern Baptist Convention's public policy commission, has sharply condemned Trump's "not-so-coded messages denouncing African Americans and immigrants."

Trump has said that "torture works" and that he would "bring back waterboarding and a hell of a lot worse than waterboarding." He has called for killing the families, even children, of terrorists—which is a war crime under both U.S. and international law.

Prominent evangelicals condemn Trump. Max Lucado has never before publicly commented on presidential candidates but this year wrote of Trump: "He ridiculed a war hero. He made a mockery of a reporter's menstrual cycle. He made fun of a disabled reporter." "His attitude toward women is that of a Bronze Age warlord," says Moore. Peter Wehner, who served in the past three Republican administrations, denounces Trump as a "moral degenerate" and "comprehensive and unrepentant liar."

Trump's boasting is breathtaking. Some of his recent comments: "Nobody's ever been more successful than me." He said he had studied the Iran deal "in great detail, greater by far than anyone else." "Nobody knows more about taxes than I do, maybe in the history of the world." "No one reads the Bible more than me." One final example: "Nobody is better on humility than me." Yet Trump has said he has never asked God for forgiveness because he doesn't need it.

WE NEED A WISE STATESMAN

Do we evangelical Christians trust Donald Trump to be a wise statesman leading the world to avoid conflict and war? The U.S. president is the leader of the democratic world and the commander of the world's largest military. A wise, thoughtful president who listens carefully to the best-informed advisers is essential if the United States and China are to avoid catastrophic conflict in the next decade or two.

Trump has absolutely no experience in foreign affairs or global diplomacy. He has repeatedly demonstrated arrogant, impulsive decision making. I can't trust him to control the nuclear trigger. In August, 50 of the nation's most senior Republican national security officials issued a public letter saying Trump "lacks the character, values, and experience" to be president, and added that Trump "would be the most reckless president in American history" and would "put at risk our country's national security."

Voting for one candidate rather than the other does not mean that one endorses all that candidate supports. It simply means that one believes the other candidate would lead to worse results.

And in 2016, there are only two meaningful choices: Trump and Clinton. One could vote for the Libertarian or Green Party candidate, but they have no chance of winning. Voting for them, or writing in someone else, will only help elect Trump.

In this unprecedented, astonishing presidential election, I have no doubt that voting for Hillary Clinton is the right choice.

Ron Sider, "Why I'm Voting for Hillary Clinton," *Christianity Today* 60, No. 8 (October 2016): 55–56.

"WHY I'M VOTING FOR DONALD TRUMP"

INTERVIEW WITH JAMES DOBSON

What are the strongest arguments for a Christian to support Donald Trump for the U.S. presidency?

First, let me say that I will respond to your questions as a private individual and not as a representative of the organization I lead.

I don't vote for candidates or political parties. I support those who will lead the country righteously, honorably, and wisely. In many ways, this is a single-issue election because it will affect every dimension of American life: the makeup of the Supreme Court. Antonin Scalia's sudden death made this election the most significant of our lifetime. The next president will nominate perhaps three or more justices whose judicial philosophy will shape our country for generations to come.

Unelected, unaccountable, and imperialistic justices have a history of imposing horrendous decisions on the nation. One decision that still plagues us is *Roe v. Wade*, imposed on America in 1973. It divided the nation and has led to the murders of 54 million innocent babies. This killing goes on every day.

That leads us to ask what the judiciary will look like in a Trump administration. I attended a June 2016 event called "A Conversation with Donald Trump" in New York, with more than 1,000 other religious leaders. Before the meeting, 30 of us met

Trump in a private session in Trump Tower. Most were evangelicals or conservative Catholics. I asked the candidate about his concerns regarding religious liberty.

I liked that he promised us emphatically that he will work to protect our religious liberties. He has since released a list of potential Supreme Court nominees that is stellar. We must pray that, if elected, he will keep his word.

Trump's selection of Governor Mike Pence as his running mate was a hugely encouraging decision. I've been a personal friend of Gov. Pence for more than 30 years. He is pro-life, pro-traditional marriage, a godly family man, a solid conservative, and a competent leader. There is no politician whom I respect more.

Many supporters of Trump believe that Clinton would be a disaster for the country. What are your concerns about Clinton?

My greatest concern is related again to the judiciary. Clinton has said she will seek to overturn religious liberty and bring the power of government against people of faith. She has made this clear on many occasions, including a comment she made during the Women in the World Summit in 2015.

Laws about "reproductive health care" and safe childbirth "have to be backed up with resources and political will," Clinton said. "And deep-seated cultural codes, religious beliefs, and structural biases have to be changed."

"Reproductive health care" is a euphemism for abortion, so that threat should send chills down the backs of every true believer in Jesus. It blatantly contradicts guarantees of the U.S. Constitution. We dare not give ultimate power to anyone who does not respect or feel limited by this historic document. It is the basis for all the freedoms handed to us by the founding fathers.

I'm convinced that with the wrong president, we will soon see a massive assault on religious liberty. Certain powerful groups and organizations seek to weaken the church of Jesus Christ and limit what pastors and ministers can say and do publicly. They believe some of our teachings represent "hate speech" and must be stifled. They seek to severely restrict the freedoms of Christian schools, nonprofit organizations, businesses, hospitals, charities, and seminaries. With Christian colleges and universities, they want to limit whom their leaders choose as professors and what their students will be taught. Government funding and accreditation will be in the crosshairs, and you can be sure that home schools will be targeted.

We at Family Talk have experienced this tyranny firsthand. The Department of Health and Human Services has mandated that Family Talk and many other Christian nonprofits cover contraceptives known as abortifacients in their healthcare plans. They include the morning-after pill and other medications that are known to prevent embryos from implanting in the uterus. They can be baby killers, and we consider them immoral. The Feds have forced us to sue to find relief. We are now in a federal lawsuit that may be decided by the Supreme Court. If we lose our case and refuse to comply, we'll face ruinous fines and will be forced to close our doors. It all will depend on five attorneys who sit on the Court.

There are many other concerns about Clinton's candidacy. She has proposed to pay for abortions in countries around the world, including generous funding for Planned Parenthood; and she is committed to the most radical demands of the LGBTQ agenda, to name but two.

Many Christians are deeply troubled by Trump's rhetoric, especially his comments about Hispanics, women, and Muslims in particular; they characterize his comments as bigoted.

Trump speaks in hyperbole, clearly. His rhetoric has been inexcusable, and I don't defend it. I hope that the criticism he has received from the public will have an influence on his speech. I think it already has.

I serve on a faith committee of 22 conservative Christian leaders, and we are working to help Trump make the right choices. I know that Franklin Graham, Jerry Falwell Jr., Robert Jeffress, James Robinson, and many other respected leaders have direct access to him. If Trump turns out to be an incorrigible demagogue, we can hope he will be reined in by the political process. There are checks and balances in our system of government.

So you don't think this a reason not to support Trump.

I don't believe for a second that Hillary Clinton isn't using equally incendiary rhetoric behind the scenes about many people, especially conservatives. Policy is what matters.

Last week, I had an appointment with an ophthalmologist for a routine eye exam. A technician pressed a metal device against my face. I looked through two holes and saw a short line of type. She then asked, "Is this good?" Then, after changing the lens, she asked, "Is this better?" I was given only two choices: number one or number two. This is where we are as a nation during this election. Is it one or is it two? There is no viable third choice.

There are obviously characteristics of Trump that I wish I could change. However, I believe he is the best candidate available, period.

Many evangelicals are critical of Trump's lifestyle, such as his pride in sleeping with many women and his investments in gambling, to name two. Do these behaviors concern you?

Of course they concern me. In an ideal world, I would want a godly man or woman for president, but there doesn't appear to be any such person on the ballot. And some of those characterizations appear to reflect Trump's past. As a Christian, I love it when people change, and I pray that he has. Evangelist Paula White says that she led him to Christ. I don't know what his commitment to Christ is—that's for God to decide. I'm not under any illusions that he is an outstanding moral example, but I do think he's a good father.

As I said in my endorsement, "Without a doubt, my decision to recommend Trump has been influenced by the way his children speak of him as a dad." As a psychologist and a family counselor, I have spent my life equipping families. I have observed that you cannot make a child talk about his or her parents the way Trump's children speak of him.

I do know that Trump has surrounded himself with many Christian leaders. Apparently, he was doing this long before he decided to run for president. He has engaged in the hard work of building relationships with the faith community and has vowed to uphold our values with his legislative and judicial priorities. It's a cliché but true: We are electing a commander-in-chief, not a theologian-in-chief.

How would you summarize your view on Trump's candidacy?

I believe this great country is hanging by a thread. If we make another tragic mistake after putting Barack Obama in office for eight years, we will never recover from it. Trump may disappoint and embarrass us repeatedly in office. But Hillary Clinton, given her lawless behavior and what she has promised to do, would be a disaster. She will build on Obama's policies to redefine marriage, expand abortion policies, assault gender identities, tax and spend our resources, appoint liberal judges and justices, and on it goes. There has to be a better person to lead us out of the wilderness. Is it Donald Trump? I pray that it is. If he turns out to be a failure, then our grandkids and future generations are the ones who will suffer. If Clinton is elected, that suffering will begin much sooner.

James Dobson, "Why I'm Voting for Donald Trump," *Christianity Today* 60, No. 8 (October 2016): 59–62.

★ *October 2016* ★

WHY I'M VOTING FOR NEITHER CANDIDATE

Both leaders fail to address the heart
concerns of black evangelicals like me.

SHO BARAKA

As a black Christian in an urban environment, I consciously
struggle to give my allegiance to either political party. In this
way, this election gives many white evangelicals a sense of what
it's like to be a black believer in America today.

As an African American, I'm marginalized by the lack of compassion the Right. As a Christian, I'm ostracized by the secularism of the Left. As a man, I'm greatly concerned by subversive
attempts to deconstruct all "classical" definitions of manhood.

I fraternize with a remnant of people who have the cultural
and theological aptitude to engage both Carter G. Woodson and
G. K. Chesterton. We walk the tightrope between conservatives
and progressives. We share an anxiety and sense of displacement
in the current sociopolitical landscape.

I have had zero interest in either candidate this election.
Many people are fearful about the next president, as they should
be. Our newly appointed chief will likely nominate Supreme
Court justices. The thought of either candidate appointing justices scares me. Many Clinton supporters seek a secular utopia

that progresses past logic. Many Trump supporters want to resurrect bigoted ideologies. Neither of these Americas is great to me.

TRUE LIBERATION

Ideally, fellow black Christians and I could thrive at the table with conservatives because we agree on a moral code. But it has been shocking to see some conservatives perform verbal gymnastics to support a candidate who has questionable character and vacillates on basic conservative principles.

Further, many of our conservative brothers and sisters have justified or ignored the deaths of Tamir Rice, Trayvon Martin, Michael Brown, and other young black men. Many claim their Republican values align with their faith, but are supporting someone who looks more like Bull Connor than Billy Graham.

Yet *both* Republicans and Democrats have supported policies that have only increased the plight of minority communities. In the War on Drugs, leaders from both parties supported draconian penalties for nonviolent drug offenses. Both parties' leaders have financially benefited from disproportionately sending folks to prison for crimes that carry far fewer consequences in affluent communities. Only recently has America witnessed what could be called the "gentrification of the drug crisis," wherein opioid addiction among whites is reaching epidemic levels. Bill Clinton's Crime Bill of 1994 escalated the arrests of people of color for nonviolent crimes. He later admitted that signing the bill was a mistake. Although I'm grateful for this revelation, some of us have carried the burdens of its implications all our lives.

I live in a part of Atlanta where African Americans make up 79 percent of the population, according to census data. If you live in a community with these demographics, you're most likely grappling with underperforming schools, anemic business districts, scarce home ownership, and nihilistic behaviors.

If I'm sensitive to this plight, then I'm compelled to partner with those who have a burden to fix these broken policies and systems. When it comes to addressing those issues, it appears that Democrats show the most compassion and desire to try to fix these problems. Yet I fear that many of our liberal pundits and activists apply wrong means that lead to a calamitous end. I often wonder if they truly want to see these communities restored and liberated. I'm even more concerned about what type of restoration and liberty they desire.

There is a distinct difference between the restoration and liberation we need and what we want. If secular humanism and all of its tenets are at the end of the liberation rope, then I refuse to grab hold. I will die a slower, more humiliating death once I'm pulled into that boat. I'd rather face my opposition knowing I never sacrificed my dignity and beliefs. I am made in the image of God. I will not forfeit that for pseudo-liberation. And liberation absent God is no liberation at all.

If the black Christian doesn't rise up with a distinct political vision, then we will find our communities under the authority of secularism. As Reformed Theological Seminary scholar Carl Ellis Jr. has noted, "Ethical content could have saved the Black Power movement. But the leaders had already swallowed secular humanism. Thus all moral decisions were left up to the individual." Individualism in a postmodern society has destructive intentions aimed at the foundations of Christian orthodoxy and natural law.

Is there any doubt that our allegiance is with the Democratic Party when the black vote has been no less than 84 percent Democrat in the past 20 years? We can discard our platitudes about keeping politicians honest when they know they have us in their pockets. Why should they submit to accountability when they know we will return to them no matter what they do? (This is not a new problem in the black community. Malcolm X's speech "The Ballot or the Bullet" addressed this blind loyalty, labeling "political chumps" those fellow blacks who support white politicians who nonetheless put black communities' needs last.)

I believe there is a third way. Urban Christians are determined to reassert ourselves into the political arena. We refuse to settle for civic engagement that forces us to either neglect our compassion or surrender our convictions. From mass incarceration to the right to life for the unborn, it's time to engage in advocacy that better reflects the love and truth of the gospel.

COMPASSION
AND CONVICTION

Allow me to quote Ellis once more:

> I believe that if we are going to move forward as a community who has distinctive concerns in America, we need to evaluate political and social ideas as they stand on their own, without regard to their ideological association.

I believe that soon there will be a movement of folks who protest both police brutality and abortions without feeling disloyal to one party or the other. These Christians comprehend an unabridged concept of life, that it is to be protected from the cradle to the grave. This is a comprehensive outlook that seeks justice in community development, education, prison reform, and job creation. These people recognize honoring humanity is a service to God and not a partisan policy.

It would be naïve to think that urban Christians are the only people who feel this disconnect. Not all Republicans are callous legalists; not all Democrats are immoral despots. I find great utility on both sides. However, who better than Christians, who have experienced persecution of all kinds, to display both compassion and conviction? Out of that experience comes the capacity to love recklessly while inviting people to a new standard.

Christ is our model of compassion and conviction. He loved Zacchaeus enough to sup with him, knowing the social stigma attached to his occupation. Zacchaeus adopted a new worldview in response to his encounter with Jesus. This worldview taught that exploiting citizens and perpetuating a system that hurt the poor was no longer an option.

Christ loved the adulterous woman enough to save her from execution. He not only cared for her immediate need but loved so perfectly that he invited her to leave a life of sexual exploitation. This is the ever-elusive balance we must try to occupy. We must show great compassion while holding to our firm convictions. We believe that the Lord can change both our hearts and our circumstances.

Instead of encouraging urban Christians to vote for a false choice this election season, my hope is that we will build a strong base, similar to the Tea Party and the LGBTQ community, that will garner attention from lobbyists, lawmakers, and pundits. The goal is to transcend political parties so that they will no longer be an obstacle. This was the posture of the civil rights movement.

This will mean *endurance* to cause political disruption. We have been silenced by liberal lobbying and frustrated with conservative complacency. Do we have the endurance of our predecessors to campaign for 384 dreadful days until we see political change, as did the Montgomery bus boycotts?

This will mean *empathy*. Though we have a heart for the truth of God, we must not divorce our ethical leanings from compassion for others.

This will mean *education* for our communities on the policies that will bring substantive change and liberty. Governance and policymaking are not results of the Fall but part of what God

intended for humans all along. So sin does not negate our responsibility to be cultivators, as artists, pastors, jurists, teachers, parents, cashiers, or students. We are a city on the hill that can no
longer lease our lot and escape to a quieter place.

Sho Baraka, "Why I'm Voting for Neither Candidate," *Christianity Today* 60, No.
8 (October 2016): 62–66.

Chapter 2

RELIGIOUS RIGHT AND EVANGELICAL LEFT

I ndividuals like presidents are important since they help to make concrete what might remain abstract, providing a focus for popular opinion in a way that a cause or a principle simply cannot. Nonetheless, we can never underestimate the role played by larger narratives. Leaders with their own set of strengths and weaknesses can end up "guilty by association" with a movement, even if that guilt ends up garnering more votes in the end.

Few such overarching stories are so potent in the public imagination concerning Christians and politics than the rise of the Religious Right as *the* voice of evangelicalism in the United States. It is less known how much this is only part of the story. American evangelicals were indeed fairly conservative, but this never really translated into a lockstep attitude toward party politics. This stereotype is even more ill-fitting before the 1970s.

Much of this is a result of historical accident. With party distinctions more subtle in the past than in recent years, it was not always unimaginable for voters to oscillate between Republican and Democrat. However, the intensity of the 1960s divided the evangelical electorate into mutually antagonistic groups, each seeing the other as compromising on key moral issues.

With the growth of evangelicalism and its increasing public stature throughout the 1970s, the numbers comprising factions on the right and left reached a critical mass where they could be more easily distinguished. These distinctions became even more apparent as leaders and organizations emerged specific to a majority "Religious Right" and minority "Evangelical Left." Between these two camps endured a remnant not quite at ease with either, but, even if it is often overstated, this bifurcation had a lasting effect on evangelical political involvement.

Most evangelicals found themselves more at home with the conservatism of Reagan's Republicans, as important concerns like abortion and religious liberty made association with the

Democratic Party increasingly uncomfortable. This was apparent particularly in the 1980s and 1990s, as open evangelicals held prominent roles in Republican administrations.

Over the years, the articles in *CT* reflected this evolution, but they never became partisan. Otherwise liberal Christians like Ron Sider and Jim Wallis were afforded ample space to remind readers of the biblical priorities for the poor and others left out of the American Dream. At the same time, those like Carl McIntire and Jerry Falwell, who were inclined to associate more closely with political conservatism, could find themselves on the receiving end of some pointed editorials.

In the end, perhaps the best thing to be said about *CT* and evangelicalism's factions is that while its articles were most often in sympathy with principles of the Religious Right, they were often quite skeptical of its methods. Conversely, while they were hesitant about the practicality of the Evangelical Left's dissident positions, they were open to giving them a hearing.

★ *April 24, 1970* ★

CARL MCINTIRE'S VICTORY: "IN THIS SIGN CONQUER"

WILLIAM WILLOUGHBY

Radio evangelist Carl McIntire doesn't believe in losing. It just doesn't fit into his or God's landscaping. On April 4 the fiery fundamentalist marched with as many as 50,000 of those who feel much the same way to the foot of Washington Monument. At his beck, the group turned to the White House and chanted, "We want victory in Viet Nam."

For McIntire, the march has to be the biggest single victory in his relentless fight against the "international conspiracy of god-less Communism." But for all his announcements that 100,000 persons would be on hand to "help turn the tide," the press paid little attention beforehand. Even after he made his point and nearly 1,000 busloads poured into the city tying up traffic for hours, reports were downplayed (despite page one stories in Washington and New York) in contrast to the splash given anti-war rallies.

Forgotten when newsmen started comparing the figures with the New Mobe's anti-war protest in the same area on November 15 was the fact that McIntire's effort was almost a solo affair—one man haranguing on 600 radio stations. Forgotten also was the fact that this was the first sizable pro-war demonstration (that was not a counterdemonstration) and that it attracted nearly twice as many marchers as the first anti-war demonstration four years earlier.

Now the time had come, said the founding president of the International Council of Churches, for the "silent majority" to make some noise; while they had been tongue-tied the Communists had taken over.

The biggest noise-maker of them all, the restaurateur who swung his way into the governor's chair in Georgia on the talking end of an ax handle, dished out the warmed-over hash that has been his and McIntire's specialty. Bible-quoting Lester Maddox told the enthusiastic crowd: "We did not lose our war over Communism in Southeast Asia. We lost it here in Washington."

Louisiana's Representative John R. Rarick earlier had scored points on much the same theme: "We are here to seek peace in Viet Nam—peace the American way—with victory." The Democrat dean of House conservatives denounced the Nixon Administration's "no-win" policy and the New Mobe's concept of unilateral withdrawal as foreign to the American spirit.

Here and there groups of hippies and others whooped it up, flashing the "V" sign and, when the Americanisms got thick, bursting out with "oink oink" and "Sieg Heil." But McIntire was not nonplused. He put static into their "V"-sign thunder when he said the youths "stole" it from patriotic Americans. Then he had his throng flash the famed Churchillian sign.

The demonstration, for all the valid or at least plausible points it was making, was an orgy of religious symbolism, patriotism, and militarism. "In this sign conquer" pins had been sold by the thousands. McIntire called on Americans to begin to wage "a holy war against Communism." He warned his audience about the history of the church in Communist countries and said it was not politics that motivated him to call the march: "One of the reasons why I'm in this fight is to keep the doors of my church open. There's not a single church in Communist China open now. ... That's what will happen in this country if they take over."

McIntire is a master at making money out of efforts to thwart him. Playing into his hands most of all was an eleventh-hour letter from the White House saying the march had been postponed. "This just simply is not so. ... This just makes my blood boil. People believe in the White House—at least they're supposed to." The White House hastily sent a correcting letter and a promise of an FBI investigation—but not before the evangelist's cries of persecution and harassment brought thousands of dollars of "the Lord's money" into his war chest.

But it was from Dixie that he drew most of his support. The Stars and Bars fluttered alongside the Stars and Stripes. The crowd sang "Dixie," and got some of the words wrong. The appeal was to causes popular in the South: Stop interference in school affairs, put Bible reading and prayer back in the schools, and get sex out. "I like our good brothers in the South," McIntire said. "It looks like they've got more fight in them than we've got farther north."

Aside from traffic problems, the marchers caused not a speck of trouble. One policeman volunteered the opinion that it had been the most peaceful march he had ever seen.

Now that the radio preacher has gained a sorely needed victory within shouting distance of the White House (see editorial, page 25),[1] there is little doubt that, if he speaks for the silent

---

1. "The Great Contender," pages 143–44 in this volume.

majority, there will be a lot more noise around Washington in
months to come.

William Willoughby, "Carl McIntire's Victory: 'In This Sign Conquer,'" *Christianity Today* 14, No. 15 (April 24, 1970): 35.

THE GREAT CONTENDER

THE EDITORS

The April 4 pro-war demonstration in Washington was a great personal triumph for Carl McIntire. It makes little difference whether the paraders numbered 15,000 or 50,000. Turnouts for such happenings hinge largely upon the extent of advance promotion. Given McIntire's meager means, a response of anything more than a few thousands must be considered successful.

Indeed, it was a moment of glory for the great contender. Only a few months ago McIntire seemed perched out on a lonely limb, isolated even from longtime friends who still shared his ideology. He surmised, however, that he could go it alone. What he needed was a spectacular achievement to show the scope of his personal influence, and he got it.

Many an evangelical groans at McIntire's success. It must be particularly difficult for those in the American Council of Christian Churches who share his theological and political views, even his separatist stance, but who had the courage to get out from under his high-handedness. These are conscientious people who deserve the fellowship of other evangelical believers.

McIntire is an intelligent man, a master of polemic, one whose convictions do not waver. Although neither a great orator nor a particularly attractive platform personality, he knows how to capitalize on restlessness and on the desire of some fundamentalists for a "king." Unfortunately, he tends to act more like a pope than a constitutional monarch.

We share McIntire's doctrine insofar as it embraces classic biblical orthodoxy, including the full authority and reliability of Scripture. We part company with him at the point of his politicking, which in theory is not different from that of the National Council of Churches, and his seeming acceptance of certain questionable social positions. Particularly abhorrent has been his appropriation of a verse on the Resurrection, "Thanks be to God which giveth us the victory" (1 Corinthians 15:57), as a campaign slogan in behalf of a military triumph in Viet Nam.

We also are turned off by McIntire's spirit, which goes beyond contending for the faith to contentiousness. He draws support for this attitude almost entirely from the Book of Jude, to the neglect of numerous other New Testament emphases. If Jesus and Paul had taken McIntire's advice, they would have devoted their lives, not to ministries of evangelism and compassion, but to campaigning for influence in Rome and drawing people out of the synagogues.

Those Christians tempted to flex their muscle at the president need to reread the Epistle of Jude. The description of heretics is strongly worded, but Jude's specific admonition to the saints is positive. The advice to "save with fear" is the last point in the list. Prior to that he urges: "But ye, beloved, building up yourselves on your most holy faith, praying in the Holy Ghost, keep yourselves in the love of God, looking for the mercy of our Lord Jesus Christ unto eternal life. And of some have compassion, making a difference ..."

The Editors, "The Great Contender," *Christianity Today* 14, No. 15 (April 24, 1970): 25–26.

★ *March 1, 1974* ★

EVANGELICAL SOCIAL CONCERN

CARL F. H. HENRY

T he Thanksgiving/73 "Declaration of Evangelical Social Concern" was significant for numerous reasons, some of which I shall indicate below.

Its importance for the future doubtless depends upon whether evangelical Christians can marshal cooperation for certain social objectives even as they do for evangelistic goals, whether some independent spirits make it an occasion of provocatory reaction, or whether others unilaterally exploit the statement for partisan purposes. No single evangelical enterprise or leader—whether *Christianity Today* or evangelist Billy Graham or whatever and whoever—today speaks definitively for evangelical social concern. Reasons for this are not hard to give, but no profitable purpose would be served by listing them here.

There is no doubt that the American evangelical outlook today is more disposed to social involvement than it has been for two generations. Yet those who have direct access to evangelical masses have not been providing principial leadership for authentic courses of action. This accommodates a great deal of confusion, the more so since ecumenical spokesmen, Carl McIntire, and others have successfully exploited mass-media coverage for conflicting positions that often have more support in emotion than in sound reason.

Whatever disposition some interpreters may have to shrug off the Chicago Declaration as saying nothing that had not already been said by denominational or ecumenical commissions on social action, negatively at least it avoided several mistakes to which contemporary religious activism has been highly prone. For some denominational spokesmen, changing social structures constitutes the church's evangelistic mission in the modern world; the call to the new birth in the context of a miraculous redemption—whether under the umbrella of Graham crusades, the Jesus movement, Key 73, or whatever—was considered a diversionary waste of time, energy, and money. The sole change demanded by the god of the social radicals is in social structures, not in individuals. The Chicago evangelicals, while seeking to overcome the polarization of concern in terms of personal evangelism or social ethics, also transcended the neo-Protestant nullification of the Great Commission.

A second defect of ecumenical social engagement has been its failure to elaborate the revealed biblical principles from which particular programs and commitments must flow if they are to be authentically scriptural. Insofar as the Chicago Declaration spoke, it attempted to do so in a specifically biblical way. The cleft between the ecumenical hierarchy and the laity, along with many clergy as well, derived in part from pervasive doubt that publicly approved socio-political particulars could actually be derived from "Christian ethics," "the Church," "the Cross," or whatever other spiritual flag was hoisted by religious lobbyists. Instead of being rallied to support specific legislative or social positions in view of hierarchical approval, a generation of churchgoers illiterate in scriptural principles of social ethics ought to have been nurtured in scriptural teaching and urged to seek a good conscience in applying the biblical principles to contemporary situations.

The Chicago Declaration did not leap from a vision of social utopia to legislative specifics, but concentrated first on biblical priorities for social change. A high responsibility presently rests on evangelical clergy to deepen the awareness of churchgoers—and their own expertise as well—in what the Bible says about social morality.

The Chicago Declaration sought to transcend the polarization of "right" and "left" by concentrating not on modern ideologies but on the social righteousness that God demands. To be sure, Chicago participants reflected a variety of perspectives, and many differences remain on specifics. Most of the biting social criticism of the twentieth century has been left to Marxists; this creates a climate in which Marxist solutions gain a hearing and prestige wider than they would have were they not permitted to preempt a field to which the ancient biblical prophets spoke boldly in a time when pagan kings were thought to be incarnate divinities and to rule by divine right.

The paramount Chicago concern was not to advance one or another of the current ideologies but to focus on the divine demand for social and political justice, and to discover what the Kingdom of God requires of any contemporary option. In brief, the Chicago evangelicals did not ignore transcendent aspects of God's Kingdom. Nor did they turn the recognition of these elements into a rationalization of a theology of revolutionary violence or of pacifistic neutrality in the face of blatant militarist aggression. Neither did they trumpet such fanfare as "capitalism can do no wrong" or "socialism is the hope of the masses." The real interest was in the question: What are the historical consequences of the economic ideologies for the masses of mankind?

To speak now of positive significance, one striking feature of the Chicago Declaration is the very fact of evangelical initiative in social action at a time when the secular and ecumenical social thrust is sputtering for lack of steam. Ecumenical activism accelerated to the peak of massive public demonstrations mounting direct political pressures upon Congress and the White House, at times involving civil disobedience and disruptive tactics. Failure of these power techniques to achieve effective social changes has understandably led to a disenchantment with public institutions, instead of reexamination of ecumenical policies, practices, and proposals for swift solution.

Evangelicals are contemplating anew the Evangelical Awakening, which is often said to have spared England the throes of the French Revolution. In that movement of social morality, evangelicals took an initiative in such matters as slavery, factory working conditions, child-labor laws, illiteracy, prison conditions, unemployment, poverty, education for the underprivileged, and much else. If ever America has stood in dire need of an awakening of both social and personal morality, the moment is now.

Another promising center of the Chicago conference was its interest in the problem of power and politics. Evangelicals see no promising way into the future of the nation unless the political scene reflects the participation of those who are involved for reasons higher than self-interest, a kind of political involvement now too much at a premium. While there is no disposition to launch an "evangelical political party," there is mounting concern for open evangelical engagement in the political arena.

If evangelical leadership means anything identifiable, it ought to imply at least that one's public moral responses in time of crisis are highly predictable. Sad to say, it does not always work out that way. But if it works out with a high degree of probability, the national scene could take a happy turn for the better.

Carl F. H. Henry, "Evangelical Social Concern," *Christianity Today* 18, No. 11 (March 1, 1974): 99–100.

★ *November 8, 1974* ★

ON BEING A
CHRISTIAN RADICAL

DAVID CLAYDON

T he modern language of "revolution," which enables us to reflect on ourselves as apart from and—if we desire—in conflict with society, finds its roots in the French Revolution, nearly 200 years ago. Here we have both a model for insurrection and a legend to which subsequent anti-society movements could appeal. Here is the source of gruesome facts and of inspiring ideals for anarchists and Marxists alike. But here too is the stark reminder that political insurrection may be little more than a myth.

Among the many modern disciples of Marx, the most widely recognized in this past decade has been Herbert Marcuse. Marcuse thinks that man has been so manipulated by capitalism that he actually enjoys affluence and its consequent values. In an attempt to climb out of his pessimism, Marcuse expresses in his book *One-Dimensional Man* the hope that youth and the intelligentsia will become radical and change society. How this could happen Marcuse doesn't tell us, but French students made a good attempt to put his words into action in May and June, 1968. The failure of what was potentially a second French revolution may in the light of history prove to be the largest single pragmatic reason for the decline of youth insurgency. In an era of pragmatism, it didn't work! But the language of the revolutionary continued to be used and was given new meaning on the university campuses, in hippie pads, and even among Christian youth.

Setting aside the problem of cultural syncretism by Christians, it appears that humanly speaking the language of the revolutionary has provided symbolic hardware that has halted the rapid decline of the youth membership of the Christian "church." I say "the language" because this symbolizes the potential dynamic and the existing doctrine of a body of people who have critically analyzed society and who are seeking to change it at the radix—the real root.

But how many of us, let alone those we lead, have solved the supposed dichotomy of personal salvation and salvation in society? In J. H. Yoder's words, how do "we choose between the catastrophic kingdom and the inner kingdom" (*The Politics of Jesus*, Eerdmans, 1972)? To me it is further evidence of God's sovereignty over history that he has used the radicalism of the sixties to radicalize a significant number of Christians.

While the events of history can trigger the process of radicalization, a radical movement will have substance only if it has a thoroughly worked-out ideological base. Yet the Christian has more than an ideal. He has the facts of God's acting in history, speaking to a nation through prophets, and then personally intruding into history.

The Scriptures teach that God created the world as an expression of his own creativity and for his enjoyment (Neh. 9:6; Isa. 43:7; Col. 1:16), that he did so freely (Eph. 1:11), and that he is not dependent on his creation in any way (Job 22:2, 3; Acts 17:28) but is sovereign over the whole of creation and sustainer of it (Eph. 4:6). We know all this because God has chosen to reveal himself to created man, and part of that revelation has been that man is created in the image of his Creator. So both man and the Triune God have personality and the potential to relate to each other.

Because of sin men were unable to relate to their Creator, but the Creator has chosen to redeem man. It is up to man to respond to this free gift. God has not discarded his creation because of sin. He continues to sustain it. He continues to allow the freedom for man to express his autonomy within history.

So we have a social reality over which God is sovereign and yet in which man has decided to be independent of God. God did not discard society for this reason but instead entered society to redeem those who would be redeemed. Those who are redeemed may see themselves either as a *remnant* or as *one instrument* through which God can act out his sovereignty over the fallen world. There are traces in the Old Testament of a remnant mentality (see Isaiah and Jeremiah) that may be understood to support the view that there are times in history when God's people are unable to speak to their society. But the very persistence of the remnant is in itself an instrument of God's sovereignty. So there is some validity in a remnant attitude, but there is a far stronger emphasis in the Scriptures on being a person through whom God can overtly exercise his will.

A study of the Old Testament prophets reveals that they performed a variety of tasks. For example, Samuel had, at least initially, a leadership role; Elijah called the people to worship the One True God; Elisha was deeply involved in politics, affirming that God is King, that God is sovereign over world politics. The integrity of our humanness does not suffer by our making Jesus our Lord. Rather, it is only when Jesus becomes our Lord that we become completely free. It is in true holiness that we find our true humanness. And it is in our humanness that we choose to let God work through us (that is, through our experience, talents, feelings, and opportunities) so that he may be glorified here on earth. Our freedom *from* the oppressor—the evil one—has meaning only in that it is freedom *to* something, namely, freedom to *be his.*

The single motive throughout the record of prophetic activity is to bring honor to God. The New Testament picks up the same theme (e.g., 1 Cor. 10:31; Phil. 2:11), that our foremost motivation is to bring glory to our King. Two other significant motives were simply stated by Jesus: "You shall love the Lord your God. ... You shall love your neighbor."

The importance of these three motives should preclude any method or style of activity that does not in itself reflect the qualities of glory and love. Failure to be motivated by these three factors can lead to disaster, as the accounts of the Kings of Israel and Judah make clear.

Was Jesus' attitude that his followers were a remnant, or did he see them as an instrument through which the Father could exercise his sovereign will over the world? Some have argued that Jesus' teaching was concerned not with society as such but only with individuals. Matthew 5 is pointed to as evidence of a position radical only for individuals. Yet Jesus called a *group* of men to follow him, and the personal radical ethics of the "Sermon on the Mount" was to be exemplified in this group. Yoder has argued from this that "to deny the powerful (sometimes conservative, sometimes revolutionary) impact on society of the creation of an alternative social group" would be "to overrate both the power and the manageability of those particular social structures identified as 'political!' " (p. 111). The very existence of a community of people who pursue a set of values different from the social milieu is radical in itself. It is not counterculture, which ultimately is a pessimistic humanism. It is, rather, the positive, affirming optimism of a God-given alternative culture.

Is the Christ-given alternative culture radical? We know that its ethics was radical in contrast to the ethical attitudes of the society of the day. But what impact was this to have on society? Jesus' instruction to his disciples in respect to society was that they were to be his witnesses. This means to declare *him*, and this must include who *he* is and what *he* has done for us. The proclamation of personal salvation includes the proclamation of the Kingdom of God. This proclamation is both personal and social.

Yet it is not a proclamation of a utopian hope for heaven on earth now; that clearly would not be biblical. It is a proclamation that God and not man is sovereign, or, to be more practical, that no one, no matter how senior or junior, in any given system need be irresistibly oppressed by the motives, ethics, values, or goals of that system (see Col. 2:13–15; Eph. 6:10–18). This seems to me to be the root, the radix, to which we as members of the Christian community must cut. To get to this radix is to be a Christian radical. The term "radical" ought to be automatically implied in the title "Christian." But to our great shame the Christian community as seen today as "the church" has been so culturally syncretistic that the radical quality, if ever evident, will be found only at the side door; the front-door appearance is that of just another comfortable institution for those who have the inclination to enjoy it.

Non-Christians will object to this Christian radical position, maintaining that the only really radical approach to society is to proclaim the complete destruction of the present "system" (that is, of government, corporation, WASP values, and so on). But we know that *any* alternative to the present system will be just as sinful. The reason for the false values is fallen man. Marx, Mao, Che Guevara, Marcuse—all these persons recognized the falseness but not the reason. But since we, through our Creator's revelation, can go one step further than Marx and Company, we do not get excited about the need for a radical change in the superstructure of society. Our lack of enthusiasm at this point reflects Christ's lack of enthusiasm for political revolution. The real revolution is that Christ is King, although his Kingdom is not "of" this world but rather is "over and above" all creation (John 18:36).

This still leaves one question. Should we be *issue-oriented*, that is, speaking or doing something about particular issues?

Jesus certainly did (e.g., his attitude toward the Sabbath, outcasts, the rich), but this is reform, not revolution. Confronting issues is a change within the system, not a change at the radix. We should surely be concerned to bring about reforms, but like Jesus and the apostles we should make our revolutionary intent clear first.

It is up to us to be his witnesses, seeking not just to stop the evil in the world, not merely to change the unacceptable into the acceptable, but first and foremost to expose the one-dimensional (Marcuse's term) foundation of our society by bringing to bear the spotlight of the second dimension, the vertical dimension of the potential God/man relationship.

David Claydon, "On Being a Christian Radical," *Christianity Today* 19, No. 3 (November 8, 1974): 6–7.

CAMPAIGN COUNTDOWN: "BLOC BUSTERS"

A nyone who expects all of America's evangelical Christians to vote the same way in the 1976 presidential election will probably be surprised when the votes are counted. As the campaign heated up during its last month it was increasingly evident that neither Gerald Ford nor Jimmy Carter could count on the highly touted "evangelical bloc."

Issues connected with religion kept popping up as election day neared, and they were alternately helping and hurting first one candidate, then the other. Abortion, the hottest religion-related subject in the early days of the presidential race, had to share attention in the final weeks with other concerns. Taxes, foreign policy, and the use of earthy language were among the topics claiming the attention of the campaigners and those who will vote for them.

Shortly after Carter drew a barrage of criticism for his income-tax proposals, attention was directed to a statement he made on curtailing church property-tax exemptions. In an interview in the September–October issue of *Liberty*, a Seventh-day Adventist magazine on church-state issues, the Democratic candidate said he favored "the taxation of church properties other than the church building itself." He was interviewed by a *Liberty* writer during the Ohio primary campaign last June.

After the Carter call for church property taxation appeared, he was attacked by Republican vice-presidential nominee Robert Dole. Declared Dole: "I find it incredible that Mr. Carter wants to impose taxes on church-owned hospitals, schools, senior-citizen homes, and orphanages. Is this really what he favors? Or is this just another case where Governor Carter has said something and may have to apologize later?"

Carter promptly issued a statement saying he never advocated taxing churches and as governor of Georgia tried to amend the state constitution so that sales taxes would not hit hospitals, nursing homes, and other church-affiliated organizations. He also pledged to try to protect the interests of charitable institutions in the tax-reform package he would propose as president.

At a White House meeting of his campaign committee on ethnic affairs, President Ford spoke to the issue: "Nothing could be worse for church-operated schools, hospitals, and orphanages, many of which face constant financial struggles to make ends meet. I can tell you unequivocally, emphatically, that this administration has neither plans nor supports any effort to tax churches beyond the present scope of federal taxation."

Foreign affairs took up much of the time when a group of thirty-four evangelical broadcasters discussed issues with Ford just a week before his second televised debate with Carter. He said there was "only a 60–40 percent chance of success" for Secretary of State Henry Kissinger's peace mission in southern Africa. He indicated it was worth the risk, saying, "If nothing were done by the United States it was likely that civil and international war would have erupted, with widespread bloodshed."

Endorsing the president's diplomatic initiatives in southern Africa during the White House meeting was Howard O. Jones, the senior black on the Billy Graham team and speaker on the "Hour of Freedom" radio program. Jones had returned to the United States the day before from three weeks in southern Africa, where he preached in Swaziland, an independent territory bordering on South Africa. "I told the president," the evangelist said after the meeting, "that thousands and thousands of Christians in Swaziland were praying his plan would work."

Carter meanwhile released the text of a cable of support that he dispatched to Donal R. Lamont, the Irish missionary bishop of Umtali, Rhodesia. The Roman Catholic prelate was convicted of aiding terrorists after failing to report the whereabouts of guerrillas who had demanded medicine at a church mission, and he was sentenced to a ten-year jail term.

Both major candidates continued to assure Jewish leaders of their interest in helping the state of Israel, but they also spoke of their support for the Jewish nation before evangelical audiences. Ford told the broadcasters that Kissinger's efforts in the Middle East "have borne fruit and the tensions have been substantially diffused."

(In the *Liberty* interview Carter said "a basic cornerstone of our foreign policy should be preservation of the nation of Israel, its right to exist, and its right to exist in a state of peace." He added that he thought its establishment as a modern state was a "fulfillment of Bible prophecy.")

The visiting broadcasters also heard a Ford pledge to maintain American troops in Korea at present levels. The president added that his administration would stand by America's treaty obligations with the Nationalist Chinese government.

Members of the executive committee of National Religious Broadcasters formed the core of the group that met Ford in the White House Cabinet Room. Other station operators and producers of religious programs were added to that group to provide geographical and denominational balance, according to Ben Armstrong, NRB's executive secretary.

Among the prominent broadcasters who came to Washington for the meeting was W. A. Criswell, whose weekly services are telecast from First Baptist Church of Dallas, Texas. Criswell, former president of the Southern Baptist Convention, had earlier been quoted as a critic of Carter's *Playboy* interview. The president was scheduled to attend a Sunday service at Criswell's church ten days after his White House session with the pastor. Criswell and other clergy among the broadcasters recounted details of their visit with Ford to their congregations.

The *Playboy* issue came up at the meeting with the president. Ford told his visitors that he had turned down an invitation to be interviewed by the magazine, which features a Carter interview in its November issue. Ford also denied any wrongdoing in the use of campaign funds while he was a congressman.

The broadcasters met with the president only a few hours before he learned of the obscene racial slur credited to Secretary of Agriculture Earl Butz. While they were waiting to see Ford, Butz and other ranking administration officials talked with them. Ford later reprimanded Butz and subsequently accepted his resignation. He also sent an apology to the broadcasters for having Butz at their meeting.

When Butz entered the Cabinet Room he asked Armstrong to tell him who was sitting in the chair he usually occupied during Cabinet meetings. Armstrong told him it was Jones, who had just returned from Africa. The then-secretary of agriculture is reported to have said, "Dr. Jones, you're sitting in my chair, and you grace it very well." None of the visitors knew at the time of the remark that was to force his resignation four days later.

The White House staffer who escorted the broadcasters to the Cabinet Room and arranged other meetings with religious leaders for Ford was Richard Brannon, an ordained Southern Baptist minister who recently moved from the White House's office of presidential personnel into the communications office. Brannon is also credited with preparations for the president's appearances earlier this year at the Southern Baptist Convention and the joint convention of the National Association of Evangelicals and National Religious Broadcasters.

While paying some attention to the nation's evangelicals, both candidates have continued to court the Catholic vote. On his way to the second debate Carter stopped in Denver for a speech at a Catholic Charities meeting. During Louisiana campaigning, Ford attended a service in the New Orleans cathedral.

Jeff Carter, the Democratic candidate's youngest son, got his father in hot water when he brought up the name of evangelist Billy Graham during an Oklahoma campaign appearance. A Tulsa radio station recorded the remarks, in which the 24-year-old suggested that Graham had bought a mail-order doctorate for $5. In a later comment in Kansas City his wife, Annette, added fuel to the fire by criticizing Graham's advice to voters to choose the best qualified candidate, whether he is a Christian or not. She said that was not "fair."

Within a week another Carter son, Chip, dissociated himself from the Tulsa remarks of his brother. He told a South Carolina audience that his father had apologized to Graham. Actually, Mrs. Carter called; forgivingly, Graham said he was unoffended.

Meanwhile Christian voters across the country were getting advice from various sources on how to make up their minds. C. Welton Gaddy, a staff member of the Southern Baptist

Christian Life Commission, wrote a series of articles for use in the Baptist press. One of his suggestions was expected to gain wide acceptance: "Southern Baptists must neither support nor oppose Jimmy Carter simply because he is a fellow Southern Baptist. Episcopalians should neither support nor oppose Gerald Ford because he is an Episcopalian."

Anonymous, "Campaign Countdown: 'Bloc Busters,'" *Christianity Today* 21, No. 2 (October 22, 1976): 109–10.

★ *November 2, 1979* ★

IS MORALITY ALL RIGHT?

The new religious lobbies say "yes"—with impact.

EDWARD E. PLOWMAN

For years, religion lobbyists have been quietly knocking on doors around the nation's capital, informing the people who run the country where churches and synagogues stand on various issues. With only occasional exceptions, though, Washington's religion lobby has wielded little political clout: legislators listen politely, but, as many of the religion lobbyists themselves wistfully acknowledge, that's about all most of them do.

This is not so, however, in the case of the newest religious lobbying force in town—the Christian allies of the political New Right. Backed by prominent television preachers and with links to both New Right political organizations and conservative members of Congress, several Christian "profamily, promorality" groups have popped into public view this year, and the political establishment—from President Jimmy Carter down—is taking note.

The new groups have Protestant fundamentalist and evangelical origins, but they are inclusivist in their political strategy, eager to recruit anyone from Mormons to Roman Catholics who will help them win their objectives. They have declared war on immorality in America's social life, on "secular humanism" in the schools and elsewhere, and on government intrusion in Christian education and other church affairs. One notable victory: Congress, under heavy pressure mustered mostly by the Christian groups and their allies, shackled the Internal Revenue Service, preventing the agency from applying new tests aimed at determining whether religious and other private schools practice racial discrimination in enrollment (see Oct. 5 issue, p. 58).

The Christian political activists have drawn a bead on legislation and legislators alike, and they intend to carry the fight into the uttermost precincts of the nation by election time next year. Candidates who don't take a forthright position against gay rights and permissive abortion, for example, or for the return of prayer and Bible reading in the public schools, may be in deep trouble.

Leaders of the Christian groups reject the accusation that they are reactionaries hopelessly mired in negativism. Earlier this year, in action described as "positive," they and their New Right allies drafted a proposed bill known as the Family Protection Act, and Republican Senator Paul Laxalt of Nevada, a Catholic, dropped it into the legislative hopper in September.

Among the dozens of provisions in the bill: a return of voluntary prayer to public schools; an end to compulsory intermingling of the sexes in sports programs; tax incentives to help families provide better care for elderly and student dependents; an end to income tax inequities for married couples (unmarried couples presently have a tax advantage); tax deductibility for a wife's housework; tightening of the food stamp program; greater freedom from federal regulations for religious organizations; withholding of funds from any entity that promotes homosexual life-styles; protection of parental rights from government encroachment; and a requirement that clinics and doctors notify a minor's parents before commencing treatment for pregnancy or venereal disease.

Two of the groups, Christian Voice and Moral Majority, are registered as non-profit, nonexempt corporations (contributions are not tax deductible). They can therefore lobby extensively and even become involved in election campaigns, unhampered by the restrictions that limit the political activities of most religious organizations.

Christian Voice was founded last January by a group of Californians headed by travel agent Robert Gordon Grant, 43, of Los Angeles. Grant, a Fuller Theological Seminary graduate with a Christian and Missionary Alliance background, served for eight years as assistant pastor under Americanism preacher W. Steuart McBirnie at the 1,200-member Glendale Community Church. He also was founding dean of the California Graduate School of Theology. More recently he founded American Christian Cause to combat the gay activist movement.

Voice, says Grant, was created out of a ground swell of interest among evangelicals who wanted to become more involved politically in shaping America's moral future. "They felt that Christians were losing by default," comments Grant. He speaks of "a tidal wave of unrest and frustration sweeping the Christian community. ... We seek to guide its power so it has a massive impact on Washington, rather than dissipating aimlessly."

He points out that Voice is actually an amalgamation of organizations that include the ACC, the antipornography Citizens for Decency Through Law, and the Pro-Family Coalition. Among the policy committee members are well-known southern California Baptist pastors Ted Cole and Jess Moody, television producer Paul Webb, and author-lecturer Hal Lindsey (*The Late Great Planet Earth*).

So far, 16 members of Congress have been recruited for the Voice's congressional advisory committee. They include four Republican senators: Mormon Orrin G. Hatch of Utah, Lutheran Roger Jepsen of Iowa, Baptist Gordon Humphrey of New Hampshire, and Methodist James McClure of Idaho. (The influential McClure chairs a group of New Right senators known as the Steering Committee.)

Grant serves as president, and a former Foursquare Gospel minister, Richard Zone, is executive director. Zone will work out of offices in Pasadena and Pacific Grove, California. The Voice's Washington office is headed by its legislative director, Gary Jarmin, a Southern Baptist who served for several years in a similar capacity for the American Conservative Union. Before that, he worked Washington's legislative haunts for six years for controversial Korean evangelist Sun Myung Moon. At the time of his defection from Moon in 1974 in a squabble over policy and beliefs, Jarmin was secretary general of the Freedom Leadership Foundation, the Unification Church's most effective front. He believes that Christians are potentially "the most powerful political force in the nation."

The Voice has budgeted $1 million for its efforts in 1979, and $3 million next year—some of it earmarked for conservative candidates. Its direct mail fundraising campaign is being handled by Jerry Hunsinger, 46, of Richmond, Virginia, a former Methodist minister whose accounts include the television ministries of Jerry Falwell and Robert Schuller, singer Anita Bryant's antigay and profamily work, Citizens for Decency Through Law, and a number of Catholic organizations and other charities. An evangelical, he also oversees fundraising for the Moral Majority.

There are at least 50 million conservative-minded church people out there, muses Grant, and he hopes to enlist many of them in Voice's promorality political crusade. Already, some 130,000 persons—including 1,200 Protestant ministers and several hundred Catholic priests—have become members, he discloses.

Voice plans to blitz millions of viewers of Christian television with spot announcements alerting them to issues in Congress and suggesting what they ought to do. There will be weekly half-hour commentary shows and a 30-minute special featuring prominent Christian and government leaders. Meanwhile, a 30-minute documentary film, *The Doomsday Report,* produced by Hal Lindsey and featuring Senator Hatch, will be promoted throughout the country. It deals with America's moral decline.

Clergy will receive a monthly legislative bulletin, complete with recommendations to share with parishioners.

At the end of the year, says Jarmin, Voice will produce the first of its morality report cards on Congress. Legislators will be rated on a "morality scale," according to how they vote on a variety of issues deemed by Voice leaders to have a morality factor.

It is this element that seems to bother critics most. For example, Voice leaders have a way of reasoning how a vote to lift sanctions against Zimbabwe is moral, while a vote against it is immoral. They apply the same sort of reasoning to other controversial issues as well, almost always arriving at the same positions as those held by New Right politicians. Like the New Right, they opposed Carter's China policy and the Panama Canal treaties.

But on many issues, the critics contend, no "Christian position" as such exists. They argue that equally devout and biblically informed Christian legislators may cast opposing votes on an issue. If that occurs, the critics insist, it is more a matter of difference in philosophy, not morality.

Moral Majority was organized last June by television preacher Jerry Falwell, 45, of the 16,000-member Thomas Road Baptist Church in Lynchburg, Virginia. His goal is to mobilize two million people to work for government policies based on traditional moral and biblical principles. One possibility: a constant bombardment of Congress with millions of letters every time an issue vital to Moral Majority is at stake.

Serving with Falwell on the board of directors are Baptist ministers Tim LaHaye of San Diego and Greg Dixon of Indianapolis.

LaHaye and his wife, Beverly, authors of books on family relationships, chair what amounts to a Christian family lobby in Washington: Family America. It disseminates advance information on family and moral issues in government, and it serves as a resource agency for family-oriented organizations needing assistance in their programs. Jay Grimstead of the International Council on Biblical Inerrancy is president, and Susan Wismar looks after legislative research.

Dixon, of the 7,000-member Indianapolis Baptist Temple, is a veteran of political wars. Earlier this year he led 400 ministers to form a human chain around Texas evangelist Lester Roloff's home for problem children, temporarily preventing authorities from closing the home. He has organized antigay and antipornography rallies, and he pushed through the Indiana legislature an omnibus bill designed to protect religious organizations from government interference.

Falwell's "Old-Time Gospel Hour" is aired weekly on more than 300 television stations and has an audience numbering in the millions. (Two million persons are on record as active donors to the telecast within the past year alone.) Falwell recalls that as he thought about his TV audience, he realized that a "moral majority" exists in America: people from many church backgrounds, concerned about the nation's moral drift and its impact upon their families, but unorganized and unable to stop the decline. Meanwhile, the "other side" was getting all the press attention.

Although from a strongly separatist church background, Falwell decided it was time for the majority to join hands, himself included. Some of his strongest support, he noted, had come from Mormons and Catholics when he preached against pornography, gay rights, abortion on demand, the Equal Rights Amendment, and on other topics that touched on family life and morality. Doctrinal differences could be thrashed out later, he concluded:

more urgent matters were at hand, and he needed all the help he could get.

Robert Billings was named executive director of the Moral Majority lobby. Billings, a graduate of Bob Jones University, was the founding president of Hyles-Anderson College, a school sponsored by well-known fundamentalist pastor Jack Hyles and his 18,000-member First Baptist Church of Hammond, Indiana.

Billings resigned his college post in 1976 to run for Congress. Unsuccessful, he moved to Washington anyway and set up shop as a consultant representing fundamentalist Christian schools in their dealings with the government. In the process, he established friendships with important people on Capitol Hill that are now paying off.

As he visited among leaders of anti-abortion and New Right political organizations, Billings discovered that many of them were as concerned as he about America's overall moral state and the alarming disintegration of traditional family values. He was soon accepted into the inner circle of New Right leadership as friend and adviser. He became treasurer of the Free Congress Research and Education Foundation, which publishes *Family Protection Report*, a conservative profamily newsletter. The foundation is headed by New Right leader Paul Weyrich, a devout Eastern rite Catholic who also directs the Committee for the Survival of a Free Congress.

Meanwhile, Billings organized the National Christian Action Coalition to research and publicize national issues of special interest to church people, and to provide a rallying point for like-minded Christians to work for change.

When Billings, who also sits on the policy committee of Christian Voice, took the helm of Moral Majority, his son William, 29, assumed leadership of NCAC. The younger Billings, likewise a Bob Jones graduate with a background in Christian school administration, has also directed another Washington-based organization, the Conservative Leadership Youth Foundation.

The elder Billings was the person most responsible for mobilizing the powerful church opposition that eventually led to the demise of the IRS's plans to make it tougher for private schools to pass nondiscrimination tests and retain their tax exemptions.

Using Falwell's 250,000-name prime donors list, Moral Majority last month raised nearly one-third of its first-year budget of $1 million. Like Christian Voice and other groups, Moral Majority will send legislative alerts to its constituency, and it may mount campaigns similar to those envisioned by Voice.

Falwell, Moral Majority's founder, has become increasingly active in political circles in the past several years. He is a familiar figure in Virginia Republican gatherings: some lawmakers say that his endorsement—or lack of it—can mean the difference in an election. At election time, politicians from both major parties beat a path to his church. He played a key role in the defeat of the Equal Rights Amendment and pari-mutuel gambling in Virginia.

Some legislators in Washington sense that Falwell, with his vast television following, is becoming a powerful figure on the national political scene as well. When earlier this year the minister taped his "I Love America" rally on the Capitol steps for airing on national television, a number of senators and representatives (including Mormons) unabashedly took seats next to Falwell, and some gave testimonials on camera supporting Falwell's antiimmorality, profamily, and pro-God views. One of the senators was Republican Jesse Helms of North Carolina, a Southern Baptist who has been trying for years to restore prayer to public schools. He is perhaps Falwell's staunchest backer in the Senate.

Liberals in and out of Congress resent Falwell's involvement in politics. Some religious leaders are upset, too. Executive James Payne of the Virginia Council of Churches has been quoted as saying that the close relationship between Falwell and Virginia Governor John N. Dalton, a fellow Baptist, comes close to infringing on the doctrine of separation of church and state.

A ruckus broke out recently over a remark Falwell made at an "I Love America" rally in Richmond attended by Dalton, Lieutenant Governor Charles S. Robb, and Attorney General Marshall Coleman. While making a strong defense of Israel during his talk, Falwell quipped that a Jew "can make more money accidentally than you can on purpose." Falwell explained to critics later that his remark was made "in jest" and was not intended to be taken as a racial slur. He promised not to repeat it. Unmoved, the critics suggested that Dalton and the other politicians should have walked out after Falwell made the remark. Dalton and Robb disagreed. Said Robb: "It was an unfortunate choice of words, but in the context in which they were spoken, I don't think it was an anti-Semitic remark."

Both on television and in print, Falwell has been blasting the SALT II arms limitation agreement as a sell-out to the Soviets, a position held unanimously by the New Right. In September, Robert L. Maddox, a Southern Baptist minister who serves on the White House staff as Jimmy Carter's liaison officer with religious groups, and a State Department official, traveled to Lynchburg to discuss SALT II with Falwell. They apparently failed to change his mind, however.

Insiders acknowledge that SALT II is in trouble in the Senate as opposition mail pours in, much of it prompted by New Right-aligned religious groups and preachers like Falwell. As part of a counterattack, the administration invited a contingent of 155 leaders representing 27 national religious organizations, including the National Council of Churches, to a White House breakfast in September. They were briefed on SALT II by Carter himself and by other administration officials.

Afterward, many of the participants fanned out among Senate offices to lobby for the treaty's ratification. Echoing some liberals on Capitol Hill, several participants said they are opposed to SALT II because they do not feel it goes far enough on the issue of disarmament. They said they were willing to back it, however, as a step in the right direction.

(In a separate development that cheered the Carter administration but dismayed politically conservative evangelicals, evangelist Billy Graham announced he'd had a change of mind and now favors nuclear disarmament and SALT II.)

Falwell and the new Christian political action movement have been receiving major press coverage over the past several months, including cover stories in *Conservative Digest* and *U.S. News and World Report*. In addition to Falwell, the cover stories featured another television personality, Pat Robertson, 48, founder of Christian Broadcasting Network and cohost of its popular "700 Club" show.

The son of a former U.S. senator from Virginia, Robertson has openly backed conservative Christian candidates in that state, and he has invited several conservative congressmen as guests on the "700 Club." The program is viewed by millions on 150 TV stations and about 3,000 cable systems.

Robertson has publicly questioned President Carter's competence, warned against the excessive influence of liberals in public policy, and suggested that the American government is really under the control of a leftist elite. Conservative Catholics and Protestants need to unite to rescue America, he says. Together, he wrote recently, "we have enough votes to run the country." To get the point across, he hopes to rally one million Christians to a meeting in Washington next year.

The broadcaster joined 17 other conservative Christian leaders in a private meeting with Republican presidential candidate

John B. Connally at Connally's Texas ranch in August to discuss issues and possible support. Others in the party included Falwell, Billings, Dixon, educator Bob Jones III, executive director Ben Armstrong of National Religious Broadcasters, Robert Dugan of the National Association of Evangelicals Washington office, Southern Baptist Convention president Adrian Rogers, and Ed McAteer, who is the national field director of the Conservative Caucus. (A member of Rogers's church in Memphis, McAteer is said to be a key figure in bringing together New Right leaders and the emerging conservative Christian activists.)

Sources say the group was more than pleased for the most part by Connally's positions on issues. The same delegation, with the addition of pastor Jack Hyles and evangelist Jack Wyrtzen, also met with Ronald Reagan, Howard Baker, Jr., and Philip Crane last month. So far, Reagan seems to be the favored candidate among the Christian leaders, with Connally a close second.

The partiality shown Reagan has caused some minor tension in New Right circles. Richard A. Viguerie, the conservative direct mail expert (he raised $8 million for Jesse Helms's 1978 campaign), recently parted company with Illinois Republican Congressman Crane and went to work for Connally. "I think the conservative movement should support him," Viguerie said. "In four or eight years, we can try to work for someone more conservative."

Viguerie, a Catholic who sends his children to a fundamentalist Christian school in suburban Washington, is part of the inner circle of the conservative Christian–New Right coalition in Washington. He controls mailing lists that contain the names of four million political conservatives, and he published *Conservative Digest.* For the first time, outsiders now have access to Viguerie's lists, and fundraiser Hunsinger is expected to use them to build support for Christian Voice and Moral Majority.

The big difference between the New Right and the Old Right is one of tone and style. The contemporary conservatives are more optimistic, more activist, and more cooperative with each other than their ideological forebears, according to analysts. In some respects, the same is true of the latter-day fundamentalists. Perhaps the most striking change from past days is their willingness to cooperate with nonfundamentalists and even non-Christians to achieve mutual objectives.

Leaders of the Christian lobbies attend weekly strategy meetings of the Kingston Group, a broad coalition of conservative political and special-interest organizations. They also attend twice-a-month meetings of the Library Court Group, a coalition of conservative religious, morality, and antiabortion lobbies. Many of the Library Court people are also members of Kingston. The coalition meetings serve as an information clearinghouse and a coordination center for lobbying and other activities. Members are pledged to maintain secrecy about what goes on in the meetings. It is known, however, that mutual-support agreements are forged at some of them (one Christian leader, for example, acknowledged that he had agreed to help out the National Rifle Association on an issue in return for backing of his causes). The "support" may involve anything from simply contacting a single congressman to mounting a major letter-writing and mass media campaign.

Comments Paul Weyrich, "This is no false unity based on papering over doctrinal differences. ... Our very right to worship as we choose, to bring up our families in some kind of moral order, to educate our children free from the interference of the state, to follow the commands of Holy Scripture and the church is at stake. These leaders have concluded it is better to argue about denominational differences at another time. Right now, it is the agenda of those opposed to the Scriptures and the church which has brought us together."

Falwell expressed similar sentiment before 12,000 at a rally in Dallas a few months ago to raise $100,000 for a legal fund for Texas evangelist James Robison. The evangelist, who preaches weekly on nearly 100 TV stations, was cancelled by WFAA-TV in Dallas for his hotly worded sermons against homosexuality. Station executives, including at least one evangelical, feared they would be forced to provide free time to gays as a consequence. (The rift was later resolved and Robison's program was reinstated.)

Seated with Falwell on the platform were ministers of varying racial, ethnic, and denominational backgrounds, including traditionalist Catholic theologian William H. Marshner (a brilliant New Right theoretician), and president Gary Potter of the Washington-based Catholics for Christian Political Action. A Jew, director Howard Phillips of Conservative Caucus, gave the opening address.

Falwell looked toward the press table and said: "The media had better understand that in another context we would be shedding blood [over our doctrinal differences]. But our commitment to the family has brought those of us of differing religious views and backgrounds together to fight a just cause ... to fight for the family."

Until Billings and the other Christian activists hit town, the Washington religion lobby was composed of about 100 persons representing several dozen organizations. Most of the big denominations and groups like the National Council of Churches and the National Association of Evangelicals have Washington staffs to look after their interests.

With several exceptions, including the NAE, their lobbying priorities have been such social issues as disarmament, poverty, hunger, health care, and racism, and their viewpoints have been mostly liberal. The only major parting of ranks occurs when the Catholics go their own way on abortion (against) and parochiaid (for).

The groups prepare newsletters, do research on pertinent issues, develop background papers, compile voting records, testify at legislative hearings, file court briefs, and jawbone with legislators and bureaucrats. Most tread lightly, in accord with IRS policy specifying that "no substantial part" of a nonprofit organization's activity should involve "carrying on propaganda or otherwise attempting to influence legislation."

Only two of the liberal-oriented religious groups have registered as nonexempt lobbies and thus are not bound by the IRS policy: the Quaker-related Friends Committee on National Legislation, and Network, an effective 4,300-member organization headed by Catholic nuns.

To coordinate their work better, and to make up for staff and budget limitations, the religion lobbyists have formed an association: the Washington Interfaith Staff Council.

Many of those in WISC are distressed over Christian Voice and Moral Majority. To them, the new conservative groups represent a cruel attempt to baptize right-wing and even extremist politics, thereby exploiting millions of uninformed believers and distorting the Christian message. "They claim they will finally get us Christian representation in Washington, but I think that shows considerable arrogance," Lutheran lobbyist Charles Bergstrom told reporters. "There are many Christians, and it's impossible to talk about one point of view representing Christian views."

The conservative Christian campaign, the critics warn, can lead to demagoguery and radical divisiveness in America's religious life. Adam DeBaugh, director of the Washington office of the predominantly homosexual Universal Fellowship of Metropolitan

Community Churches, sees it as a direct threat to the civil rights of homosexuals and possibly other minority groups.

Nonsense, says Senator Hatch. He says he sees nothing wrong in fundamentalists and other conservative Christians making up for a lack of representation of their views in traditionally liberal religious bodies like the NCC and denominational lobbies. "The other side has been working too long without opposition," he says.

A Washington columnist suggests that the liberals have only themselves to blame. He asks: "How can you be so concerned about the sugar-coated cereal that goes into a kid's mouth without also being concerned about the filth that goes into his mind?"

The NAE's Robert Dugan, a Baptist minister from Colorado who failed in a bid for Congress, says he sympathizes with many of the goals of the conservative Christian lobbyists, but he hopes they do not mistakenly attach religious labels to issues that should have none. He also hopes they will broaden their concerns to encompass more of the spectrum of human need.

Partially in response to the formation of Christian Voice and similar groups, the Christian Life Commission of the 13-million-member Southern Baptist Convention launched the Christian Citizenship Corps. Spokesman William Elder said that the corps will be an alternative to organizations that have "wedded conservative politics and conservative Christianity."

The goal of the program is to enlist "a grassroots network of Southern Baptists" who will become involved in political action "to promote public righteousness." The commission will collect and channel information on legislative issues "and their ethical implications" to corps members, primarily through a "Moral Alert" newsletter when fast action is called for on special issues, Elder said. Although headquarters may take positions on issues, he indicated that corps members will not be told "what they should think and how they should vote."

According to an SBC news release, formation of the corps marks the first time the nation's largest Protestant denomination has attempted to mobilize political action through an organized structure.

It may or may not remove some of the heat from the Southern Baptist who occupies the White House.

Edward E. Plowman, "Is Morality All Right?" *Christianity Today* 23, No. 25 (November 2, 1979): 76–85.

THE CHRISTIAN AS CITIZEN: THREE VIEWS

Charles Colson, Jerry Falwell, and Jim Wallis represent three widely divergent views concerning the Christian as citizen. Each interacted at length with *Christianity Today* Institute participants, clarifying their views through a question/answer session.

1: A VIEW FROM THE EVANGELICAL CENTER

CHARLES COLSON, CHAIRMAN OF THE BOARD, PRISON FELLOWSHIP MINISTRIES

How would you respond to those who say an elected official's faith is a private matter and should not be implemented in his public life?

This is the view advanced by Gov. Mario Cuomo and others. If they mean that we can't impose what we may think is God's will upon a pluralistic society, I would agree. But Cuomo went beyond that. He argued that he was under no obligation to help create a consensus toward moral positions in the society. If as Christians we privately believe something but it has no effect on our actions, we have a dreadful denial of the lordship of Christ.

Are you then more attracted to some of the organized Christian political movements?

The danger with Christian political movements per se is that they tend to make the gospel hostage to a particular political agenda. You may wrap the cross in the flag and make God a prop for the state. This is a grave danger.

How can the Christian community determine the public issues worthy of their energies at any point?

I think if you start reading the Bible you will see that there is a whole agenda that God has laid before us on the makeup of a righteous society. Obviously the abortion issue has to be at the top of everyone's list because we are dealing with human life, and the sanctity of life is such a fundamental biblical principle.

Perhaps a threshold question would be laws that in any way restrain or interfere with the proclamation of the gospel, and I mean not merely its verbal proclamation. The Soviet Union in 1928 made worship officially legal, but they abolished the church's role in help to the poor, church schools, aid to the needy, and other social functions. "Go ahead and worship, sing your hymns—that's fine. But if you start helping people, you're invading the priorities of a sovereign state."

Do you see this today anywhere in North America?

We see some freedoms being chipped away. A local zoning board in Fairfax County, Virginia, threatened to rescind the zoning of a church because it houses indigent people at night. And the basis for their stand was that it is not the responsibility of the church to take care of people at night. The church should only conduct Sunday morning worship services. So the zoning officials are writing the agenda for the church.

Then you have the Marian Guinn case in Oklahoma, a case of church discipline over sexual morality. The church withdrew fellowship from her and she won a $390,000 judgment against the church for invading her privacy. One of the jurors said, "Well, what right does the church have to tell a person how to live?"

There is, then, a mindset gradually evolving in America that says the church doesn't have any real relevance to how people live.

When you advocate criminal justice legislation, what argument do you make to the non-Christian for support?

We're in a society in which 91 percent of the people say they believe in God, 81 percent say they are Christians. So when I argue for restitution in criminal justice policies I never fail to say that it is not only working now, that it is not only less expensive than incarceration, that it is more redemptive to the individual and pays back the victim, but—by the way—that it is what God in Exodus 21 instructed Moses to do first at Mount Sinai.

A congressman was asked in the last election, "If you were elected to represent the people, and your will differs from the people's, will you vote your will or the will of the people who elected you to office?" How would you answer that?

Do we have a republic or a pure democracy? If we have a republic, the elected office holder is given certain responsibilities to lead the people and sometimes to make decisions that are contrary to the prevailing climate. It is the politician of courage and conscience who can stand between the mob and justice.

Can principled Christians survive in politics?

I don't believe you can privately believe one thing and publicly act another way. If you believe one way you must take your stand, follow your conscience and God's leading, and attempt to get the public on your side. If you fail and still feel as a matter of conscience that you then cannot discharge the law, then you have got to resign. God ordained government. The opposite is anarchy, which is worse than sinful government. But in being involved, we need to be free to pursue biblical righteousness as we're best able to understand it, either as officials or as citizens.

Looking back on your own career in politics, could you have survived as a Christian?

I've thought, "Could I—believing what I believe today—have served four years as special counsel to President Nixon?" And the answer is, categorically, no. I would either have resigned or been exiled to the outer circle.

On what points would you have felt the pressure?

The whole way you fight your battles. Telling the truth. It wouldn't have come up frontally on religious issues because Nixon happened to believe most of the things we evangelicals believe on fundamental values. It would have come up in one's demeanor toward other people. Politics is a brutal game—particularly brutal at that level.

Does that mean we should discourage Christian people from going into politics?

Oh, no. We must just get better people in there who will be able to withstand those pressures and survive as long as they can.

2: A VIEW FROM FUNDAMENTALISM

JERRY FALWELL, PRESIDENT, MORAL MAJORITY

You are widely perceived to be intent on installing a theocracy, similar to the Puritan colonies in Massachusetts. How do you deal with that?

I don't think anybody who believes his Bible would want a theocracy or believes there is going to be one until Christ returns. I think that, because the national media has intentionally painted this picture, the general public looks on Bible-believing Christians as people who want to do what the ayatollah has done in Iran.

I personally could vote for a Jew for president or any other political office, or a Roman Catholic or Protestant as quickly as I could a fundamentalist as long as the person was competent to fill that office, was committed to the principles and values that I believe in, and had a track record of personal behavior and conduct that was becoming to that office.

On a moral issue like abortion, on what grounds do you ask non-Christian people to stand with you against it? Do you appeal to Scripture, or is there some other argument?

I would stand the same way Charles Finney did in the slavery debate of the 1850s, arguing that we're dealing with the lives of real human beings. Most of the American people are, unfortunately, totally unconcerned about what the Bible says; but I think there is plenty of support for the dignity of human life beyond the Bible. I work very hard at quoting no Scripture when, for example, I am on *The Phil Donahue Show*, so the secular audience won't tune us out. Yet I want to say scriptural things. I think you can avoid Scripture without violating Scripture.

You avoid Scripture so that you won't be tuned out. That's very pragmatic.

I don't think that pragmatism is always compromise. If you have a planeload of hijacked people—men, women and children—and the hijacker agrees to let the women and children go, you don't say, "No—either everybody or nobody."

I think you can state principles in modern terms that meet the criteria of all sides (or almost all) and thereby bring in a much-larger coalition toward a desired goal than if you decide, "I'm just going to bring the fundamentalists in." To do that on an issue like abortion, we're going to have to give a little—exceptions for rape, incest, and the life of the mother. Slowly, we're educating our people to a kind of pragmatism that doesn't violate their conscience and accomplishes by consensus a general good—not an ideal good—but a general good. And in the meantime, in our pulpits we can stand for the ideal.

Do you expect an issue such as abortion to be solved on the legislative or the judicial level? Or should it be addressed in the culture?

I think we have a lot to do before we can turn to the justices in the courts and say, "Change the law."

Twenty-five years ago Bishop Fulton Sheen said the church has no right to tell a teenage girl who is pregnant out of wedlock, "You cannot have an abortion," unless, when she asks, "Who is going to take care of me?" the church is willing to say, "We will."

This is why in the past three years we have started 191 Save a Baby Centers nationally. We plan to start a thousand in the next five years. We've worked with 11,000 pregnant girls in the past 35 months, and not one has had an abortion after the first counseling session, and not one has left us without accepting Christ as Savior.

I think in this decade we will have some kind of court ruling on the abortion issue, even if it will never be as absolute as it once was. But when that happens and convenience abortions are history, we've got to have in place a structure to handle the 1.4 million girls who are pregnant without any money so they will have an alternative to the back alley abortionist.

The literature of Moral Majority does not present that emphasis.

Moral Majority is a political organization that is involved in one thing only—political change. While we continue that emphasis, we in the churches have got to be consistent in our ministry and go after the creation of the structure I've just described. If we do, I think we will succeed on both sides.

In your statements on nuclear defense you appear to have written off those fellow Christians who may believe in defense but who reject the extremes of a nuclear solution.

It's just that I disagree—not that I think they are heretics. I personally think that conventional defense is not adequate to prevent nuclear blackmail.

I feel the president's position is not a warlike one. I really believe that the best deterrent to war, and the best guarantee to peace, is a strong defense. If we had all of the young men in this nation under arms, with every conventional warfare ability at their disposal, we'd be nothing compared to the nuclear might of the Soviets.

Even though on a personal level you are known to be likable, your whole style of political confrontation is perceived to be that of a political hornet. Some people feel this is wholly incompatible both with democratic dialogue in a pluralistic society and with your profession as an ambassador of the love of Christ.

I hope in my own life there is a growth going on that leads away from some of that unnecessary stridency. I think you can go too far in the other direction, however, and become ineffectual, afraid to step on ants. Finding the middle has not been easy for me.

3: A VIEW FROM THE EVANGELICAL LEFT

JIM WALLIS, EDITOR, SOJOURNERS

Although you are not formally in politics, you are mainly known for your political positions. How do you unite your biblical and your political interests?

At the heart of everything else, I'm a pastor in a local congregation in Washington, D.C. The gospel has a personal and a public meaning. And we're trying to understand what that meaning is both on a personal level in our own lives and on the public level.

How does the Bible inform the public side of your Christian mission?

If we want to be biblical, our views and politics should be profoundly shaped by the priority of the poor. In my seminary days, we made a study of the Bible to find everything it said about the poor. We went through the entire Bible to find every passage about poor people. We found the Bible literally filled with the subject, second only to idolatry.

One of us took scissors and cut out of a Bible every reference to poor people, love for enemies, and reconciliation. It took him a long time to do it, and when he was done, the Bible that he was using was falling apart. I used to take that old Bible out with me to preach. I used to hold it high in the air and say to congregations of Christian people, "Brothers and sisters, this is the American Bible, full of holes from all we have cut out, all we have ignored. Our Bible is full of holes."

How would you answer those who say you impose your political ideology on the Bible just as Jerry Falwell imposes conservative politics?

It is dangerous to go to the Bible with any ideological framework. I don't believe that any ideological system or perspective can be justified from the Bible. I think the priority of the poor in the Bible is as clear as anything there, but that it does not prescribe specific solutions.

Those who believe in a liberal welfare state, for example (which I don't), or a Marxist reordering of things, or the laissez-faire capitalist system have difficulty deriving any justification from the Bible. But the priority of the poor is clear. And that raises a question about our response to the poor in concrete ways.

How consistently can you distinguish biblical politics from ideological politics? An article in *Sojourners* before the 1984 presidential election presented Reagan as the worst political option. It predicted "his second administration will be free of whatever restraints public opinion may have placed upon the greed and militarism of the first, a long-term crisis facing the U.S. economy will continue to deepen, the military budget will continue with its lunatic spiral." Is this not the language of ideological politics?

Sojourners is a journal of opinion, and this article reflects our opinion about what we can expect from the second Reagan term in the White House.

If the poor are the biblical priority, then we have to make a political judgment about how the poor will fare, specifically, in the second Reagan term. That same article is also very critical of the Democratic alternative of Walter Mondale around many of these same questions.

This was our opinion about what was going to happen. And it was not governed by, for example, a Marxist perspective. There are people who root themselves in the Bible who condemn the injustice of the American system not because of Marx, but because of the Bible. Others may disagree with us, but to simply call that "ideological" or Marxist misses the point. My objection to the American system of wealth and power is not because of Marx but because of the Bible.

Your rejection of nuclear weapons is total. You make it a test of Christian faithfulness. But how realistic is this in today's international scene? Surely there is no way to roll back history and banish nuclear weapons.

I do believe that, by the grace of God, things are possible that Christians don't believe are possible. Most people once believed that slavery was inevitable. Now, looking back, that view seems nonsensical to us. Most Christians thought slavery was so bound up in the fabric of society, and that the economy depended on it. Only a handful of Christian visionaries could, through the eyes of faith, see a world without slavery.

Are you urging unilateral disarmament?

We have always said that nuclear weapons must be abolished everywhere and anywhere they are. We have called for unilateral initiative on the part of the U.S.

And the time has come for the church to say as the church, unequivocally, that nuclear weapons are morally unacceptable and can never be sanctioned.

That's a faith position; governments are not bound by these things. So we will have to propose what ethicists call "middle axioms," steps toward a moral position that secular governments will feel are reasonable while there is moral persuasion going on.

I think it is very possible for nations, just pursuing their own perception of self-interest and survival, to begin to take steps away from the brink of nuclear confrontation and military build-up. And finally, I don't believe nuclear weapons will be abolished without a spiritual awakening.

Where do you stand on the abortion question?

Christians must stand up in defense of life everywhere it is threatened, whether it be unborn lives, whether it be peasants in Central America feeling terror and death, whether it be lives of enemy populations under the shadow of our missiles, or whether it be those on death row.

The polarities of this question have been so painfully tragic; the Left is concerned about nuclear weapons and seems not to care about abortion, which has resulted this past year in 1.4 million aborted lives. On the other hand, many of my friends on the Christian Right are concerned with abortion, as I am, but seem not to draw connections between the defense of the unborn and the defense of the lives of children impoverished in my neighborhood. We need to be prolife across the spectrum.

Charles Colson, Jim Wallis, and Jerry Falwell, "The Christian as Citizen: Three Views," *Christianity Today* 29, No. 7 (April 19, 1985): 24–27.

DEAR PAT: WINNING ISN'T EVERYTHING

CHARLES COLSON

In 1976, America felt the first tremors of Christian political activism. Many Christians lined up behind a candidate who announced he was born again. Carter's success emboldened evangelicals to forge a powerful new coalition for the 1980 election.

Now, a decade later, those tremors have become an earthquake. The Christian New Right has become a formidable voting bloc; and, to cap it off, a leading evangelist has become a serious contender for president.

Many who firmly believe God will bless the nation and reverse its moral descent through Christians in political office are wildly enthusiastic about Pat Robertson's all-but-announced candidacy. Finally, in the words of Jimmy Swaggart, we can back "one of us."

But for others, Robertson's announcement was the "last straw," unleashing ten years of pent-up resentment against growing Christian political influence. Michael Kramer, for example, wrote in *New York* magazine that Robertson is the "latest in a long line of religious leaders who've craved control of the secular world," and concluded that "Robertson's main problem is that he preaches resentment and intolerance." So much for journalistic objectivity.

The backlash was evident as well in the Michigan Republican primary. Bush supporters passed out cards reading, "Help keep religion out of politics ... fundamentalist supporters of Reverend Pat Robertson are trying to take over the Michigan Republican party!" The strategy apparently worked: only nine percent of GOP registrants voted for Robertson—and even among those identifying themselves as born again, less than one quarter voted for him.

Even friends of the Religious Right are concerned. Sen. Bill Armstrong warned that "for Christians to assume for the church a role of being power brokers ... is not only untruthful to the faith but invites a backlash, and properly so." Education Secretary William Bennett accused Robertson of "invidious sectarianism and intolerance." Strong words among friends.

The cause of all this is not so much Robertson, who with but a few slips has avoided triumphal language. Since the Constitution allows no religious test for office, he has just as much right to run as anyone else.

No, the real problem is that by stepping forward, Robertson inherits the sum of ten years of excessive rhetoric and thus draws fire on all sides from secular critics. He will be blamed for everything, including such ridiculous proposals as the religious affirmative action program advocated a year ago by a Christian leader: If, say, 24 percent of the people are born again, 24 percent of office holders should be born again.

Robertson will also have to bear the baggage of his own overzealous supporters, who have claimed that "America is ready for a president who will speak for God as well as for the American people," and that "the ability to hear from God should be the number one qualification for the U.S. presidency."

Such talk curls the hair of secularists (and thinking Christians), conjuring up images of religious ayatollahs and Cromwell's Commonwealth.

Whether in the guise of Christian theocracy or liberation theology, there have always been those who have confused the kingdom of God and the kingdoms of this world. But we need to remember: the kingdom of God is not built by man, nor does it rest on anyone's ideological platform.

The Robertson campaign puts evangelicalism to its toughest test in decades—for if the triumphalism continues, the backlash will intensify, diminishing Christian influence in society. On the other hand, the exposure could provide an opportunity for Christians to articulate a responsible view of political involvement.

It will not be easy to reverse ten years of misdirected rhetoric, but I believe it is possible. Whether he has asked for it or not, the mantle to do so now falls to Robertson: What he and his supporters say and do (assuming the dubious proposition that they are fairly reported) will help shape what influence evangelicals have in American politics for the next generation. It is a heavy responsibility, but Pat Robertson, who is intelligent and articulate, can do it—if:

- He steps out of the pulpit and drops the "Reverend." He has already wisely resigned as "The 700 Club" host. Not only is there a deeply ingrained tradition against clergy in politics, but for Robertson to run as a reverend creates the impression that he represents the church as a corporate body.

- He makes clear that he is running on his abilities, not on divine mandate. The biblical function of government is to preserve order and promote justice. The first test, therefore, should be as it was when Jethro advised Moses to choose "able men who fear God." When it comes to whose finger is on the nuclear

button, most Americans would agree with Martin
Luther's assertion that he would rather be ruled by
a competent Turk than an incompetent Christian.

- He articulates a responsible Christian view of justice, which is little understood by the secular world.
He must make clear to both his supporters and his
detractors the distinction between the responsibilities of Christians as private citizens and Christians
as office holders.

The private citizen is obliged to evangelize, to be salt and light,
to "Christianize" his society. But the Christian serving in government, while maintaining his first allegiance to God, has a different
public responsibility: it is not to take dominion, it is to preserve
evenhanded justice, to protect religious liberty and responsible
freedom of all citizens.

Christians are not simply one interest group among many,
pursuing their own advantage while others are left to fend
for themselves. Biblical justice, in the words of James Skillen,
involves "principled pluralisms; and the 'Christian' state is one
that gives no special public privilege to Christian citizens but
seeks justice for all as a matter of principle."

If Robertson can get this message across to the millions who
are now listening, it may be a far greater contribution than anything he could achieve if he won the Oval Office.

Charles Colson, "Dear Pat: Winning Isn't Everything," *Christianity Today* 30, No.
17 (November 21, 1986): 60.

HOME TO LYNCHBURG

Assessing Jerry Falwell after Moral Majority and the PTL

TERRY MUCK

J erry Falwell's announcement that he is leaving the Moral Majority came as no particular surprise. Yet coupled with his recent severing of ties with Jim Bakker's scandal-ridden PTL ministry, Falwell's announcement takes on greater significance. Although he will not be totally removed from the political scene (what pastor or college chancellor can?), his withdrawal from the Moral Majority and PTL provides an opportunity to assess his accomplishments with each.

THE MORAL MAJORITY

If simply getting the dust to fly were the criterion by which a movement like the Moral Majority can be graded, Falwell would get straight As. He has accomplished everything leaders of great movements have done: he mobilized the masses, used the media masterfully, and made enemies galore.

But just getting the dust to fly by having the guts to state an opinion honestly and uncompromisingly should not be the standard by which Christians judge movements. We demand that goals be worthwhile, means honorable, and motivations selfless.

Yet, even measured against those goals, Falwell gets better than passing grades.

To be sure, the Moral Majority has not been a perfect model of Christian political involvement. Even though it disavowed being a strictly fundamentalist Protestant movement (it also includes Catholics, Jews, and anyone else concerned about the issues it supports), the vast majority of its supporters have been fundamentalist Protestants. Questions have also been raised about fundraising and partisan politics, some of which even now demand fuller answers:

- Are the Moral Majority's accountability structures adequate to supervise the financing of such an enterprise? Indications point to Falwell making all major decisions. Should one person have that kind of control, given the massive amounts of money involved?

- Why has the Moral Majority allowed itself to become virtually identified with the Republican party? Falwell has seemed, at times, nothing more than a political bellwether for the current administration, too eagerly flying trial balloons on South Africa, Israel, and defense spending. Not all Christians, even grassroots, conservative Christians, agree on how to solve those problems. The Moral Majority's potential for conscientious comment on these value-laden issues has been made somewhat sluggish by the necessities of partisan politics. Thus, it has occasionally been forced to trade ethical force for power and influence. Perhaps that is an inevitable result of getting involved in the political process. But it has a number of Christians less eager to endorse

wholeheartedly the Moral Majority's efforts, even
though many of its causes are right on target.

• Should an organization of this scale even exist?
Since most of the money needed to do the work of
the Moral Majority comes from small donations, are
local-church contributions diminished in any way?
The Moral Majority's protestations notwithstanding, most people regard it as simply an extension of
Falwell's overall ministry, a church in political cloth-
ing. Does that put it in competition with smaller,
more personalized ministries?

On balance, though, the Moral Majority has done what it
intended to do: give grassroots conservatives a voice. And it mobilized two million of these voters, giving them a chance to fight the
encroaching relativism of our culture.

Perhaps Falwell's greatest accomplishment, however, was
getting Protestants, Catholics, and Jews to work together on
common causes. The Moral Majority is a coalition of groups
that heretofore had let theological differences stand in the way
of coordinated activity on shared concerns like abortion and pornography. It stands as a model of ecumenicity of the best sort—an
agreement to work together on issues without trying simply to
gloss over theological differences.

That such a foray into the dangerous waters of ecumenical
action should come from a fundamentalist pastor is remarkable.
It took laudable courage for Falwell to disavow the strict sepa-
ratism of his roots. Having the courage to speak prophetically is
usually associated with someone espousing extremely divisive
opinions rather than someone looking for the common ground
that our Judeo-Christian heritage provides, and then working

together with all who will support such action. Rarely is enough credit given to such consensus builders.

PTL

No case illustrates this better than Falwell's audacious attempt to short-circuit Jim and Tammy Bakker's commitment to self-destruction at Heritage Village. By placing himself squarely between the fundamentalist and Pentecostal camps, Falwell opened himself to public vilification by the Pentecostals, and to the risk of further alienating the strict separatists in his own camp who had never quite adjusted to the Moral Majority's philosophy. It was a courageous position, yet one consistent with the scripturally mandated goal of unity in the body of Christ.

The space between one Christian's truth and another Christian's truth is a no-man's-land, dangerous even if one continually shouts the agreed-upon truths of Scripture. We need some people willing to live life between the shifting tectonic plates of modern denominationalism—people willing to forge brave new alliances while resisting both uncharitable fanaticism and unfaithful liberalism. Falwell was willing to do that, and he paid a price for his effort.

The extent of the price is still to be determined. The "Old-Time Gospel Hour," Falwell's television ministry, recently announced that 50 stations were being dropped. Whether due to the more general public suspicion about television evangelism (all the major televangelists report cutbacks and reduced viewer support) or a realigning of Falwell's audience in particular, it is too soon to tell.

WHAT JERRY LEARNED

The lesson of Falwell's PTL and Moral Majority involvement is a good one. We simply cannot make progress in discipleship and evangelism by being timid and withdrawn, by hardening positions that need less to be frozen than to be melted and recast. The world is a constantly shifting place. It demands the very best from the whole church, not just little pockets of isolated firefighters. Through the Moral Majority and his PTL adventure, Jerry Falwell has added a piece to the puzzle of how we can evangelize the bewilderingly diverse world we live in.

Perhaps Falwell himself evaluates his PTL experience best. Regarding the task, he felt progress was made: "We brought some semblance of order out of chaos." But he also recognizes the personal effect on him: "By training, Baptists distrust Pentecostals. As time went on, we came to love and respect one another. I'll never again be as tough on Pentecostal issues as I have been in the past."

Add one more good thing. Jerry Falwell is not leaving PTL and cutting back on his Moral Majority involvement to start a new, bigger, better organization. He returns to the local church pastorate. That in itself gives us a clue to Falwell's priorities. It also is a shot in the arm to all of us who think the local church will play a crucial role in fighting the secularism of the twenty-first century.

Terry Muck, "Home to Lynchburg," *Christianity Today* 32, No. 1 (January 15, 1988): 16–17.

QUICK CHANGE ARTISTS

"Republican Revolution" becomes a reality
with the help of conservative Christians.

RANDY FRAME

Ralph Reed, executive director of the Christian Coalition, and Kate Michelman, president of the National Abortion and Reproductive Rights Action League, do not agree on much. Yet their capsule analyses of last month's elections are identical: Democrats got hammered, and the Religious Right, spearheaded by the coalition, deserves much of the credit.

Indeed, few around the country would challenge this analysis. The Republicans took control of both houses of Congress for the first time in four decades. Not a single incumbent Republican senator, representative, or governor lost, while Democratic institutions such as New York's Gov. Mario Cuomo and House Speaker Tom Foley were ousted.

In state after state, candidates supported by the Religious Right emerged victorious. In Pennsylvania, conservative pro-life candidate Rick Santorum, 36, won in his Senate race against incumbent liberal Democrat Harris Wofford, 68. Re-elected candidates favored by politically conservative Christians included, in the House, Baptist pastor and Christian bookstore owner Ron Lewis (Ky.) and Gary Franks (Conn.), an African-American

Republican. In the Senate, newcomers coasted to victory, including Spence Abraham (Mich.), Mike DeWine (Ohio), and John Ashcroft (Mo.), a former governor who is an outspoken Assemblies of God gospel singer.

Reed's organization distributed 33 million voter guides—nearly all at churches on the Sunday before the election. He believes the "conservative religious vote was decisive—the swing vote" in the Republican takeover.

According to the coalition's exit polls, 33 percent of those who voted were "born-again evangelicals," defined as people who attend church at least four times a month and profess to a personal conversion experience. This compares to 24 percent two years ago, 18 percent in 1988, and just 10 percent in the last midterm election, 1990.

Reed's claim that the Christian Right made the difference takes on credibility given surveys indicating that religious conservatives voted between 65 and 70 percent Republican and only about 25 percent Democratic.

In South Carolina, Republican David Beasley beat Democrat Nick Theodore in a close gubernatorial race, 50 to 48 percent. A born-again Christian, Beasley ran what he called a "pro-family" campaign, opposing abortion, homosexuals teaching in schools, lotteries, and seven other issues targeted by the Christian Coalition.

"Christians [in South Carolina] have a tendency to come out and vote in greater numbers than other groups, and I think that's one of the things that pushed us over the top," said Mark Chambers, Beasley's campaign manager.

One of the few outcomes that bordered on disappointment for candidates favorable to the Religious Right came in Virginia, where Oliver North lost in his Senate race to incumbent Democrat Charles Robb. Even at that, Reed cited exit polls indicating that only 8 percent voted against North because of his stands on the issues. A majority rejected him due to his role in the Iran-contra affair.

Even with a campaign war chest of $20 million, North won only 43 percent of the vote. Robb, who was plagued with his own personal scandals, received 46 percent, while independent Marshall Coleman received 11 percent.

BAD YEAR FOR INCUMBENTS

A strong distaste for the politics of big government characterized this year's election season, boding ill for Democratic incumbents. "I've never before felt this level of cynicism toward politics and government," says *Sojourners* magazine editor Jim Wallis, who spent much of the election season on a book tour around the country.

Such a mood was exemplified in Chicago, where Dan Rostenkowski, the powerful former House Ways and Means Committee chair under a 17-count criminal indictment, lost after 36 years in Congress. Many who voted for his Republican opponent, 32-year-old Michael Flanagan, probably did not know he is a pro-life Catholic.

Some Left-leaning spin doctors have suggested that had Republicans made up a congressional majority, they would have been thrown out this year. But, says Wallis, "the Democrats will miss the lesson if they don't see that this was a vote against them, against Clinton, against old liberal approaches, against big government in particular." Wallis, a social activist, added that, by and large, "Democrats won only where they were running against weird or weak candidates."

Some entrenched Democrats will return. In Massachusetts, Ted Kennedy won with a late surge over multimillionaire venture capitalist Mitt Romney, a Mormon. In California, seven-term incumbent congressman Vic Fazio, who earlier this year convened the Radical Right Task Force to counter the effects of the Christian Right, defeated Christian businessman Tim LeFever by a slender margin of 3,000 votes.

LOOKING TO '96

While the Democratic party is licking its wounds, the Religious Right is licking its chops in anticipation of imposing yet another term limit, this one on the nation's leading Democrat: President Clinton.

In looking forward to the next presidential election, however, religious conservatives will face perhaps their biggest political test: a struggle for the soul of the Republican party.

Republicans agree widely with the principles expressed in Congressman Newt Gingrich's much-publicized Contract with America: Get tough on crime, cut taxes, and reduce government spending except for defense. However, other planks in the GOP platform—a pro-life stand on abortion, for example—may be in jeopardy.

On the GOP horizon are such potential presidential contenders as Sen. Arlen Specter of Pennsylvania and California Gov. Pete Wilson, two abortion-rights advocates who could gain votes by appealing to moderates.

Gary Bauer, president of the Family Research Council, has been in the political trenches in the family-values debate. Bauer observes, "Many 'big tent' Republicans maintain that they can combine liberal social policies with conservative economic policies and, by some sort of political 'averaging,' claim the mantle of moderate." If that's the direction Republicans go, Bauer says, they will merely "join yesterday's ranks of defeated Democrats."

At the same time, Bauer is urging legislative action on more than the family-values agenda. He supports quick congressional action on a balanced-budget amendment, term limits, and a line-item veto—all off-the-shelf Republican proposals.

For Reed's part, he is confident that the GOP's new identity is strongly conservative. "This was not just a victory for the Republican party," he says. "This was a landslide for a particular kind of Republican party: pro-life, pro-family, unapologetically positioned in support of religious conservative themes and values." Reed notes that the Senate has gained 8 pro-life Republicans, the House has gained 45 pro-life Republicans, and states have gained 8 pro-life governors.

Reed acknowledges that "the Supreme Court appointments of the Reagan-Bush era were a missed opportunity" in terms of overturning *Roe v. Wade.* He blames a Democratic Congress, not the former presidents. As for the 1996 presidential race, Reed says he is satisfied that potential Republican candidates Bob Dole, Phil Gramm, and Jack Kemp are solidly in the pro-life camp.

"I'm grateful for the stronger pro-life voice, and I hope they will successfully promote family values," says Evangelicals for Social Action president Ron Sider. "But I wonder if [Republicans] will live family values as well as preach them. I wonder if the Republican agenda will serve everybody or just white, middle-class constituencies."

Jim Skillen, executive director of the Center for Public Justice (CPJ), maintains that Republicans' insistence on increasing defense spending is misguided. "We are at a point in history where the kinds of battles the U.S. faces are not the kinds that require a push in defense spending," Skillen says. Citing the federal deficit as an example of such a battle, he added, "If we do face a military threat, we can recharge, but you don't just spend money to stay ahead."

Wallis is dismayed both with traditional liberal and proposed conservative responses to the problem of the poor. "Liberal solutions want to control the poor. Conservative solutions want to abandon the poor," he says. There are some Republicans who do not just toe the party line, Wallis says. "At least Jack Kemp talks about racism as if it's real. He talks about poor people as if they exist. By and large, his Republican colleagues don't."

ADVICE FOR THE RIGHT

Even though the Christian Right has not asked for any advice, some within the evangelical camp are offering it anyway. Despite Reed's interpretation of North's defeat, the CPJ's Skillen maintains that Christians should be careful "not to wrap the American flag and the Cross together."

Skillen believes conservative Christians should realize that "we have to make some distinctions" between what the Bible truly teaches and legitimate differences of opinion on political matters.

Christian Legal Society attorney Gail Jansen believes the Christian Right is "fast becoming just another special-interest group with its own list of litmus-test issues." She adds, "The Christian political perspective has to be much more than issue-oriented. We need to identify political principles of justice that apply to the broad spectrum of society."

Wallis says, "If there is any religion left in the Religious Right, they must resist and refuse this Republican agenda of social abandonment of the poor, which is morally unacceptable."

This year a new organization, the Interfaith Alliance, formed, hoping to be a counterweight to the power of the Religious Right. Prior to the elections, the alliance, a national organization of religious leaders representing mostly mainline denominations, alleged that the Christian Coalition voter guides were "shamelessly slanted."

204 Religious Right and Evangelical Left

TIME FOR NEW MODELS?

CLS's Jansen believes that many Christian voters are frustrated at having to choose between two political parties that emphasize two different visions, both of which have appealing components. She says Democrats offer a social conscience but little else, while Republicans are more open to "Christian values in the political realm."

"Our two-party system as currently constructed does not give people enough options," Jansen says. "I sense that many people are casting about for a new model, one that can produce candidates who are concerned about the poor and about balancing the budget."

In a similar vein, Wallis maintains that Republicans and Democrats each speak to a part of a biblical vision for society.

"Conservatives talk about cultural breakdown in terms of the decline of family and moral values," Wallis says. "Liberals talk about oppression, which is a biblical word. There is a relationship between the two, and Christians ought to be speaking to both."

Randy Frame, "Quick Change Artists," Christianity Today 38, No. 14 (December 12, 1994): 50–53.

PUTTING OUT
A CONTRACT

Christian Coalition's vision for America takes a hit.

CAROLYN CURTIS

Ralph Reed, Christian Coalition executive director, may have taken a seat at the Washington table of power, but it quickly turned into a hot seat. For a variety of reasons, moderate, liberal, and even some conservative Christians have lambasted the coalition's Contract with the American Family.

Reed unveiled the contract to Congress on May 17, flanked by House Speaker Newt Gingrich and GOP presidential aspirant Sen. Phil Gramm (R-Tex.). Reed, head of the 1.6 million-member Christian Coalition, has the attention of conservative Republicans, many of whom credit evangelicals with the GOP landslide victory last November. The coalition scored more points by waiting to introduce its agenda while the GOP negotiated its own Contract with America (*CT*, March 6, 1995, p. 42).

While insisting the contract is not a threat or an ultimatum to lawmakers, Reed made it clear that Christian conservatives could no longer be ignored in policymaking.

"As religious conservatives, we have finally gained what we have always sought: a place at the table, a sense of legitimacy, and a voice in the conversation that we call democracy," Reed declared. "This is not a Christian agenda. It is not a Republican agenda. It is not a special-interest agenda."

Reed claimed the vast majority of Americans support the 39-page document. "Our purpose is not to legislate family values. It is to ensure that Washington values families."

Several of the proposals already have been introduced in Congress. Points include restoring religious equality in public places; returning education funds to local control; promoting school choice; protecting parental rights; eliminating the marriage tax penalty; protecting states' rights not to finance abortion and to place limits on late-term abortions; restricting pornography on the Internet and cable television; and trimming public funding for the arts.

Some pro-family groups, such as the Traditional Values Coalition and National Right to Life Committee, welcomed the initiative. But by devising a contract, the Christian Coalition caused some other organizations to bristle.

"For the Christian Coalition to claim the ideological and spiritual endorsement of 40 million Christians is not only ludicrous, it is inexcusable," said Interfaith Alliance chairperson Herbert Valentine.

"It's a sad day in American politics when a TV preacher's political front group dictates the agenda for the United States Congress," said Barry Lynn, executive director of Americans United for Separation of Church and State.

POLITICAL PARTISANSHIP RESISTED

A week after Ralph Reed's congressional appearance, a group representing more than 100 religious leaders issued a "Cry for Renewal," challenging the Christian Right.

"The moral authority necessary to mitigate the excesses of power has been replaced by a thirst for political influence," read the statement, crafted by *Sojourners* editor Jim Wallis and Eastern College sociologist Tony Campolo. "The almost total identification of the Religious Right with the new Republican majority in Washington is a dangerous liaison of religion with political power," the document said.

"Cry for Renewal" does not single out the Christian Coalition or the Contract with the American Family. Signers include InterVarsity Christian Fellowship president Stephen Hayner, Habitat for Humanity founder Millard Fuller, theologian J. I. Packer, religious broadcaster David Mains, Episcopal Presiding Bishop Edmond Browning, and National Council of Churches General Secretary Joan Campbell Brown.

James Skillen, executive director of the Center for Public Justice, called "Cry for Renewal" "a reactionary document, a plea to be heard and get attention by people who fear that—because of the Christian Coalition's newly achieved clout—they are no longer viewed as significant voices in the public dialogue."

Diane Knippers, president of the Institute on Religion and Democracy, agreed. "The Religious Left's rhetoric against the Republican agenda is no less a liaison of religion with political power than the Religious Right's support for it."

QUESTIONS FROM THE CHOIR

The Christian Coalition's proposal also drew flak from some conservative groups. The American Life League (ALL) urged the coalition to withdraw the contract, saying the abortion plank compromises too much. "Under scrutiny, this flowery preamble is deceptive and misleading," ALL president Judie Brown said.

Even conservative Christian organizations have not given the proposal glowing reviews, because it fails to call for banning abortion and opposing special rights for homosexuals. "As an overall pro-family agenda, I think it's unduly modest," Gary Bauer, president of the Family Research Council, told *CT*. "We hope to get a larger agenda on the table before the year is out."

Other conservative groups have spawned look-alike contracts. The Christian Action Network (CAN) issued its own ten-point Pro-Family Contract with America in May. CAN spokesperson Allison Woodburn told *CT* the group's proposal—which includes a call for a school prayer amendment and a ban on homosexuals in the military—"reflects the views of its members and not just what politicians want to hear."

In April, televangelist Jerry Falwell asked congressional representatives to sign a "Moral Contract with America" that contains seven principles, including endorsement of the family as a husband and wife, not "gay, lesbian, or any other strange combination," and a call for the United States to "stand firm in our ties with the State of Israel if we expect God to bless our nation."

Carolyn Curtis, "Putting Out a Contract," *Christianity Today* 39, No. 8 (July 17, 1995): 54–55.

★ *October 5, 1998* ★

EVANGELICALS ARE NOT AN INTEREST GROUP

CHARLES COLSON AND NANCY PEARCEY

As the election approaches, politically minded conservative evangelicals are discovering they are not involved in the issues so much as they are the issue. "Religious Right Shows Its Muscle" reads a headline in the *Chicago Tribune*. The *Arizona Republic* warns that "the religious right is causing near-civil war in some campaigns." The buzz on Capitol Hill is that the Religious Right is splitting conservative ranks.

But this bellicose imagery could cause real harm to evangelical political activity.

The latest round of press attention was triggered when Jim Dobson gave his celebrated speech threatening to abandon the Republican party. Worried party leaders convened a Values Summit and agreed to take action on such things as abortion and the marriage penalty.

Dobson did a noble service in jarring Congress out of its lethargy, but nothing sets off alarm bells in the press faster than political stirrings among the Religious Right. Journalists immediately warned in apocalyptic tones that religious conservatives were "marching on Washington" and "demanding their due." Articles described Christians as a powerful voting bloc that delivered 45 percent of the vote in the 1994 Republican sweep of Congress. Many alluded to Ralph Reed's phrase that Christian conservatives are demanding "their place at the table" and depicted them in the same terms used for a labor union or any other special-interest group.

Sadly, Christians have sometimes contributed to this image. Of course, we have a right to a place at the table, like any other citizen. And yes, we have political clout because millions of Americans share our moral concerns. But that can never be the basis of our political stance. We contend for certain truths in the political arena precisely because they are true, and because these transcendent truths are crucial to public justice and freedom.

Our message is not, We put you in office, now pay up; but rather, This should be done because it is right, it is a principle that undergirds any well-ordered civil society. We must be clear that the moral positions we urge are not partisan; they apply to Democrats and Republicans alike.

Our principles are derived from Scripture, but in a pluralistic society they must be translated into terms nonbelievers can understand, language that appeals to the objective moral order recognized by the ethical systems of all great civilizations—what C. S. Lewis called "the Way" or "the Tao."

For example, when we work to change abortion laws, we appeal not only to divine revelation but also to the most fundamental duty of government: to defend the defenseless. Our nation was founded by a generation willing to fight and die for the "inalienable" right to life. Both Christian believer and Enlightenment deist agreed on the rights that government must protect.

Or consider assisted suicide and eugenics. The reason we oppose legalization is that these things are contrary to the fundamental duty of government recognized since our founding.

As G. K. Chesterton writes, eugenics "is chiefly a denial of the Declaration of Independence. It urges that so far from all men being born equal, numbers of them ought not to be born at all."

Finally, when we oppose gay marriage and domestic-partner laws, our purpose is not to punish homosexuals but to preserve the unique legal status of the heterosexual family. This is not some theocratic power grab; it is asking government to recognize a fundamental social pattern that has undergirded every successful society throughout history.

In seeking limits on government, our motivation stems from a rich tradition of political philosophy rooted in the Reformation—a tradition that made constitutional democracy possible. It rests on the recognition that every sphere of society has its own function, its own authority, which government may not usurp but rather must protect. Dutch statesman Abraham Kuyper coined the phrase "sphere sovereignty" to assert that the individual, family, church, school, and business enterprise all owe their origin to God, not government. Therefore, their proper function and structure comes from God; there are lines that government may not cross in its social-engineering schemes.

As Kuyper put it, we live "coram Deo" (before the face of God), and we are directly responsible to God in each area of life. For Christians, politics is the high calling of ensuring that government protects the pre-political institutions and preserves the moral order.

This is why it is so crucial not to allow ourselves to be tucked into any party's hip pocket, or cast as just another political interest group in the ideological struggle. Our concern is on a higher level: that all spheres of society are free to fulfill their God-ordained function. At times we may represent a majority, at other times only a small percentage of the vote, as in the early abolitionist movement. But our position remains the same: that there exists a natural order that government is morally obligated to respect.

Our task is to serve as society's conscience, seeing all of life from God's perspective and interpreting that vision in prudential terms for our fellow citizens. We don't seek power; we seek a society where government promotes justice in all spheres of society and protects the public good.

Charles Colson and Nancy Pearcey, "Evangelicals Are Not an Interest Group," *Christianity Today* 42, No. 11 (October 5, 1998): 160.

SPOILS OF VICTORY

Pro-life Democrats hope party's
takeover will remove stigma.

SHERYL HENDERSON BLUNT

I n the immediate aftermath of the 2006 Democratic takeover
of Congress, conventional wisdom said many evangelicals had
abandoned the GOP.

News outlets and analysts eagerly described a "seismic
shift" that pointed to the "end of the conservative pendulum
swing" and a weakened Republican base. In a widely publicized
Beliefnet poll, 30 percent of 771 evangelicals reported voting for
fewer Republicans than in past elections. Early exit polls showed
almost a third of white evangelicals had voted for Democratic
Congressional candidates, some of whom touted pro-life views.

"The Religious Right's dominance over politics and evangelicals has come to an end," Democratic adviser and Sojourners/
Call to Renewal leader Jim Wallis told *Christianity Today* the day
after the election.

But a closer look at the results suggested something else:
White evangelical Protestants, who have recently bolstered the
GOP base, did not desert the party. Republicans actually captured 70 percent of their vote, while Democrats received 28 percent. Compared to the 2004 House races, when evangelicals cast

74 percent of their ballots for Republicans and 25 percent for Democrats, the small shift suggested the party's base had stayed home—with the GOP.

"We didn't really see a lot of change in the voting patterns of evangelicals," said John Green, a senior fellow at the Pew Forum on Religion and Public Life and co-editor of *The Values Campaign? The Christian Right and the 2004 Elections.* Green said the bigger swings for Democrats involved white Roman Catholics, 55 percent of whom voted for Democrats versus 44 percent for Republicans, along with less religious and non-religious voters. "That's where Democrats had their biggest gains," Green said.

Nevertheless, evangelicals did express dissatisfaction with the Iraq war and political scandals, according to Green. "All kinds of things were going wrong for the Republicans," he told *CT.* "Maybe the remarkable thing was that [evangelicals] stayed as Republican as they did, given all of this discontent."

HEARTLAND VALUES

National figures don't show the whole story. Even with a small overall change among evangelicals, pollsters say shifting allegiances could have made a difference in states like Ohio, Pennsylvania, and Missouri. Many Democratic candidates in these heartland states who talked about faith and values declared victory on Election Night.

Democrats dominated in the bellwether state of Ohio. Governor-elect Ted Strickland collected 51 percent of the white evangelical vote and 58 percent of the Catholic vote. The ordained Methodist minister trounced conservative Republican Secretary of State Ken Blackwell, who boasted of strong connections with the Religious Right.

Rich Nathan, senior pastor of Vineyard Christian Fellowship, a Columbus megachurch, believes the Religious Right inspired a backlash.

"I think there is some sense that the Religious Right has been engaged in hubris, and evangelicals are reacting to that," Nathan said. "There is concern about the over-identification of evangelicalism with the Right's politicizing of the message."

Pollsters say moderate Republicans in suburbs are distancing themselves from the party's social-conservative wing by voting Democrat. Key examples include large suburban areas in Virginia, Missouri, and Pennsylvania.

"There has been a growing division between the more mainline Protestants and the ideologically driven evangelicals," said G. Terry Madonna, director of the Center for Politics and Public Affairs at Franklin and Marshall College. "This has particularly affected suburban, Republican voters, and is certainly making them less willing to vote Republican."

Nathan believes the backlash comes as more evangelicals are beginning to re-examine their political priorities.

"There is a growing trend toward the broadening of the evangelical agenda beyond the hot-button issues of abortion and gay marriage," said Nathan, who sees evangelicals and other conservatives rethinking their views on the Iraq war, poverty, and the environment. He said Vineyard's attention to social justice and outreach programs for the poor have also "really resonated with dyed-in-the-wool evangelicals."

"I would say the evangelical political conscience is maturing, and it could be that we are beginning to see the emergence of what Carl Henry talked about 60 years ago in *The Uneasy Conscience of Modern Fundamentalism*—a full engagement on the issues, as opposed to a single litmus paper test," Nathan said.

HOLDING CONGRESS
ACCOUNTABLE

This broadened agenda is what activists like Wallis have been working for. But it remains to be seen how Democratic Party leaders will react to new congressional members who don't vote pro-choice.

Kristen Day, executive director of Democrats for Life of America, said Democrats learned in 2004 that discouraging pro-lifers was not helping their party. So Democratic strategists recruited a few social-conservative candidates for 2006. Day believes the change started when Democratic Senatorial Campaign Committee chairman Sen. Charles Schumer supported Bob Casey Jr. in the Pennsylvania Senate race.

"He was the test case that proved successful," Day said. "The DNC was behind Casey and other winning pro-life Democrats 150 percent. It's very encouraging to see that you no longer have to support abortion to get the support of the party."

Day said the growing coalition of pro-life Democrats in the House and Senate—a new total of about 36—will make it more difficult for party leaders to "strong-arm people into voting pro-choice."

John Green said pro-life Democrats did help the party take several key races. But he cautioned that party divisions over abortion could make the big-tent strategy less appealing.

"It depends on how the Democrats act," said Rep. Lincoln Davis, D-Tenn., an evangelical. "If they tend to the left, it won't take them 12 years to get kicked out. Nancy Pelosi is Speaker because pro-life, conservative Democrats have won, and I think she realizes that." Davis said voters and unyielding pro-life Democrats have sent the party's leadership a powerful message. "It tells Nancy Pelosi that if you don't have the pro-life Democrats in Congress, you can't be Speaker. You can't govern. You can't talk about the minimum wage" and other priorities.

Linking pro-life measures to these platform priorities could be effective. Davis, sponsor of the Pregnant Women Support Act, said he is planning to re-introduce his legislation with one major difference—a $2-per-hour increase in the minimum wage. "This will help allow a young lady to afford to keep her baby," Davis said.

But as many conservatives can attest, propelling a party to victory and actually shaping legislation are two very different challenges.

"The Religious Right and the secular Left both lost on Election Night," Wallis said. The goal now? "We have to hold the new Congress accountable."

Sheryl Henderson Blunt, "Spoils of Victory: Pro-Life Democrats Hope Party's Takeover Will Remove Stigma," *Christianity Today* 51, No. 1 (January 2007): 54–55.

Chapter 3

COMMUNISM AND FOREIGN POLICY

I nternational affairs have a way of distilling the essence of political philosophies and emphases, as competing ideas battle not
in rhetoric or votes but in human lives. With the stakes being
more obvious, if not actually higher, foreign policy was a regular
topic of discussion in *CT* articles during these years. With few
exceptions, such pieces fell within the broad range of support for
American foreign policy and traditional just-war ideals.

During the late twentieth and early twenty-first centuries,
international tensions were centered on two great global and
existential threats—Communism from the superpower of the
Soviet Union and Islamism from terrorists out of the Middle East.
More than the "ordinary" concerns of national pride and dynastic
advancement, world-encompassing new ideologies vied for control of every aspect of life. Christians could not remain neutral
when faced with the demands of this new era.

The early part of this period was arguably the most dangerous time in recorded history. For the first time ever, human
beings possessed the power to annihilate human civilization, and
there were two warring camps seemingly willing to do just that.
Discussions of primordial floods and eschatological destruction
could remain safely abstract, but from the 1950s to the 1990s, the
prospect of a nuclear holocaust was all too real.

Wars of smaller scope, but greater realized destruction, were
endemic. From 1956 to 2016, the world was wracked by the Suez
Crisis, the Cuban Revolution, the Vietnam War, the Six-Day
War, the Yom Kippur War, Afghanistan, Grenada, the Falklands,
Lebanon, Libya, Panama, the Gulf War, Rwanda, the Balkans,
9/11, Afghanistan again, Iraq, Syria, and others too many to
count. The last three decades have, if anything, been more peril-
ous than those before. Indeed, there has been less fear of a world-
ending cataclysm, but hardly a year has gone by since the end of

the Cold War where Americans were not in combat somewhere in the world.

Individual conflicts play a big role, but the question of Communism loomed even higher. Whether during the high Cold War of the 1950s and 1960s or during the time of collapse in the late 1980s, columns and news items emphasized greatly the threat posed by the Hammer and Sickle, not just to American interests but to human rights. This is a fundamental distinction that is often missed in retrospective studies. Communism was not seen as just another rival power or alternative system of government; it was a rival religion, complete with prophets, saints, and an eschatological hope. It was not an equal to the American system but an intrinsically oppressive and tyrannical caricature of Christian principles.

★ *October 29, 1956* ★

CHRISTIAN RESPONSIBILITY AND COMMUNIST BRUTALITY

THE EDITORS

E vents of the last few weeks are causing many Christians to experience an "agonizing reappraisal" of their concept of world order. How are the demands of an enlightened Christian conscience to be met when confronted by the situation in Hungary? When men are dying in their desire for freedom; when God-given aspirations for self-determination are being brutally crushed; when a reign of terror of unexceeded rigor is being perpetrated even as these lines are written, what should be the reaction of Christians who are living in freedom and peace?

Is the Christian approach to expend itself in resolutions of disapproval? Is a renewed statement of the principles of Christian freedom and human justice a sufficient answer to the willful destruction of a nation?

A relatively small number of trucks carrying Red Cross supplies does not solve the problem, although it is a part of our responsibility and can and will be amplified as opportunity presents itself. Nor will expressions of sympathy mean much unless sympathy is implemented by action.

The philosophy: "Anything short of war," can do irreparable harm, for it gives the aggressor a sense of security which itself begets aggression. We believe just such a situation has developed.

The rape of Hungary may be the desperate act of a tottering regime which was born in terror and which has continued to exist in the same manner. But America and other free nations share the blame insofar as they have sustained that regime by recognition and given it a forum of respectability in which to operate.

A slap on the wrist is not the answer to what Russia has done in Hungary. Expulsion from the United Nations, with its accompanying disintegrating effect on world Communism, is the least Christians should demand in way of punishment.

Which shall take precedence—the preservation of an organization, or the certifying of a moral principle?

The Editors, "Christian Responsibility and Communist Brutality," *Christianity Today* 1, No. 4 (October 29, 1956): 25.

September 2, 1957

CHRIST AND
THE ATOM BOMB

THE EDITORS

To preserve the universe from capitulating to pagan views of origin and existence, each generation must delineate and declare the relationship between Christ and the atom. Development of the atomic bomb, and of its even more monstrous successors, imposes on our own generation particularly an unprecedented urgency to meet this task. In fact, for us the challenge may already involve retrieving as well as withholding the atom from Satan and his destructive purposes.

During the past decade, atomic energy's military significance received man's concentration far more than its peacetime potential. But relegated to even less consideration than the link between the atom and peace has been the link between the atom and God. The long overexposure (and double exposure) to evolution and naturalism has obliterated, at least skewed, the present generation's recognition of the Christian doctrine of origins and being. Unfamiliarity with Christian thought patterns is prevalent. The comfortable assumption of Christianity as a permanent, all-inclusive Western tradition has inured modern man to a purposeful personal investigation of religion. Within his remnant of theological categories, the average man, therefore, can only associate the atom bomb with the Devil, rather than the atom with God.

Communism drives relentlessly toward world revolution. The political absolutism of "might makes right" perils millions with barbarian mass destruction. Atomic fall-out and radiation mean yet unplumbed hazards. Must not the Christian conscience speak to the world's conscience about the atom and its uses? Not to do so is a shirking of responsibility. Indeed this silence of a Christian community grants to alien philosophies permission to interpret the atom and its serviceability in wholly secular and arbitrary terms.

But silence is not the only charge to be leveled at the Christian community. What is spoken in the name of the church, often by its cursory nature, and sometimes by its narrow and even mis-guided phrasing, is hurtful to Christianity and helpful to paganism.

Monstrous as it is, the atomic bomb is but a part of a much vaster, more important concern, that of the atom itself. To con-fine the problem to the atomic bomb is unfortunate both for the proclaiming church and for the listening world. Largely inun-dated by naturalistic ways of thought, twentieth-century cul-ture needs from the Christian churches a more comprehensive approach to the atom than merely pronouncements on the bomb.

Basic to Christianity's philosophy of life as it relates to war is the Christian doctrine of origin and existence. While a generation may perpetuate its survival by restraining the atom bomb, that survival may be within a pagan concept of life that brings its own and worse final doom. At every moment the Christian movement must primarily engage in a total battle for the souls of men and not simply in lesser endeavors that spare life unchanged for the pagan world. The contemporary church needs to proclaim the comprehensive message of the God of the atom when it issues its subordinate proclamations on the atom bomb.

In this connection, some of the recent programming of the Voice of America has reflected a deeper sensitivity to spiritual realities than have the massive church organizations. The U.S. Information Agency's approval of Moody Institute of Science films such as *God of the Atom* for international educational purposes is commendable, since such material lifts the question of the use of the atom beyond the elemental issue of the peaceful or destructive employments of nuclear energy to the higher principle of the spiritual purposes of the universe. If the primary basis of the Communist philosophy is evolutionary naturalism, as indeed it is, then no decisive blow has been dealt to the Communist program for the use of the atom while this basic philosophy is unassailed. The neglect of the Christian doctrine of creation within the churches is due largely to the infiltration of evolutionary naturalism into the religious as well as the secular centers of Western thought and life. This deficiency is a current factor that nullifies the churches' own efforts to champion the peaceful over the destructive use of nuclear energy. To borrow a warning from the recently published symposium on *Contemporary Evangelical Thought* (Channel Press, 1957), the unchallenged revolt against the God of creation provides modern man with leverage for his revolt against the God of redemption.

If the subject of Christ and the atom is urgently vital, the subject of Christ and the atom bomb is an appropriate and crucial problem as well. If the church is properly concerned with why Christ made and preserves the atom, it is also properly concerned with why man splits it.

Christianity is not a religion of war; it is on the side of peace among men. Today when so much of the initiative for world peace is carried by secular agencies, when the warring chapters in the history of Christianity are exploited by anti-church movements, it is especially necessary for Christianity to entrench in man's conscience the fact that the tidings of the incarnation are those of "peace on earth" and that Christ's beatitudes include a special designation of his disciples as peacemakers. Above all the symbols of warfare and strife in the world today, the church of Christ should tower as a symbol of peace.

Alien conceptions of peace, so often today defined as mere cessation of outward hostility, can easily mislead Christian leaders, however. A striking feature of the New Testament is that despite its emphasis upon the peace of God in human life, the early church was not drawn into political dispute with the Roman empire, the mighty military power of that day. The Apostle Paul wrote to the Romans of the mighty *dunamis* of God, and of Christians being "more than conquerors," but whatever may have been the perils of mankind and of the scattered Christian communities, the early Christians felt no constraint to chart a military program for the Roman Empire. The early Christian concern for peace on earth was linked exclusively with the necessity for spiritual and moral regeneration of individuals, not primarily with programs of action whereby unregenerate men might assure mankind's survival. The followers of Jesus Christ never understood their task to be the promotion of survival programs for unregenerate men who sought physical security while persisting in rejection of the Redeemer; rather, they ministered to the sick and to the dying by way of spontaneous commentary on their living faith, and they preached Christ the Savior and Lord before whom even the Roman emperor must be counted a doomed sinner needing salvation (cf. Rom. 3:20, 23). Although it insisted upon the universal validity of the biblical revelation, the early church did not foster resolutions to reform unregenerate humanity.

Leaders in the World Council of Churches have frequently pleaded for suspension of all current tests of nuclear weapons.

Such a demand was voiced to the American government at the WCC New Haven meetings in August. An adopted report of its Commission of the Churches on International Affairs urged that "governments conducting tests should forego them at least for a trial period, either together or individually, in the hope that the others will do the same, a new confidence be born, and foundations be laid for reliable agreements."

Entrance of churchmen into the political order in the name of the church frequently has the effect of ascribing to multitudes of parishioners opinions which they as individuals do not in fact entertain, and for the propagandizing of which they have no mandate. Organized Christianity thus may become enmeshed in questions that go beyond the scope of the church's legitimate function. In demanding that the United States unilaterally suspend all current tests the WCC's recent action on nuclear weapons actually supported present Soviet Russian policy. This shocking situation coming from the most representative gathering of Christendom apart from the Papal See supplies a tremendous asset to the Russians in their present jockeying for world sympathy and international support. Although motivated by quite other considerations, the WCC action nonetheless climaxes a Communist drive begun in the Stockholm Peace Conference, namely, by mobilizing and utilizing pacifist sentiment in the non-Communist world to deter the development of new atomic devices in the West thus to alter the balance of power between the Communist and non-Communist worlds. One of the program's most zealous proponents has been Professor J. L. Hromádka from Communist-dominated Czechoslovakia.

While some dissent was evident at the New Haven conference, the recommendations of the executive committee were never effectively challenged. Professor Florovsky, Russian Orthodox Church official, publicly abstained from support of the atomic tests statement because he considered it a political issue. Dr. P. O. Bersell, Augustana Lutheran leader from Minneapolis, publicly declined to support the re-election of Dr. Hromádka to the executive committee but finally yielded with the explanation: "If the executives are satisfied, knowing the nature of this election, I am satisfied." Archbishop Geoffrey Fisher of the Church of England was criticized when he suggested that the World Council should not take sides in international disputes, but confine its pronouncements to "fundamental spiritual principles." Mayor Charles P. Taft of Cincinnati, a leader in the Protestant Episcopal Church, cautioned against pronouncements without the aid of experts, indicating that this is a common failing in church groups. But executives of the central committee received overwhelming endorsement in virtually everything they proposed. The result of the New Haven sessions may well be that, in the months and years to come, the political program of the WCC will receive more scrutiny than ever before. The great tragedy of the twentieth century would be if, in the effort to conserve the creative power of the atom for Jesus Christ, the atom bomb should unwittingly have been given in to the destructive service of Karl Marx.

The Christian churches have adequate reason to warn the nations of the world of their moral accountability to the Living God, to condemn the evil of aggressive warfare, to protest the one-sided enlistment of scientific genius to what Pius XII has called a "race toward death," and to show concern for the well-being of the race in view of the perils of radiation. The Christian community has good reason also to disown a fatalistic view of the inevitability of war, and to emphasize the crucial role of spiritual decision upon the flow of history.

But what mandate do the Christian churches have for instructing any nation that it ought in the name of political righteousness to desist from testing its military defenses? If God wills the state as a political order to promote justice and to restrain injustice in a sinful society, is not a state precondemned to suicide if it is deprived of the right to test its weapons of defense in a century in which one world power, operating on the thesis of state absolutism, makes no pretense of its goal of world revolution?

The usual reply, that a halt must be called in the bomb race because of the vast destructive capacity of nuclear energy, is not decisive. No clear case has been made out for a qualitative difference between nuclear bombs and other weapons of warfare; the difference, however great, remains quantitative. Eliminate the bombs, and terrible though more conventional weapons of war remain. Does the church bless these? Does it condemn their use under all circumstances also? Is experiment with tactical atomic bombs (limited to battlefields and used against cities only along the front lines of land fighting) approved as moral? Can this qualitative line really be drawn in warfare?

Is not an organization that intrudes into such questions in the name of the church confused about the weapons of the church's warfare? Are we not driven to ask whether behind the WCC action there still lurks the optimistic hope of the now discredited social gospel of Protestant liberalism, that by the reorganization of unregenerate mankind on ostensibly Christian principles a warless world will be inaugurated?

No Christian—indeed, no human being—can fully escape agony of soul over the death-dealing prospect of modern warfare. The Christian churches are rightly driven to assure themselves that they are making their fullest contribution to world peace. But what scriptural license has a resolution to end the testing of the bombs, even for a trial period, as a strategic Christian contribution to world peace? As a venture of political idealism it may perhaps be justified, even perhaps as a military maneuver, but that is a decision which statesmen charged with the destinies of the political order need to make. When Christian churches speak, are they not obliged to stress that man's only guarantee of survival is his devotion to the commandments by which God judges the race; to stress the connection between the social evils of the world and the master passions of individual life (cf. James 4:1, "From whence come wars ... Come they not hence, even of your lusts that war in your members?"); and to stress the contribution to peace made by the regenerating power of the gospel? Doubtless it is superficial to hold that, in a sinful order, the preaching of the gospel is the only contribution that Christianity can make to promote world peace. But, if anything, it is superficiality compounded to seek a Christian solution while neglecting the gospel, and venturing simply to reorganize an unregenerate world order on the basis of romantic idealism.

Progress in disarmament hinges upon a sense of mutual trust among nations. Even unchurched leaders today ask what basis exists for trusting a Communist leadership that acknowledges no objective moral principles, let alone the reality of the Living God and the validity of his commandments. Is not the gospel the best weapon the church knows for restoring these dulled spiritual and moral sensitivities?

The Christian community is profoundly right in its warning to the world that nuclear war will provide no solution to world problems, but will bankrupt modern history. But if Christian forces hope to show the way to peace, they had best not concentrate their efforts on dubious vulnerable techniques for avoiding war. Worldly organizations may busy themselves with delaying actions for postponing doom, but the church's primary role is to call a new race of men into fellowship with Christ as Lord. The cessation of nuclear bomb tests is no more the world's real hope for peace in this decade than the organization of the United Nations was in the last. That great hope is Jesus Christ. And it is time professing followers of Christ clarify this hope in a world of peril. The modern man's one great prospect of peaceful existence in these dark decades lies in the recognition of the lordship of Christ, in the reaffirmation of the Judeo-Christian view of life, and in the dedication of the atom and the atom bomb to the service of righteousness and love.

The Editors, "Christ and the Atom Bomb," *Christianity Today* 1, No. 23 (September 2, 1957): 20–23.

WHY COMMUNISM IS GODLESS

G. AIKEN TAYLOR

To most Americans today the word "communism" suggests all manner of evil. You need but whisper, "He is a Communist," and, if your neighbor believes you, the alleged Communist could next be charged with almost any crime whatever and your neighbor would not be surprised. The Communist has the role of international villain once held by the Fascist, except that the Communist enjoys an even worse reputation. He would rob his own brother blind; he would betray his own parents to the police; he would delight in desecrating churches, for he is an atheist.

Even after making allowances for the excesses of some Communists, most people would indict the Communist philosophy itself for certain basic wrongs. It reduces all men to a common political denominator, it destroys individual initiative and private enterprise, and it takes away the basic freedoms that Western democracies prize. Worst of all, it is godless.

Now there is an interesting combination. How did "godless" get into that line-up? Because, most will say, it belongs there. But why? The other indictments clearly do, of course. Any ideology that seeks to erase all distinctions between men is bound to have a low view of the worth of the individual. Any political system that reduces all its citizens to a common denominator necessarily discourages private enterprise. But why must such a system be godless?

Few people, I dare say, have given much thought to the matter. If we ever notice how often communism shows its atheistic stripe, we probably explain the fact to our satisfaction by saying that it just happened that way: the spread of communism has been controlled by godless men. But, we hasten to add, if the leaders of world-wide communism could be influenced by the gospel, Western democracies (even if not wholly identical with Christianity) could then co-exist with the disciples of Marx and Lenin. In other words, if the occupants of the Kremlin were Christian, cold war would end.

Such wishful thinking fails to take into account the possibility that the nature of communism may be such that were the leaders of Russia Christians, they could no longer be Communists. What if communism is necessarily godless? What if atheism follows logically upon its ideological premise—or, what if its ideological premise is the natural expression of atheism?

Socially and ethically, Christianity and communism appear deceptively alike. The surface similarity has often been noted, occasionally with confusing results. Not long ago certain enthusiastic patriots entered a hue and cry in the national press, charging that the Sunday School literature of a large denomination was Communistic. The literature in question advocated the sharing of one's worldly possessions with one's neighbor as a worthy principle of life.

Now you cannot decide that a literature is Communistic or Christian just because it advocates sharing. It could be either or neither. The point is, however, that some identify the principle of sharing with both.

In this connection, responsible commentators have occasionally taken the experience of the first-century Christians in Jerusalem to indicate that the New Testament church practiced communism until it found that it could not make it work. But many thoughtful people are not convinced that it could not have been made to work. They find it hard to condemn any philosophy that teaches the support of the weak by the strong, that seeks to eliminate poverty by drawing upon the "haves" on behalf of the "have-nots."

As the world-wide struggle continues, Christian spokesmen often fail to make their case against communism, and some seem secretly to wonder if the ideological issue is really crucial after all. The agents of the Cominform, meanwhile, reap an increasing harvest of converts.

To an unbeliever, Christianity indeed looks something like communism. He may wonder whether the latter, stripped of world-wide ambitions and controlled by less greedy men, would not be a similar force for good in the world.

But how could that be? If a Christian society reflects the ethics of godliness, then communism reflects the ethics of ungodliness. The church is the community of the redeemed in Christ Jesus. Opposed to the ideal society represented by the church stands the Communistic society, inevitably godless.

And why inevitably? Because its aims are contrary to the Godward orientation of the Christian society. The difference is one of motivation, of inner spirit.

Both Christianity and communism preach doctrines of neighborliness, but with important differences. Communism believes the supreme good to be the betterment of Man; Christianity wants only to glorify God.

The Communist reasons somewhat as follows: this world is here for the benefit of man, who really owns no part of it for it was here before he came and will be here when he is gone. I, of course, am man. Moreover, all men are equal. I, therefore, am equal to any. Now all men (and I) deserve an equal share of this world's benefits and, until equality is achieved, a sort of natural law applies (such as that water seeks its own level), which brings down the rich and elevates the poor (me).

The Communist is a dedicated person because he sees a better world for himself when the equalization process is completed. The share-and-share-alike program is for his betterment. He wants to divide up the available wealth because he expects thereby to have more. "I," he says to his neighbor, "am as worthy as you. You, therefore, must share with me that I may be better off."

The Christian, on the other hand, no longer a "natural" man, reasons somewhat as follows: this world and all upon it exists for the glory of God. Man enjoys the world's goods, which were here before he came and will be here when he is gone, only by permission, not by right. Within the community of the redeemed, the Christian views has brother as his equal. But his perspective is not that of an underprivileged man claiming equality with a privileged, it is that of a privileged man willing to count his lesser brother equal to himself.

The Christian also is a dedicated person. He sees better things for his brother when his own will is surrendered to God, and he expects it to happen at his expense. The share-and-share-alike program he practices is for his brother's betterment, not his own. "You," he says to his brother, "are as worthy as I. I, therefore, am willing, for Christ's sake, to share with you in order that you may be better off."

In short, communism is the natural expression of selfishness—politically the practice of the philosophy that "the world owes me a living." Christianity, on the other hand, is the earthly expression of love—the practice, among men, of unselfishness.

The Communist expects to make a profit from life; the Christian is willing, for Christ's sake, to take a loss. The one looks for gain, though it disclaims the profit motive; the other is happy to sacrifice.

Communism exalts the self; Christianity bows before God. There is nothing naturally wrong with putting my self first. That is what the natural man does instinctively. In fact, it is contrary to sinful nature to think of others first. Only the redeemed man seeks his treasure in heaven rather than on earth.

By now it should be clear why Christianity and communism can never meet in the same person. No Christian can be dedicated to a way of life which exalts man above all other considerations. Conversely, no Communist can be truly Christian. If he acknowledges God above, he loses the heart of his materialistic orientation.

It is one thing to say, in the abstract, that there are too many inequalities in the world. It is another thing to equalize the distribution of wealth, for purposes of advantage, by fiat or by force. The Christian may say to his unredeemed neighbor, speaking of another, "See that I am willing to give what I have so that our neighbor may have enough." But the Christian cannot say, with quite the same justification, "I am willing to give, but because you are not willing to join me, I will force you to give so that our neighbor may have enough."

The use of force inevitably accompanies communism because selfishness and sharing are incompatible. If goods and services must be divided to make the system work, then the man who has more or produces more must continually sacrifice a part of what he has or produces in order that his neighbor may have more. This does not make the human spirit happy. It also contradicts the first promise communism makes: that if one enters into a communal agreement, one will become better off. Thus force must be used, and Communist states inevitably become total-itarian dictatorships.

Finally, communism cannot logically stop short of a total world view any more than Christianity can. There can be no such thing as active communism without the goal of world domination. No possible limit can be set beyond which communism can be expected to agree it has no interest. If every man has a right to a portion of his neighbor's goods, then why not any neighbor and every neighbor? This, of course means anywhere and everywhere. As long as inequality exists anywhere in the world, as long as any man owns anything which is not—theoretically, at least—available to every man, communism would be denying itself if it did not recognize the fact and seek to do something about it.

As long as human beings live together in the world, they face the problem of social and economic relationships. The Christian, whatever his political philosophy, will never make material gain the chief end in life, for he looks toward a city whose builder and maker is God. The unbeliever, on the other hand, will doubtless seek some form of dominion whenever he is superior to his fellows; some form of communism, whenever he is inferior and in the natural struggle for the best in view. The trouble with the Communist is that his view does not extend beyond the horizon.

G. Aiken Taylor, "Why Communism Is Godless," *Christianity Today* 3, No. 6 (December 22, 1958): 13–15.

THE COMMUNIST MENACE: RED GOALS AND CHRISTIAN IDEALS

J. EDGAR HOOVER

At the invitation of Christianity Today, *the distinguished director of the FBI, J. Edgar Hoover, speaks his mind on the Communist threat to the Christian heritage. Based on his long experience in dealing with subversive forces, Mr. Hoover here relates for* Christianity Today's *wide readership how the Communist Party operates against the American religious heritage. He expresses some firm convictions on how churchmen and churchgoers may effectively confront the Red menace in prayer, thought, and action. Scheduled in three successive issues, Mr. Hoover's future themes are "Communist Propaganda and the Christian Pulpit" and "Communist Domination or Christian Rededication." Readers of Mr. Hoover's best-selling book* Masters of Deceit *have found it to be a definitive analysis of the Communist menace facing the world today.*

The twentieth century has witnessed the intrusion into its body fabric of a highly malignant cancer—a cancer which threatens to destroy Judaic-Christian civilization. One-fourth of the world's land surface has been seared and blackened by this cancer, while one out of every three human beings is caught in its tentacles. At this very hour, some are wondering whether we as a free nation can survive the frontal and underground assaults of this tumorous growth of communism.

Just 100 years ago communism was a mere scratch on the face of international affairs. In a dingy London apartment, a garrulous, haughty, and intolerant atheist, Karl Marx, callous to the physical sufferings and poverty of his family, was busy mixing the ideological acids of this evil philosophy. Originally of interest only to skid row debaters and wandering minstrels of revolution, Marx's pernicious doctrines were given organizational power by a beady-eyed Russian, V. I. Lenin, who, with his Bolshevik henchmen, seized state power for communism in 1917. From that wintry day in St. Petersburg, communism began to flow in ever greater torrents. After Lenin came the crafty and cunning Joseph Stalin and now the ebullient master prevaricator, Nikita Khrushchev. Communism is today literally a violent hurricane, rocking not only the chanceries of the world but seeking to capture the bodies, minds, and souls of men and women everywhere.

UNIVERSAL DOMINATION THE GOAL

The full implications of the Communist challenge are shocking. The ultimate Communist goal—as defined by Marx, Lenin, and other Communist leaders—is the ruthless overthrow of our Judaic-Christian heritage and the establishment of a world-wide Communist society. By its very nature, communism is expansionist and universalist. In fact, the Communists feel that they can find their true fulfillment only by conquering non-Communist areas and bringing the whole planet under their dominion.

This overriding Communist goal of universal domination becomes the key to Party activities. Feeling that history has destined communism for ultimate victory, the Communists believe that permanent peace with non-Communists is impossible, that life must be an inevitable struggle between the two. "It is inconceivable," Lenin proclaimed, "that the Soviet Republic should continue to exist for a long period side by side with imperialist states. Ultimately, one or the other must conquer."

REJECTION OF OBJECTIVE MORALITY

Hence, there arises the ugly manifestation of Communist "ethics"—namely, the Communist belief that morality must be subordinated to the class struggle, the inevitable conflict between communism and its opponents. What is moral? Anything which serves to destroy the enemy and promote communism. Lenin was most explicit: "Morality is that which serves to destroy the old exploiting society and to unite all the toilers around the proletariat, which is creating a new Communist society."

Communist morality, of course, is rooted in total rejection of a belief in God and in the values of the Christian moral code. Supernatural concepts and divine revelation play no role in communism. "We repudiate all morality that is taken outside of human, class concepts," Lenin proclaimed. "We, of course, say that we do not believe in God, and that we know perfectly well that the clergy, the landlords, and the bourgeoisie spoke in the name of God in order to pursue their own exploiters' interests."

This rejection of God gives communism a demonic aspect—transforming it into a fanatical, Satanic, brutal phenomenon. Morality is not determined by ethical standards grounded in an Absolute, but in the expedient interpretations of the Party—meaning, in actual practice, the whims and desires of the ruling clique or

Party leader. This leads to the terrifying doctrine that "the end justifies the means." Proof of the cynical ruthlessness of such morality is the following description by long-time American revolutionaries:

> With him the end justifies the means. Whether his tactics be "legal" and "moral," or not, does not concern him, so long as they are effective. He knows that the laws as well as the current code of morals, are made by his mortal enemies. ... Consequently, he ignores them in so far as he is able and it suits his purposes. He proposes to develop, regardless of capitalist conceptions of "legality," "fairness," "right," etc., a greater power than his capitalist enemies ...

A SOCIETY WITHOUT GOD

Hence, under communism we see a decisive break from and thrust against the Judaic-Christian heritage. Communism is not just another political party, social organization, or economic philosophy which can be understood within the framework of our traditional Western heritage. So to regard communism is radically to misunderstand its terrific driving power, insidious persuasion, and terrifying intent. The Communists are not interested in remodeling or reforming our society, but in organizing a completely different society—a society which by denying God hopes to create a new type of man: Communist Man. St. Paul, the great Apostle, could say, "If any man be in Christ, he is a new creature." The Communists would pervert this profound truth to say: "If any man be in the Communist Party, he is a new creature."

CONFRONTING THE RED CHALLENGE

The question arises: how can a philosophy so anti-God, anti-religious, anti-human be so provocative and appealing to some people in our country? Perhaps in this strategic question we can find some of the challenges of—and answers to—this demonic way of life.

Let's take a look at some of the Communist challenges today and see what we as Christians can do about them.

1. *The Communists appeal to man's idealism, and ask the very best of his life.* Communist propaganda proclaims Marxism-Leninism "the greatest cause in the history of mankind," worthy of man's highest devotion. The Communist appeal is always to the noblest, the best, the most admirable in man. "The great vision and courage of us Communists has never been matched by that of any past heroes in the annals of mankind. In this respect we have every reason to be proud ..."

   Answer: Have we in America and in the church given sufficient emphasis to Christian ideals, and called for heroic effort in the attainment of great goals? In particular, have we imbued our young people with the moral idealism which helps to mold their lives for Christ? Perhaps we have contented ourselves with catering to man's mediocrity, rather than attempting to bring out the noblest and deepest strands of character. Like Isaiah of Jerusalem, we must ever keep the awe, the majesty, and the holiness of God before us—and call men to ever greater efforts in His service. Are we pressing on toward the high calling in Christ, toward the goals of a Christian society? The Christian church—as history has proved—has the power to capture men and lead them to divine levels. By exalting God and His purposes in the lives of men, the church can unmask the utter falsity of communism's siren calls.

2. *The Communists do not doubt the validity of their cause; they press ever onward for their secularized Utopia, confident of ultimate victory.* "We Communists must possess the greatest courage and revolutionary determination of mankind. ... While we clearly see the difficulties confronting the cause of communism, we are not in the least daunted by them ..."

Answer: Are there too many pessimists, waverers, and people of little faith in the ranks of the church today? Is there the enthusiasm among our people to match this Communist aggressiveness and certainty? The church of Christ has a great message to sing, a great responsibility to fulfill. Never must she feel pessimistic, daunted, or uncertain.

3. *The Communists expect from their members a deep sense of personal sacrifice and dedication.* "To sacrifice one's personal interests and even one's life without the slightest hesitation and even with a feeling of happiness, for the cause of the Party ... is the highest manifestation of Communist ethics." This is a sacrifice of the members' time, talents, and personal resources, financial and otherwise. Casual effort is not a Communist trait.

Answer: Do we in the church and society really expect a deep sense of personal sacrifice and dedication? Do too many individuals come to church exerting only a "casual effort" and not giving sacrificially of their time, talents, and personal resources? The Communists have discovered that a demand for the very best actually brings forth the very best from the individual. If the Communists can create such responses on the basis of a cold, cynical materialism, just think of the accomplishments which can be wrought by the power of the Holy Spirit!

4. *The Party stresses the need for fidelity and loyalty to the mission of communism and the necessity of members to shun all temptations which would distract them from their assigned tasks.* "But if for the sake of ... the Party ... he is required to endure insults, shoulder heavy burdens, and do work which he is reluctant to do, he will take up the most difficult and important work without the slightest hesitation and will not pass the buck."

Answer: In our society today is there too much tendency to "pass the buck," to let George do it? Do we not often start out enthusiastically in civic or church work, and then let temptations sidetrack us from our task? Are we embarrassed when we are criticized for doing Christ's work? Are we ready to shoulder heavy burdens? Are too many following the easy road of conformity with secularism and not holding sufficiently high the banner of Christ?

5. *The Communists proclaim that working for the Party brings internal peace, joy, and happiness to the member.* He finds here creative achievement and self-fulfillment. "He will also be capable of being the most sincere, most candid, and happiest of men."

Answer: The Christian gospel tells of the deep joy, peace, and blessings which come from belief in Christ as Savior and Lord. Is the church doing enough to overcome the loneliness of contemporary man, his feelings of insecurity and frustration in a world growing more secular every day? Fear, personal unhappiness, and uncertainty stalk the streets today. Crime, juvenile delinquency, and disrespect for law and order are rife. Are we meeting these challenges in the Christian spirit, offering with maximum effort the true answer of the gospel, telling people that belief in God is the true way to a peace of mind which passes all understanding?

PERVERSION OF THE TRUTH

These are some of the challenges of communism today, and the problems they pose for Christians. Communists, in fact, attempt to capture the historic values of Christian civilization, such as love, mercy, and justice, and after grossly perverting their true meaning, they actually turn these values against their parent!

With shameless perfidy, the Communists hail themselves as the great exponents of love—most truly, one of mankind's most sublime virtues. Under communism, it is proclaimed, "there will be no oppressed and exploited people, ... no darkness, ignorance, backwardness. In such a society all human beings will become unselfish. ... The spirit of mutual assistance and mutual love will prevail among mankind." We know, in fact, however, that communism means terror, fear, and slavery. Communism represents a new age of barbarism, which is repealing the centuries of progress of Western man toward tolerance, understanding, and human brotherhood. Communist Man—the product of this system—is a brute, ideologically trained, who unhesitantly conducts purges, runs concentration camps, butchers the Hungarian Freedom Fighters. He is immune to the emotions of pity, sorrow, or remorse. He is truly an alarming monster, human in physical form, but in practice a cynically godless and immoral machine.

ROLE OF THE MINISTRY

If communism is to be defeated, the task must rest largely upon the theologians and the ministers of the gospel. Communism is a false secular religion with pseudo-theological explanations of the great verities of life, such as the creation, life on earth, and the world to come. Communism is an all-encompassing system with explanations—though wrong ones—for this great universe of God. The Party offers answers—though perverted ones—for the hopes, joys, and fears of mankind.

In the final analysis, the Communist world view must be met and defeated by the Christian world view. The Christian view of God as the Creator, Sustainer, and Lord of the universe is majestically superior to the ersatz approach of dialectical materialism concocted by Marx and Lenin. The task of our clergy today is to translate this Holy Truth into the daily lives of our men and women. This truly is their responsibility as Christian clergymen.

Strong, responsible, and faithful Christians, wearing the full armor of God, are the best weapons of attack against communism and the other problems of our day. "Seek ye first the kingdom of God, and his righteousness." In this way you will be playing a vital role also in helping defend our cherished way of life.

J. Edgar Hoover, "The Communist Menace: Red Goals and Christian Ideals," *Christianity Today* 5, No. 1 (October 10, 1960): 3–5.

FACING THE ANTI-GOD COLOSSUS

BILLY GRAHAM

T he American people have been buoyed up by Khrushchev's backdown in Cuba and by the apparent split between China and Russia.

This may be false security. An official high in the Kennedy administration told me, "This could possibly be a trap to lull us to sleep again while the Communists consolidate their positions, heal their differences, and plan new strategy for world domination."

Who would have thought three years ago that Russian generals would command a well-armed and well-disciplined army only 90 miles from American shores? Who would have thought that the four-power government of Berlin would be split by a wall, or that American troops would be fighting in a Southeast Asian war, or that China would dare to attack neutralist India?

I have just returned from touring most of the countries of Latin America, where we encountered some harsh facts. Castro's agents are busy everywhere, and in some places such as Venezuela and Guatemala they have resorted to terrorism. I was in Latin America during the Cuban crisis, and I found leaders were not so much afraid of the rocket and missile bases as they were of the continued Communist subversion activities.

Few of the articles which I have seen lately have emphasized one very important point. In spite of a few recent reverses, the Communists have been winning during the last 15 years. This is the unvarnished truth, and it is time we faced it squarely. It is difficult for us Americans sitting in the quietness of our living rooms watching television to comprehend what has been taking place in other parts of the world. Because of America's heritage of political freedom and our long-standing respect for constitutional law, both of them by-products of the Christian faith, we have thus far been spared the chaos and confusion that Communism has engendered in many parts of the world.

From my vantage point of world travel, the view is far from encouraging. During the past few years I have talked to a number of Communist leaders in several parts of the world. I am convinced that we face a titanic, self-confident movement that may never take "No" for an answer, that in its drive toward world domination it has little intention of stopping or giving up. While there may be a vast difference between the Soviet and Chinese brands of Communism, yet when the chips are down they will probably be united. The thing that unites them is their ultimate goal of building a kingdom on earth without God. They plan to build a world totally unlike anything history has ever known. Their methods of obtaining this goal may differ, but their objective remains the same. During the past few years, when the free world finally struck back after a long series of aggravations in such places as Guatemala, Berlin, Korea, and even Cuba, the Communist machine has merely paused, regrouped, and started using other tactics. They have often used smiles—employed "peace"—which led to Western relaxation, only to frown suddenly and resume aggression. These situations have not upset the table of conquest; they have only slowed the pace of operation temporarily.

We of the free world can discuss, we can debate, we can suggest, we can appease, we can exchange notes, we can beat our breasts, we can analyze our failures, we can issue ultimatums, but not a single one of these things has managed to halt the Red Tide during the past 20 years.

When we seek summit meetings to reduce international tensions, we realize the Communists have little intention of making concessions unless it is to their advantage to do so. We have also learned from sad experience that they do not tell the truth. Mr. Gromyko sat in Mr. Kennedy's office and brazenly told him there were no offensive weapons in Cuba when American intelligence already had proof that there were.

When we try to increase mutual understanding through the churches, we often find our Christian efforts treated like imperialist propaganda. A European bishop and respected leader in the ecumenical movement told me that the World Council of Churches has become in measure one more theater of conflict in the Cold War. This was certainly evident both at New Delhi and at the Central Committee's recent discussion of the Ghana problem in Paris. The World Council finds it difficult to rebuke the Communist world for fear of "offending" the churches in Eastern Europe.

Thus at every turn Western man finds himself frustrated in his efforts to maintain his freedom and identity in the oncoming tide. His appeals to reason are lost in the verbal avalanche that sweeps from the other side. His outlays for needy neighbors are often used to turn these neighbors against him. The words "freedom" and "democracy" and their defense have become confused by the other side's use of the same terms to explain its plan of enslavement. Very little seems to work.

In the face of such a juggernaut what shall we do?

SEARCHING THE FUTURE

Many Bible students are beginning to search the Scriptures anew in terms of eschatology. Dr. Markus Barth of the University of Chicago recently startled a chapel audience at Harvard University with an address on "The Second Coming of Christ."

The question that many students of the Bible are asking is simply this: Are the present days of crisis prophesied in Scripture? Even a casual investigation would seem to indicate that the Bible warns of a time of turmoil and trouble such as the world has never known. A predicted period of crisis was the burden of Christ's prophetic ministry. He even ventured so far in the Olivet discourse as to look ahead through the centuries and mark out the major movements that would transpire throughout the entire age of the church. As one theologian summarized his words: "The age would start with bitter persecution of His followers. There would be wars and commotions, but this would be no indication of the imminence of the end. The age would conclude with the return of the Son of Man with power and great glory."

Christ warned the disciples not to be deceived; he exhorted them to possess their souls in patience, and when certain predicted events came to pass to look up, knowing that their redemption was drawing nigh. In this same passage Jesus warned against our "hearts being overcharged with surfeiting." He urged us to be ever watching and praying. He indicated that "those who become involved with the sin of the present order will neither watch nor pray, and their spiritual senses will be overtaken with sluggishness. They will be unable to peer through the darkness of the midnight and catch the first faint glimmer of dawn." There is no doubt in my mind that the great upheavals predicted at the climax of history will be preceded by certain manifestations that indicate their nearness. Spiritual Christians who search the Scriptures will be able to read the signs of the times.

Up to now the church—particularly in the United States—has tended to live in a dream world. I find that the church on the rim of the Communist world is far more "aware" than we are.

Are we perhaps under the spell of some diabolical spiritual power? There is an unmistakable mystery in all this. The Bible speaks of the "mystery of iniquity," and the power of antichrist. Could it be that our apathy is a strategy of those principalities and powers that war against the souls of men? The Scriptures teach, "Because they received not the love of the truth, that they might be saved ... for this cause God shall send them strong delusion, that they should believe a lie" (2 Thess. 2:10b, 11).

Could it be that Communism is some vast judgment that God will allow to fall on the West for the deep moral rot that has infected almost every country? Will history repeat itself? Concerning Israel, who had rejected the truth and gone into immorality and idolatry, 2 Chronicles 36 says: "God sent his messenger the prophet to warn the people because of his great love for them, but they mocked the messenger of God, despised his word, and misused his prophets, until the wrath of the Lord arose against his people till there was no remedy." Therefore "he brought upon them the king of the Chaldees." In other words, God allowed a great pagan king to bring judgment upon his own people. Jesus said, "To whom much is given, much is required." The English-speaking world and Western Europe have had far more spiritual light than any other nations in the world's history. Except for a dedicated minority, we are rejecting that light intellectually and morally.

Events of the present hour should shock the church into renewed dedication and vigorous action. It is reported that on the day that the Bolshevik Revolution began in Russia, church leaders in Moscow were wrangling over what color to paint the walls of a certain cathedral.

LOSS OF INITIATIVE

My second observation concerning Communism and the present world crisis is this: It seems to me that in the face of materialism's appalling gains the church has retreated into a defensive position. Some of us have panicked as we have viewed with horror the rise and spread of the anti-God colossus of materialism at home and of Communism abroad. So we have become defenders rather than crusaders. We are on the defensive rather than the offensive. I personally think we have spent far too much time in apologetics, and not enough in declaration. The early church did not defend the faith; they propagated it. Christ needs no defense. He needs to be proclaimed! He needs to be exemplified in human personality. He needs to be lived!

This genius marked the early church. They took Jesus' words literally: "And I, if I be lifted up, will draw all men nigh unto me."

Rome was the "Moscow" of Christ's day, and the goal of Roman imperialism was to bring the world under its dominion. In many ways, of course, Communism cannot be compared to Rome. For one thing, Communism has all the modern psychological techniques of "brainwashing." It also has modern weapons whereby a relative few can control an entire nation. (Only 3 percent of the people of the Soviet Union are Communists.) Despite the tyranny of Rome, however, I read no speeches in the Bible by Peter, John, or Paul against the political regime of their day. They preached Christ and they preached Christ alone. They declared his Lordship and his Redeemership, and did it within the context of a tyranny that eventually imprisoned and killed them. Their powerful Christian thrust was shortly to shatter the Roman imperial colossus, and to inaugurate the Christian era.

We are living in one of the most challenging periods of history. It has been my privilege to preach the gospel in every part of the world, and in every area I have found dedicated followers of Jesus Christ. I have seen thousands of all races and speaking many languages march forward on every continent to receive Christ as Savior. This age is a great time to be alive. These are days of unusual opportunity. Never before have we had such wonderful tools for propagating the faith.

Dwight L. Moody once said: "I look upon this world as a wrecked vessel. Its ruin is getting nearer and nearer. God said to me: 'Moody, here is a lifeboat; ... rescue as many as you can before the crash comes.' "

THE LORD OF HISTORY

Another thing we must remember is that Christ is the Lord of history. "He is the same yesterday, today, and forever." The calendar cannot contain him. Nothing takes him by surprise! Kingdoms are shattered, nations crumble, systems fall in the wake of him who is King of Kings and Lord of Lords. He shall have the final word, the final reign, the final glory, and the final judgment! Nothing, not even the gates of hell, can prevent his triumph.

Even today, in the Soviet Union, Jesus Christ is causing trouble! *Newsweek* recently reported: "American church leaders have been returning from the Soviet Union with reports of unexpected vitality in Russian religious worship. But the trend may be a fleeting one. The Communist party announced last week an accelerated drive against religion, including a major campaign for the popularization of atheism."

The atheistic regime is disturbed by the undercurrent of Christian belief that persists despite redoubled efforts to stamp Christ out of the people's conscience. Thus, by asserting his mastery of the present, Christ again vindicates his Lordship of history.

Until the day of his final victory and consummation there will be many upheavals and wars and rumors of wars. The church may undergo persecution to an extent and with an intensity the world has never known. It is not impossible that the tide of Communism and materialism now sweeping the world may be motivated by the winds of divine judgment. In turn, however, God's judgment will also descend upon the world of atheism, materialism, and worldliness. If the Scriptures are clear at all, they are certainly clear on this point: "The kingdoms of this world shall become the kingdoms of the Lord and of his Christ."

The Holy Spirit has kept me from the horrible abyss of thinking that man by his own accomplishment would bring all things to perfection. Instead, the Bible teaches that left to himself, sinful man will bring about all the disasters announced in its pages. It could well be that the weaknesses of the West, together with the failure of the church, have made possible the strength of Communism.

The Christian posture should be one not of defense, but of preparation for "that day." These should be days of personal rededication; of retreat into the closet of prayer; of girding our children for days of possible persecution because of their faith. I personally find myself studying far less for sermon preparation these days and more for devotional purposes, and pray that I may be worthy to suffer for him if he so decrees.

The church needs to develop an atmosphere in which martyrs are made. As Lester DeKoster has said, "The church's whispers must become shouts; her lethargy must become enthusiasm; and her subdued light must become a beacon set upon the hilltops of the world."

While she still has opportunity, the church should evangelize with new vigor and call nations to repentance from sin to avert the coming crisis. The progress of history is not inevitable. Not even the progress of judgment is inevitable. When God decided to judge Nineveh, he sent Jonah to preach repentance. Nineveh repented of her sin and judgment was spared. Said Isaiah the prophet: "Except the Lord of hosts had left to us a very small remnant we should have been as Sodom, and we should have been like unto Gomorrah."

When and in what measure judgment shall fall will be determined by the depth of the church's dedication to her Lord. Can we say that the church as it exists in the United States is made up of God's people? Are we the ones of whom the Scripture declares: "And they overcame him by the blood of the Lamb, and by the word of their testimony; and they loved not their lives unto the death" (Rev. 12:11)?

Billy Graham, "Facing the Anti-God Colossus," *Christianity Today* 7, No. 6 (December 21, 1962): 6–8.

HALTING RED AGGRESSION IN VIET NAM

THE EDITORS

S peaking of the Roman patriot Cicero, Sulla, the Roman military dictator, said two thousand years ago: "There are soldiers who never bore a sword, and brave men who died in no battle." Against a backdrop of international proposals that America pull out of Viet Nam and pressures by press and pulpit to negotiate in the face of Communist aggression, President Johnson has spoken to the American people as a brave soldier.

The president has placed the Viet Nam situation in proper perspective. Simply stated, the problem exists because North Viet Nam coveted control of South Viet Nam and viciously breached that country's sovereignty by naked aggression. The United States is fighting to fulfill its pledged word of honor to defend South Viet Nam against such aggression. In this fulfillment, Mr. Johnson affirmed, "We will not be defeated. We will not grow tired. We will not withdraw, either openly or under the cloak of a meaningless agreement." Behind these words lie three sound ideas: (1) South Viet Nam has the right of self-determination; (2) Communist aggression in Southeast Asia must be resisted; (3) world order must be strengthened. American policy does not yield one inch to those who want peace at any price, and who never seem to condemn Communist aggression or even understand the nature of its threat.

The United States has no ulterior motives, wants no territory, and is willing to help in the development and growth of Southeast Asia. But to Hanoi and Peking the message was loud and clear: There will be no withdrawal. No possibility exists of military successes for aggressors. Only the thinnest edge of American power has been unleashed.

The aggressors would be foolish indeed not to take a close look at the offer of unconditional discussion, although the Chinese, expectedly, rejected it at once. This offer was accompanied by the promise of a billion-dollar American investment in the economic development of the crowded Asian sector of the world. The president challenged Russia to join in this peaceful development by investing its own resources in plowshares rather than in swords. Russian response to this overture will test the sincerity of her professed "peaceful" aims in what may be a choice between the olive branch and the bomb. Moved by idealism, the president called for food to feed the hungry, taken from the overflowing American granaries, and looked to a time of peace when medicine and education would improve the lot of the hard-pressed millions. In support of this idea he quoted from the Scriptures. But his moving challenge to accept either life or death fell short of the biblical truth that God sets eternal life and eternal death before all men—and that the best things in life are assured only to those who choose eternal life.

The present situation is not without irony. Some say Mr. Johnson's policy is the one represented by Barry Goldwater and repudiated by the electorate in the choice of Johnson over Goldwater. This is a gross oversimplification. It may indeed be true that Mr. Goldwater read the signs better than Mr. Johnson a year ago. What Goldwater feared has happened. But the president now discerns what he may not have seen then.

In a democracy, the right to dissent is ever present. Always there will be those who disagree with any policy formulated by the party in power. It may be hoped that Mr. Johnson will not yield to opponents of a sound policy in Viet Nam—those who neither sense nor see the true nature of our present dilemma, and whose hopes for withdrawal would precipitate another Munich. America is still the greatest bastion for freedom, and it holds the greatest military power in world history. This power must be used responsibly when principle, freedom, and truth are at stake.

The Editors, "Halting Red Aggression in Viet Nam," *Christianity Today* 9, No. 15 (April 23, 1965): 32.

REFINING CZECH COMMUNISM

THE EDITORS

T he Soviet-led invasion of Czechoslovakia will take memories back thirty years, when the same small country became the victim of another aggressor. That aggressor's emblem was the crooked cross. Britain and France stood by consenting, and Chamberlain's infamous treaty with Hitler made a pretense of ensuring "peace in our time." Whether military intervention then would have stopped the Nazis is questionable; now, in a nuclear age, it seems folly to confront the Soviet bloc with force. The inaction of Western democracy in 1938 did nothing to commend it to the Czechs, and was probably a major factor in their entering the Communist camp a decade later.

To regard last month's events in isolation would be a mistake, for Soviet uneasiness about its satellites had been growing for some time. Yugoslavia broke with Stalin in 1948. Successive years saw trouble among the workers in East Germany, the crushing of a more serious revolt in Hungary, and the Albanian defection to Red China, with whom the rift has widened to such an extent that Peking condemned the latest invasion as a "shameless act." During the past months Rumania has evinced an increasingly independent spirit, but it was Czechoslovakia that gave most concern. Its break from Moscow would have opened a corridor from free Europe into the Ukraine, probably the most restless of the Soviet republics. Moscow's swift and brutal plugging of the gap would have outraged world opinion still more had Americans not been in Viet Nam. There is little doubt that the Communists considered this an important factor in timing, just as the British invasion of Suez twelve years ago encouraged Soviet suppression of the revolt in Hungary.

In the 228 days available to him since the overthrow of hardliner Antonín Novotný, Alexander Dubček seemed to be advocating everything that Stalinist Communism stood against: free speech, a free press, secret balloting, the right to emigrate and travel abroad, greater industrial independence, decentralization of government, questioning minds, the right to demonstrate. Under Dubček, several bishops were reinstated in this land where 15 percent of the 14.4 million population are practicing Roman Catholics. Forty other offending priests had their convictions set aside. Intending ordinands became so numerous that Bishop Frantisek Tomasek, apostolic administrator of Prague, planned to open a second seminary, and was optimistic that the Dubček regime would grant permission for this. The bishop saw new signs of religious fervor. "We are no longer a silent church," he said.

Another mistake, however, would be to think that Czechoslovakia was rapidly becoming a non-Communist state. It was regularly supplying arms to the North Vietnamese. Josef Cardinal Beran, the 79-year-old Archbishop of Prague, long a prisoner of Novotný, is still in exile in Rome. About 1,500 priests are still consigned to secular employment. All priests must take the oath of loyalty to the Czechoslovak Socialist Republic. The government will not return church property confiscated two decades ago.

Josef Hromádka, leader of the Prague-based Christian Peace Conference, had earlier claimed to see encouraging portents.

Marxists were now acknowledging that a changed society does not produce changed men, he told the World Council of Churches' Central Committee in Crete last year. He urged discussions between the 100-percenters on each side. "Half-Marxists and half-Christians," he explained, "don't do much." The erstwhile Princeton seminary professor has always held that believers should contribute actively to the development of socialism.

In any event Hromádka had long ago forfeited his right to speak for orthodox Christianity. At the WCC's Amsterdam Assembly in 1948, he denied that Communism was either total-itarian or atheistic. "Its atheism," he insisted, "is rather a prac-tical reaction against the forces of the pre-socialist society than a positive philosophically essential tenet." He suggested that it was in many ways "secularized Christian theology, often furi-ously anti-church." The vision of Marx, Lenin, and Stalin as Christians unawares is as intriguing and theologically confus-ing as the Archbishop of Canterbury's expectation of meeting atheists in heaven. Both interpretations would tend to rile a Party member. The Christian Peace Conference might even have been embarrassed by any new liberalism in Czechoslovakia that could have moderated its customary pro-Communist, anti-American pronouncements. At the CPC gathering in Prague four years ago, the largest foreign delegation was the British, and it was led by a Church of England priest, the Rev. Paul Oestreicher. Now a senior staff member of the British Council of Churches, Oestreicher attended this year's WCC assembly at Uppsala as correspondent of the *Morning Star*, Britain's official Communist daily. The 1964 Prague meeting looked upon Eastern criticism of the West as wholly justifiable, while Western criticism of Communism was regarded as a misuse of Christianity.

A measure of religious freedom in Czechoslovakia would make it difficult to retain strict controls on neighboring regimes fed for so long on atheistic propaganda. The Czechs were heading toward a middle position in this as in other areas. Said one of their diplomats just before the August invasion: "Good Catholics in Czechoslovakia are dead serious today when they pray for the welfare and victory of their Communist government." Of that government's officials, 70 percent reportedly spent time in jail under Stalin and after. It is not surprising that the Soviets had no substantial fifth column in Czechoslovakia to ease the aggressors' entry and settlement.

Clearly the Soviets cannot understand or tolerate any brand of socialism other than their own. To them, moderate socialism is a dangerous dilution. Those who disagree are classed as "evil-breathers"—that is, enemies of the Soviet Union. An editorial in *Pravda* on August 20 said: "Marxists-Leninists are not and can never be indifferent to the fate of socialist construction in other countries and the general cause of Socialism and Communism on earth." There is logic here. Those who feel that the future belongs to Marx consider it a duty to sweep away anything that stands on their road to world domination on Marxist lines.

It is unthinkable to them that Communism has been tried and has failed. So the situation naturally demands that an imperialist threat be posited, and an invitation invented. That the Czechs had requested military aid was dismissed as "an inept and obvious fraud" by George W. Ball, United States representative to the United Nations. He called it a "document of treason invented and written by frightened men in Moscow, reacting to their own dark nightmares." The threat-and-invitation formula had been useful in Hungary twelve years ago. All this reflects reversion to a hard line that must be a setback for liberal tendencies within the U.S.S.R. itself. The sun may be steadily sinking on Stalin's empire, but the Marxist myth survives. Says Professor Zbigniew Brzezinski, a Columbia University expert on Soviet affairs: "This is a victory for Oriental Communism over Western Communism, which was always attracted by social democracy while Oriental Communism was attracted by despotism."

Last month's "pre-midnight sneak" violated the United Nations Charter and shocked world opinion. The *mot juste* came from an unlikely source when Walter Ulbricht described the invasion as "a shining example of socialist internationalism." Even those who had supported the Soviet Union over Hungary in 1956, among them the French and Italian Communist parties and the Indian Government, joined the chorus of condemnation. A *New York Times* editorial suggested: "The United Nations could and should defy that illegal act of detention by inviting President Svoboda, Premier Cernik and Communist party chief Dubcek to come to the U.N. and state their nation's case. This could be done as a procedural matter, exempt from the veto; the invitation so extended would immediately put Moscow to the test."

But Russia was not alone on trial in this crisis. What of the World Council of Churches, which has spent an inordinate amount of time on condemnatory resolutions on American involvement in Viet Nam? Now, if ever, was the time to recall Dr. Eugene Carson Blake's words at Crete. He said that if the WCC "acts timidly and by compromise rather than courageously and by principle," many Christians would look elsewhere "for the dynamism and the faithfulness that the ecumenical movement requires." The Central Committee at that Crete meeting had much to say about the violations of human rights in those nations that could be criticized with impunity. By a piece of colossal hypocrisy, however, and under coercion by Archbishop Ieronymos of Athens, it said nothing about the untried prisoners of the Greek junta. The rejoicing attendant upon Orthodox entry into the WCC in 1962 was evidently not to be jeopardized for the sake of 3,000 dissident Greeks.

How has the WCC reacted to the Czech situation? At Uppsala, with matters steadily deteriorating, it said nothing—just as it continued to say nothing about Greece. No outraged protest was conveyed from Uppsala to the Soviet Union via the Metropolitan Nikodim, a perennial and vociferous figure at these ecumenical occasions. In response to the *fait accompli,* a month after Uppsala, the director of the WCC's Commission of the Churches on International Affairs sent a message to the CCIA's commissioners and national commissions. It begins promisingly: "The reported military action in Czechoslovakia ... creates a tragic situation for the people of Czechoslovakia and constitutes a threat to world peace and good will."

At last the nettle was going to be grasped! The Soviet bloc was to be censured, just as the United States, South Africa, Rhodesia, and Portugal had regularly been! But was it? "At this initial stage it may be helpful to remind ourselves of statements relevant to the present situation which the WCC has issued on previous occasions," continued the director, Dr. O. Frederick Nolde. "I send these to you after consultation with the General Secretary of the WCC and CCIA colleagues." There follow five quotations from previous WCC assemblies, dealing with such matters as human rights, religious liberty, and peace appeals. Then comes a sixth quotation, this time from Uppsala, which says: "We Christians who have often lived in hostility toward one another see how the nations in order to avoid wars of inconceivable dimensions seek the way to co-existence. This challenges us to creative 'pro existence' with the welfare of our neighbor in view." Whatever this means, the Czechs in their present plight will find it as irrelevant to their condition as mere words addressed to the poor and needy (cf. James 2:16). Where was that contemporary "costly word" of which we have heard so much?

Days passed while the WCC claimed to be seeking advice from its membership, including the churches in Bulgaria, Poland, East Germany, Hungary, the Soviet Union—and Czechoslovakia. It seemed a bizarre, needless prelude to humanitarian protest. Meanwhile the Soviet Union made a tactical reversal of policy, and this got the hesitant ecumenists at least partially off the hook. They then issued a statement that said, *inter alia*: "We deplore the military intervention" by the Soviet Union and her allies. The tardy statement came, it was made clear, "not only because of the grave issues of peace, human liberty and dignity at stake, but also in response to a plea indirectly forwarded to us from one of our member churches in Czechoslovakia."

Although belated and weaker than many friends of freedom would like, it was, nonetheless, the clearest and most unambiguous criticism of the Soviet Union ever ventured by the World Council of Churches. Any lesser response would have reflected the decline and disintegration of more than international Communism!

In joining the concern for the Czech people, the WCC had after its fashion jettisoned timidity and compromise, and evinced a measure of that courageous and principled action for which Dr. Blake had pleaded last year in Crete. The WCC pronouncement admittedly has mystifying overtones that await further clarification; but if member churches behind the Iron Curtain recommended or even tolerated the protest, this may be hailed as an ecumenical gain, and could signal the dawning in Geneva of a new spirit in which deference to Communism has less place.

The Editors, "Refining Czech Communism," *Christianity Today* 12, No. 24 (September 13, 1968): 33–35.

PLAIN TALK ON VIET NAM

THE EDITORS

After years of asserting that no North Vietnamese troops were engaged in South Viet Nam, the Hanoi government suddenly launched a full-scale invasion on several fronts, using a greater mass of armor than Hitler had for his invasion of Russia in 1941. A few weeks later, President Nixon announced that the United States was mining North Vietnamese harbors and would interdict ships loaded with military supplies for the North. He indicated that he does not want to provoke a confrontation with any other nation.

Mr. Nixon's actions have aroused a storm of criticism and protest. A few voices—but only a few—have noted the perplexing fact that while many have condemned Nixon's actions in the most sweeping terms, very few critics have been honest enough to place it in the context of the *Blitzkrieg* to which it is a response. As president and commander in chief, Nixon has the responsibility of making the decisions on Viet Nam. Rallies, threats of impeachment, and the like will not deter him—nor should they. Under our system of checks and balances, the president's power is not absolute. The Congress has the authority to tie his hands and change his policy. All it need do is cut off all spending for Viet Nam. Of course, if Congress were to take this step, it would have to assume the responsibility for the consequences, including the impending military debacle that the president, by his controversial actions, is trying to prevent. It is highly unlikely that Congress will so act, though some of its members may talk themselves hoarse.

No one can predict with any certainty whether Mr. Nixon's decision will check the North Vietnamese offensive. What does appear certain is that Hanoi will remain intransigent unless it suffers a decisive military defeat. From its own point of view, this is only logical.

We need to remember that all of us, from the president down, are finite and fallible. History is replete with examples of men's tragic blunders committed through ignorance, miscalculation, venality, naïveté, or plain stupidity, sometimes with the best of intentions. History also teaches us that no one can foresee all the contingencies; sometimes bad decisions yield good results and good decisions seem to turn out badly.

It is widely questioned whether we should ever have gotten into Viet Nam in the first place. After all, we chose not to intervene in the abortive Hungarian revolution of 1956 or in the massive military occupation of Czechoslovakia by the Soviet Union in 1968. But we are already in Viet Nam, and Mr. Nixon has been trying desperately to extricate us from this entanglement. Anyone who thinks he hasn't is blind to reality. It certainly is in the president's own political interest to do so. But getting out is incomparably harder than getting in.

Whether we approve or disapprove of the president's conduct of the war, we are going to have to live with what he has chosen to do, because he is president and the Congress as a whole has shown unwillingness to take steps that could negate his actions. However, the people will have their say in November. At that time the electorate can return Richard Nixon to the White House or send him home. If they do the latter, they should send home a lot of senators and congressmen as well for permitting the president to continue a policy they had the power but not the civic courage to stop. To attempt to pressure the president into backing down without actually ordering him to do so—and thus incidentally to encourage the other side to persist in the aggression he is trying to suppress—may be prudent electioneering tactics, but it can hardly be called responsible statesmanship.

Meanwhile all Americans, and especially Christians, should stand by the president, even if they think his policy is mistaken. Every Christian should pray that what is being done will lead to peace and justice.

The Editors, "Plain Talk on Viet Nam," *Christianity Today* 16, No. 17 (May 26, 1972): 27.

★ *August 29, 1975* ★

THE DEMANDS
OF DÉTENTE

THE EDITORS

Richard Nixon and Henry Kissinger were the architects of détente between the United States and the Soviet Union. Its purpose was to keep these two superpowers from bringing on World War III. The assumption was that peaceful co-existence is possible and is necessary to avoid a nuclear holocaust. No one really expected that this would end the struggle between capitalism and Communism; the motive was to assure that the war would be fought with political, economic, and social weapons, not with bombs and guns.

Détente has encountered strong opposition from some Americans, such as Senator Henry Jackson and Governor Ronald Reagan. Russians like Alexander Solzhenitsyn and Andrei Sakharov have made plain their opposition to détente in their powerful critiques of the brutal Soviet system. They and many others argue that détente has been a one-way street with the advantages going mainly to the Soviets. They can point to the recent Helsinki meeting, where President Ford signed an agreement interpreted by Leonid Brezhnev as an acceptance of the Soviet conquest of such countries as Hungary, Czechoslovakia, and Poland.

Brezhnev, who like us has his problems, said: "No one should try to dictate to other people, on the basis of foreign policy considerations of one kind or another, the manner in which they ought to manage their internal affairs." This was almost laughable considering the open or clandestine activities of the Soviets in other countries such as Italy, Portugal, Viet Nam, Chile, Cuba, and the nations of Africa.

We are at a point where economics and politics may intersect. A bad harvest has come to the Soviet Union. The Soviets badly need grain, and they have made substantial purchases in America with more to come. Undoubtedly Brezhnev fears that the grain may come with strings attached. American labor leader George Meany, head of the AFL-CIO, has expressed himself about this and about Communism in general. The appearance of Solzhenitsyn on the labor union's platform and the wide acceptance of what he said by labor leaders and workers is certain to have caused Brezhnev more concern.

Détente is one form of the continuing war between capitalism and Communism. We can be sure that the Soviet Union is attempting to use détente to further its own purposes in this struggle. Therefore we think that the United States too should employ détente to accomplish certain long-range goals, goals that are in the interest not simply of America but of mankind.

More than anything else the Soviet leaders fear the free movement of persons and ideas. The Soviet Union is a closed society in which dissent is suppressed and the movement of citizens is severely curtailed. Never has the Soviet Union practiced what it committed itself to in signing the Geneva declaration on human rights. Demands for liberalization made by persons within the Soviet Union will have little success. Pressure must come from the West. The refusal of President Ford to invite Solzhenitsyn to the White House when he first came to Washington several weeks ago lost him a chance to promote the cause of freedom in the Soviet Union.

Why not use the Soviets' need to purchase grain as an opportunity to extract concessions that will extend human freedom in that closed society? Why not insist on the right of every Soviet Jew to emigrate to Israel or elsewhere? Why not demand that the Soviets cease to harass and persecute its citizens who dare to criticize the Soviet system? Why not demand real religious freedom for Soviet citizens? Why not insist on the free flow of literature—including Bibles—into the Soviet Union for distribution to all who wish to read what the West has to say? Why not require the Soviet Union to intervene on behalf of the missionaries detained in South Viet Nam so that they may come home at once?

The United States will be making a great concession in selling grain to a nation that has made no secret of its hostility to capitalism and its plan to annihilate it. The least we can do is require that some concessions be made in return.

The Editors, "The Demands of Détente," *Christianity Today* 19, No. 23 (August 29, 1975): 26.

IF COMMUNISM FAILS, DO WE WIN?

CHARLES COLSON

Time magazine called last May "the most momentous month" in the second half of the twentieth century.

That may be no overstatement. Consider these extraordinary scenes: thousands of students marching on China's Tiananmen Square calling for democracy and freedom; Polish citizens streaming to the polls to defeat Communist-party officials (which has led to the appointment of a non-Communist prime minister); open elections in the U.S.S.R. in which Andrei Sakharov, who spent six years in exile, was elected to the Congress of People's Deputies.

In China, however, the fresh hopes of May had wilted by summer. The white statue toppled beneath mud-caked tank treads; we will never know how many students fell beneath the force of the "People's" Army, nor how many citizens died, single bullet to the head, by the executioner's revolver.

But the truth is, while China's leaders may have cleared Tiananmen Square, they cannot clear the winds of democracy from Chinese air. These new winds sweeping the East may well signal the culmination of the great ideological struggle of the twentieth century.

LOSING LUSTER

These past nine decades have been dominated by the confrontation between two competing political systems: the utopian vision of a workers' state versus the liberal democratic tradition.

The communist movement began in 1904 when a Russian exile converted Karl Marx's humanistic philosophy into a revolutionary scheme of totalitarian power. And by 1917, Vladimir Lenin's Bolsheviks swept to power, seizing the hearts and minds of Russia's deprived peasants.

Communism also seized the hearts and minds of romantic idealists in the West. In 1919, after visiting the Soviet Union, journalist Lincoln Steffens summed up the trendy view: "I have seen the future and it works."

Within a few decades, Stalin's eradication of millions of his countrymen exposed communism's moral vacuum; yet it still sustained momentum with subversive expansion in Asia, the overt annexation of Eastern Europe, and the embrace of Third World nations eager to throw off Western colonialism.

Surprisingly, it also continued to enjoy support on some Western campuses and churches. Some modern liberation theologians sounded no less effusive about Marxism than Hewlett Johnson, the "Red Dean" of Canterbury, who in the 1930s described the Soviet Union as the "salvation of the world."

But in just this decade, communism has begun to lose its luster. Third World guerrilla movements now oppose Marxist oppressors; Solidarity has both challenged and humbled the Communist government of Poland.

Meanwhile, economic resurgence in the U.S., Europe, and Japan has proved free-market capitalism superior in meeting human needs than the utopian rhetoric of communist bureaucracies. In desperation, the Soviet Union instituted glasnost and perestroika; China began massive economic reforms. But, as we saw in Tiananmen Square, those reforms spawned something more.

Many observers have interpreted these tumultuous developments in the communist world as being the result of economic unrest. But that, according to a long-time missionary to China, is to miss the point entirely. "The real forces here are more than economic. They are spiritual. These people who have been non-persons for so long are finally saying, we want to be persons again even if it costs us our lives." As a banner in Tiananmen Square put it, "We love our rice, but we love democracy more."

Alexander Solzhenitsyn foresaw this same point in 1976 when he wrote, "We are approaching a major turning point in world history" caused in part by the "process of spiritual liberation" in the Soviet Union and other communist countries. Solzhenitsyn believed that economic freedom would lead to demands for political freedom. Manifested in the refusal to bow to oppression any longer, this spiritual upheaval would rock the very foundations of the communist world.

SPIRITUAL EXHAUSTION

There is an understandable temptation to conclude that this upheaval signals the demise of communism and victory for the West. But I believe such a judgment is overly optimistic.

For coupled with his vision of spiritual impetus in the East, Solzhenitsyn foresaw a concurrent spiritual emptiness in the West. In his controversial 1978 Harvard University commencement address, Solzhenitsyn decried the "spiritual exhaustion" and "decline in courage" of the West.

Among the many signs of Western decadence he cited was the loss of the resolve necessary to preserve our social contract: "To defend oneself one must be ready to die, but there is little such readiness in the society raised in the cult of material well-being."

A recent *Rolling Stone* poll of the baby-boom generation bears this out: Asked whether there was any cause for which they would be willing to fight to defend their country, 40 percent replied, none.

Here is the irony: At the very time the titanic economic and political battle of the twentieth century seems headed toward its grand dénouement, the forces that will shape that outcome are less economic and political than spiritual. The real issue will be whether the "spiritual liberation" beginning in the communist world will throw off the chains of oppression with a bang before "spiritual exhaustion" finishes the West with a whimper. What a tragedy if, at the very moment the oppressed masses of the East reach for the torch of democracy, the West disintegrates, morally unable to sustain the spirit by which democracy must be fueled.

What message is there in this for Christians?

Christians are charged with bringing a Christian witness to bear on all of life. If our society is in spiritual decline, then the church has failed to make a Christian impact on our culture.

If we care about the survival of the West—and there are those of us who feel strongly that the liberal democratic tradition offers humanity's best hope for human freedoms—then it is our task to inject spiritual vigor into a morally exhausted body politic.

That is no small task for an already enculturated church in America. It demands a level of courage and commitment no less than that demonstrated by the students of Tiananmen Square.

Charles Colson, "If Communism Fails, Do We Win?" *Christianity Today* 33, No. 14 (October 6, 1989): 64.

January 14, 1991

WAR CRY

While forces in the Middle East gather
behind a line drawn in sand, the church
will draw the line with tears.

GEORGE K. BRUSHABER

On November 19, in Paris, 34 member nations of NATO and the Warsaw Pact signed the European Security Agreement. After more than 40 years of East-West confrontation, the danger of the Cold War seems finally to have given way to peace.

By contrast, that same day in the Persian Gulf region, war came a giant step closer. Saddam Hussein matched George Bush's military escalation with his own announcement that he would now send another quarter-million troops to the Saudi Arabian border. Though we pray it never happens, at press time war seems imminent.

As the president struggles to make clear his case for direct action, most Americans agree Iraqi aggression must be resisted. For the U.S. and its allies to have the power to restore justice and not to do so may actually be immoral, which is why we sympathize with our president when he draws the line against Iraqi aggression. But the tremendous cost of human life that comes with war should lead us, as Francis Schaeffer suggested, to "draw the line only with tears." As Christians, we need to urge caution against chauvinistic nationalism and ethnocentric pride. We must guard against the seductive euphoria of war, especially techno-war in a faraway place against a people we don't understand very well. But beyond that, what is our message to the church? And from the church to the world?

First, we must acknowledge that two major wars and hundreds of regional conflicts have not improved human nature. Individuals and nations remain locked in the iron grip of sin with all of its cruelty. The next war may protect territorial interests, but only the redeeming and transforming power of Christ will change hearts on both sides of the battlefront.

Second, we must recognize that God is sovereign; his purposes ultimately prevail. His demands are mercy and justice and faithfulness to him. It is righteousness alone that exalts and preserves a nation, not military strength. Even as we are comforted that God expresses his love and mercy through his sovereign might, we must strengthen our resolve to live as he demands.

Third, we must be careful about attaching undue eschatological significance to this crisis (Matt. 24:6–7). However, to live expecting our Lord's return—whether we are at peace or war—is our reassuring privilege and inescapable obligation.

Fourth, we must exercise responsible citizenship. Profound moral and political judgments do not come easily; as we work toward settled convictions of our own about U.S. involvement in the Persian Gulf, we should participate in the public debate and the political process with humility, gentleness, and grace. Regardless of our views, our troops deserve respect and support. They serve because their leaders and their country have called them. We dare not inflict the lasting damage on these military men and women that we did on their counterparts in Vietnam. As we pray for their safety we must be prepared to suffer with those who suffer, and grieve with those who grieve.

Finally, we must call the church to prayer. It is in such times of testing and crisis that the church has often been its most effective in expressing the will and character of God. If the tanks rumble and the rockets fire, Christians everywhere ought to "pray without ceasing" for our leaders, for the safety of our troops, even for the enemy (Jesus died for Saddam, too).

War tears our souls; victory is often hollow. That is when the church's weapons of love, compassion, service, and prayer— bathed in tears—are needed most.

George K. Brushaber, "War Cry," *Christianity Today* 35, No. 1 (January 14, 1991): 14–15.

TYRANNY BY ANY OTHER NAME

CHARLES COLSON

I t would be hard to imagine a more visually engrossing year than 1991. Television screens throbbed with the dramas of war and peace; Operation Desert Storm, the bombing of Baghdad, the ground war, surrendering Iraqis, burning oil wells, and then troops coming home, families reunited, hugs on the tarmac.

But the most dramatic spectacle was the war that ended not with a bang, but a whimper. During the failed Soviet coup last August, we saw tanks in the streets of Moscow, then flags flying as the people resisted.

As I watched, my mind flashed back over my own life. I suddenly realized that much of it had been devoted to fighting a cold war that was now over.

As a marine lieutenant, I trained to fight the "communist hordes" invading South Korea. As a Senate aide, I worked through all-night budget sessions to fund the American rocket program and missile race after the Soviets' surprise launch of Sputnik. In the White House, I was dazzled by weekly military briefings on megatonnage, throw-weight, and strategic targeting.

I remember one night in the Oval Office in 1971, alone with President Nixon as we discussed how to get a critical antiballistic-missile program through the Senate. Nixon said somberly, "You know, Chuck, I hate spending money on all these missiles. My mother was a Quaker. I want peace. But if we don't do it, America will fall behind. The balance of power will shift; we will lose to the Soviets. Twenty years from now this world will not be safe to live in."

Such considerations influenced almost every policy decision. The fate of the world hung on nuclear deterrence.

Or so we thought. Those 20 years have now passed. And without a missile launched, we won.

ULTIMATE BETRAYAL

Clearly, deterrence was important. President Reagan upped the ante in the eighties, calling the Soviets' hand. And, as we always believed it would, the free market eventually whipped the heavy-handed socialist-state system.

But those factors alone could not account for what we witnessed in Moscow. Something more than economics moved those crowds through the streets, something that cold-war politicians in the U.S. had scarcely considered. How could we have missed it?

Christian friends, now officials in Eastern European governments, told me they had alerted U.S. officials back in 1987. They felt spiritual pressures building; they saw disillusionment on the faces of their Soviet oppressors. But the U.S. shrugged off such information.

I've encountered this mindset. While in Moscow last year, I was asked to come to the American embassy to calm a crowd of protestors.

At the embassy, I was ushered into a senior officer's suite. "Who are these people?" I asked.

"Oh, Baptists," he responded. "No, Pentecostals. I don't know, religious people of some kind."

I was stunned at how little our officials knew. He explained that these people wanted preferential treatment to get exit visas.

"They need them," I said. "They have been persecuted for their faith."

"Oh?" said the officer, throwing up his hands. "Well, they have to get in line like everybody else."

I believe we missed the real momentum in the East because the West was distracted by politics. Government officials were so involved in grand diplomatic and military strategies that they were blind to far grander spiritual forces. And our satellites, so sophisticated they can count the bolts on a tank, could not see inside the human heart.

The temptation now is to declare victory and enjoy a peaceful world happily ever after. Maybe Francis Fukuyama, the former State Department official who wrote "The End of History," is right. Democracy has won. The great world struggles are over.

But succumbing to that illusion is the greatest danger of this watershed moment. Communism failed because it was built on the false premise that man is good and utopia can be achieved. Its tyrants went on to repress the people. And it preached economic determinism, a doctrine that history is shaped not by spiritual, but by economic forces.

If we now conclude that the West won solely because of the superiority of the free market and our expensive weapons, we too will have fallen for the myth of economic determinism—and we will repeat the mistake that I and other policymakers made 20 years ago. That would be the ultimate betrayal of those heroes who risked their lives to bring democratic principles to the East.

TOTALITARIAN CONSUMERISM

The crucial concern today is not that we meet Eastern Europe's economic needs. There is a desperate need for food—and we should help, though only if we are assured of continuing reforms. The greatest need, however, is not for material bread, but spiritual bread. And satisfying the deepest longings of the human heart is something that government, or for that matter Western culture at large, cannot do.

No, that is the job of the church. Rarely have we had a greater opportunity. I was recently in Hungary and Czechoslovakia; believers there need whatever we can supply them: Christian literature, Bibles, training materials. Christian leaders in those countries recognize what the people need most—to rebuild the church and to give hope to the heart.

In Czechoslovakia I met Václav Maly, the priest who led thousands through the Prague streets during the uprisings of 1989. When Václav Havel was elected president, he offered Maly any position he wanted. But, as Maly told me, "All I want to do is preach the gospel because that's what our people need more than anything."

He's right. If the West declares victory and believes that economic abundance (the first signs of which are the VCRs, and the many pornographic magazines I saw in the streets of Prague) will meet the needs of the hungering East, we will squander the opportunity of this moment in history.

And if all that is offered to those who risked their lives to resist totalitarianism is self-indulgent, Western materialism—what Václav Havel calls "totalitarian consumerism"—then they will soon discover that they have changed one form of tyranny for another.

Charles Colson, "Tyranny by Any Other Name," *Christianity Today* 36, No. 1 (January 13, 1992): 72.

DOES KOSOVO PASS
THE JUST-WAR TEST?

CHARLES COLSON AND
NANCY PEARCEY

The scenes are as vivid in my mind as though they were yesterday: crowds of antiwar demonstrators circling the White House in a haze of spent tear gas and marijuana smoke. Watching from my office, I was struck by the large number wearing clerical collars, symbolic of the active role played by the mainline churches. The biggest march was led by the Episcopal bishop of Washington.

These memories flooded back as American pilots began bombing Belgrade. As we write, U.S. troops, escorted by Apache helicopters, are massing on the Serbian border.

Is it Vietnam redux? The parallels are disturbing. But there is one conspicuous difference: churchmen are strangely silent. Bombers even flew raids on Easter Sunday with nary a word of protest. The church's earlier call to conscience has been muted.

Yet a military engagement this serious raises moral questions that the church should address. Moreover, the war in Yugoslavia highlights a profound shift in U.S. policy toward military engagement in the post-Cold War era. Here, as in Somalia, Haiti, and Bosnia, America is not defending vital national interests but seeking to halt ethnic cleansing and terrorism, brought to our living rooms in full color by CNN. The military is being employed as a humanitarian rescue unit, dispatched to halt other nations' internal conflicts and help troubled peoples get along.

But is this a morally justifiable use of force? I'm no isolationist, but this new role for the U.S. needs to be examined and debated. And Christians have the best tools for doing so in traditional just-war theory. First articulated by Augustine in the fifth century, the theory has informed Western reflection on the ethics of war and peace for 1,500 years.

Armed force is justified, according to the theory, only if it meets several criteria, such as: It has a just cause; it is a last resort; it is declared by proper authority; its effects are proportionate (the evils caused by war itself are less than the evils to be righted); and it has a reasonable probability of success. Measured against that moral grid, how do our policies in Yugoslavia fare?

First, a just cause is self-defense or righting a grievous wrong. There is no question of self-defense here: Slobodan Milosevic's butchery is taking place within Serbia's sovereign borders and he is not attacking any other nation. But we are seeking to right a terrible wrong; President Clinton even described his policy as "humanitarian bombing." So one could argue that the first criterion is met. Yet questions remain. Why intervene in Yugoslavia and not Sudan or East Timor or countless other places torn by civil strife? There seems to be no rhyme or reason to our selection of which thugs to "punish."

The second criterion is that armed force must be the last resort. Yet reportedly, the Joint Chiefs of Staff argued for economic sanctions instead of bombing—advice that went unheeded. Clearly, NATO did not exhaust nonmilitary forms of coercion.

Third, the war must be declared not by private groups but by sovereign authority. The authority in this case was NATO, which arguably meets this criterion; yet tricky constitutional questions remain. The Constitution gives only Congress the authority to declare war; both Presidents Johnson and Bush sought congressional approval before going into Vietnam and the Persian Gulf. Yet President Clinton committed forces without congressional sanction.

Fourth, proportionality: Do our tactics create more evil than they stop? The painful irony is that as NATO began bombing, Milosevic intensified his reign of terror—killing more civilians and driving them from their homes. In the short term at least, NATO bombing has increased death and suffering.

Finally, the policy must have a good chance of success. According to news reports, before the president proceeded, the Joint Chiefs informed him that bombing alone would not do the job. Yet he went ahead with such a plan. Moreover, even if Milosevic caves in and peace talks resume, will this be genuine success? Milosevic is unpredictable, and the situation will remain volatile. Having committed the military, we will have to keep it there to maintain peace. As one who wore my country's uniform during the Korean War, I support our troops. But supporting them in this case means warning of the great risk they will be mired in protracted guerrilla warfare. (We forget that several of Hitler's crack divisions were pinned down in Yugoslavia trying to rout guerrillas out of the mountains.)

One thing is certain: U.S. foreign policy has embarked on uncharted waters, employing military force not in response to a military threat but to achieve social and political goals. This introduces moral questions that the church ought to raise now, not waiting until the body bags start coming home and the nation grows disillusioned. In the Gulf War, clerics led protests, waving placards that read, "Blessed are the peacemakers." And in World War II, British bishops denounced their own government's bombing of German cities. Where in this conflict are Christians pressing a moral perspective?

The Christian church must assert its historic position as the conscience of society and bring a moral grid to bear on post-Cold War foreign policy.

Charles Colson and Nancy Pearcey, "Does Kosovo Pass the Just-War Test?" *Christianity Today* 43, No. 6 (May 24, 1999): 96.

★ *October 22, 2001* ★

INTO ALL THE WORLD: THINK GLOBALLY, LOVE GLOBALLY

Our era of isolationism is over. It's time to join the world.

MIRIAM ADENEY

How do we respond to the devastation of September 11, the deadly attacks on the World Trade Center and the Pentagon? Many responses come to mind: Prayer. Care for the injured and bereft. Increased security, increased vigilance. Just punishment for the masterminds behind the carnage. Sharper on-the-ground intelligence-gathering. Stronger international cooperation against terrorism. Congregational immersion in Scripture stories of God's people who lived through radical loss and destabilization, from Joseph to Daniel to John, Peter, and Paul.

But there is one more response: American Christians will want also to become better global citizens.

HIT IN THE SOLAR PLEXUS

Since the so-called end of the Cold War, many of us have not given much thought to the rest of the world except as occasional business, tourist, or short-term mission connections. Those days of ignorance are over. We have been hit in the solar plexus with the truth that we are globally connected and cannot cut loose.

In his bestseller on globalization, *The Lexus and the Olive Tree*, Thomas Friedman describes a label on a computer part that reads, "This part was made in Malaysia, Singapore, the Philippines, China, Mexico, Germany, the U.S., Thailand, Canada, and Japan. It was made in so many different places that we cannot specify a country of origin." We are globally integrated as never before. Yet many of us have continued to live cocooned in our own little circle of friends, walled off from people who are different. To think about the rest of the world overwhelms us. Masses of data pour over us, jumbled in sound bites that juxtapose great human tragedies with beer ads. We know that even the internationally minded— American expatriates and missionaries—have made mistakes. How can ordinary citizens like you and me know enough to make intelligent comments on global issues?

"Whenever I think about those people over there, I worry," one churchgoer said recently. "And I know God doesn't want me to be worried. So I've decided he doesn't want me to think about them." Another Christian says that's why she doesn't read the newspaper anymore. The news disturbs her, and surely that isn't the will of God.

PRAY THROUGH THE NEWSPAPER

Christians should be different. Of all people, Christians are to love our neighbors. When our neighborhood expands to include the globe, then we're called to love globally. How? Some of the most important steps may be some of the simplest:

- Pray through the newspaper, especially the world news section.

- Befriend foreigners who live in your city.

- Develop strong relationships with your church or denominational missionaries.

- Ask members who are business owners to talk about their global involvements.

- Go to a local college and find out whether there's a group of local "friends of international students."

- Ask your high-school and college youth what they're studying about global issues.

- Teach a church class on the biblical basis of mission, tracing global issues from Genesis to Revelation.

And we should strive to do this without a patronizing smile, at arm's length. Loving our neighbors means something more. It means being vulnerable. It means entering into their pain. When God in Jesus came to live among us, he shared our troubles and felt our hurts. Do we empathize with those in other countries?

Globalization has hurt a lot of people. Although transnational business has brought a lot of wealth to other countries, people in those countries suspect that transnational corporations—most based in America—are reaping the lion's share of the benefits. This breeds a love/hate feeling toward America.

In the article "Globalization as a Challenge to the Churches in Asia Today," published in the October 2000 *Asia Journal of Theology*, Yong-Hun Jo of Korea writes that poverty levels in Asian countries have worsened as globalization has bloomed. Although the article's tone is moderate, and recognizes the benefits of a vigorous economy, it also speaks of bankruptcies, destruction of jobs, massive unemployment, a sharp rise in prices and decline in wages, capital flight into tax-free zones, the reduction of public services, environmental degradation, and a growing distance between the rich and the poor. At present 34 percent of the children under age 5 in Southeast Asia are underweight, as are 50 percent of the children in South Asia. Half the people in the world live on $2 a day or less.

And when labor must follow jobs in a borderless world, many leave behind spouses, children, and parents with whom they would have traditionally spent much time. Globalization obliterates family closeness.

Do we feel that pain? The prophet Amos blasted God's people because they did not grieve for hurting people: "Woe to you who are complacent in Zion and to you who feel secure on Mount Samaria, you notable men of the foremost nation. ... You lie on beds inlaid with ivory and lounge on your couches. You dine on choice lambs ... but you do not grieve over the ruin of Joseph" (6:1–6).[1]

"Suppose a brother or sister is without clothes and daily food," writes James. "If one of you says to him, 'Go, I wish you well; keep warm and well fed,' but does nothing about his physical needs, what good is it? In the same way, faith by itself, if it is not accompanied by action, is dead" (2:15–17).

There are many macrostructural and microstructural ways to reach out to these needs, and we must develop skills in these areas. At the same time, we must never forget evangelism. Economic programs may teach methods, but evangelism will unleash the meaning and the motivation to use those methods conscientiously.

THE HEALING OF THE NATIONS

Our government and military is responding to the devastation of September 11 at several levels, but for cozy and complacent

---

1. NIV here and in the next paragraph.

Christians, this tragedy has been a personal wake-up call. There's a big, real world out there and it is not negligible. We cannot ignore the pains of other peoples without danger to ourselves—from huge hungry populations, from environmental degradation, from religious terrorism.

Becoming global Christians does not mean a paternalistic relationship with believers in other countries. It means being siblings under a heavenly Father. We have much to give in answering some needs, but our brothers and sisters have resources we can no longer live without. We must listen, for example, to how believers in Indonesia, Sri Lanka, and Malaysia have learned to live with the constant threat of terrorism (see "The Hard-Won Lessons of Terror and Persecution," p. 20). We must learn from believers in Rwanda and Croatia about forgiving known and unknown enemies. And believers in the Near East have much to teach us about responding to extreme forms of Islam.

The Earth—all of it—is the Lord's. All of Scripture rings with this. God's concern for global issues didn't begin when Jesus said, "Go into all the world" or "You shall be my witnesses." Thousands of years earlier, Abraham heard God call his name, saying, "I will bless you, and in you all the families of the earth will be blessed" (Gen. 12:2, 3).

Isaiah saw the people of God as a light to the nations (42:6). Habakkuk saw the "earth full of the knowledge of the LORD as the waters cover the sea" (2:14). Micah saw that "his greatness will reach to the ends of the earth. And he will be their peace" (5:4–5). Jonah, Daniel, Esther, Nehemiah, and even Naaman's slave girl saw God's care for the nations. All of Scripture resonates with God's absorbing interest in the whole Earth. We cannot be healthy American Christians today and ignore the world. A global concern is not optional. It comes from the heart of God.

In his brief commentary on Revelation, *For the Healing of the Nations*, Justo González paints two biblical futures. Glimpsing them may help us find a place to stand in the wake of these attacks:

> There is a vision according to which all peoples and nations and tribes and languages must bow before the beast and worship it. This is the vision of Nebuchadnezzar: "You are commanded, O peoples, nations, and languages, that ... you are to fall down and worship the golden statue that King Nebuchadnezzar has set up" (Dan. 3:4–5). There is a vision that takes for granted that there will always be a great harlot who sits upon many waters; and these waters are the many nations and tribes and languages and peoples who must bring their wealth to her. ...
>
> But that is not the vision of John of Patmos. According to his vision, out of these many nations and tribes and peoples and languages, God will build a kingdom in which all have royal and priestly honor. According to that vision, a great multitude, from all different nations and cultures, will jointly sing, "Holy, Holy, Holy, Lord God Almighty."...
>
> We must be multicultural, not just so that those from other cultures may feel at home among us, but also so that we may feel at home in God's future ... because like John of Patmos, our eyes have seen the glory of the coming of the Lord; because we know and we believe that on that great waking-up morning when the stars begin to fall, when we gather at the river where angel feet have trod, we shall all, from all nations and tribes and peoples and languages, we shall all sing without ceasing: "Holy, holy, holy!"

Miriam Adeney, "Into All the World: Think Globally, Love Globally," *Christianity Today* 45, No. 13 (October 22, 2001): 14–16.

★ *December 9, 2002* ★

JUST WAR IN IRAQ

Sometimes going to war
is the charitable thing to do.

CHARLES COLSON

When the war began in Afghanistan, Defense Secretary Donald Rumsfeld asked a handful of religious leaders to brief him on just-war doctrine. Most of us gave high marks to the administration's efforts to meet just-war standards. I asked, however, the one discordant question: "How would the administration justify a preemptive strike on Iraq?" Without hesitation, Rumsfeld cited the precedent of Israel's attack on an Iraqi nuclear plant in 1981.

One year later, the question is no longer hypothetical. As I write, U.S. forces are massing for war with Iraq. By the time you read this, troops may be in Baghdad. But whatever happens, the morality of a preemptive strike will continue as a hot debate. Last September, the president drew the battle line, boldly declaring preemption as a national policy.

This issue is of particular concern to Christians since we are the heirs of the just-war tradition formulated by Augustine 1,600 years ago. Historically, the doctrine's requirement of just cause has been defined as responding to an attack.

But has terrorism changed the rules? Should the doctrine be "stretched," as just-war expert George Weigel argues? Can a preemptive strike be morally justified?

The first response from the church was negative. U.S. Catholic bishops oppose an attack unless Iraq can be linked to the September 11 terror strikes. One hundred Christian ethicists announced opposition; so did the general secretary of the Middle East Council of Churches. The new Archbishop of Canterbury and Pope John Paul II both expressed reservations.

But I think this reflects too narrow an understanding of just war. Our attitudes may be unduly influenced by Cold War memories. For four decades, the world was kept in relative peace—at least from nuclear holocaust—by nuclear checkmate. The West and the U.S.S.R. embraced the policy of Mutual Assured Destruction, in which both sides targeted the other's cities. Neither side dared attack, fearing a hugely destructive retaliatory strike; with civilians deliberately targeted, preemption was unthinkable.

But this was not the case before the Cold War. Proponents of "anticipatory self-defense" frequently cite a famous precedent of the British attacking across Niagara to prevent an invasion by Irish revolutionaries in Canada. And no less a Christian eminence than Sir Thomas More wrote, "If any foreign prince takes up arms and prepares to invade their land, they immediately attack him in full force outside their own borders."

In the run up to World War II, many argued that Hitler should not be appeased. European leaders engaged in extraordinary—and we now realize counterproductive—diplomatic efforts to avoid war. Had the allies had the weapons, would a preemptive strike against the Nazis have been justified before they overran Poland? In hindsight the answer is clear, as it was to the Christian pastors who were executed for conspiring to kill Hitler.

The question of preemptive strike turns on facts. For 12 years, Saddam Hussein has mocked the United Nations and the world. If he is, as the U.S. and British believe, stockpiling weapons of mass destruction and acting in concert with terrorists, he forfeits claims of sovereign immunity.

Unlike the Cold War, when early warning systems could detect missile launches, terrorists give no warning. If Saddam Hussein were to prepare a missile for launch, the U.S. would certainly be warranted in firing in self-defense. Giving a terrorist a dirty bomb to be delivered in a suitcase is no different—except for delivery time—from a missile launch.

Of course, all of this presupposes solid intelligence and the goodwill of U.S. and Western leaders. I find it hard to believe that any president, aware of the awesome consequences of his decision and of the swiftness of second-guessing in a liberal democracy, would act recklessly.

Christians should remember that the just-war doctrine is not grounded in revenge, punishment, or even justice. Thomas Aquinas discussed it in *Summa Theologica*—not in the section on justice but in the section on charity (that is, the love of God). As Christian scholar Darrell Cole writes, "The Christian who fails to use force to aid his neighbor when prudence dictates that force is the best way to render that aid is an uncharitable Christian. Hence Christians who willingly and knowingly refuse to engage in a just war ... fail to show love towards their neighbor as well as towards God."

Out of love of neighbor, then, Christians can and should support a preemptive strike, if ordered by the appropriate magistrate to prevent an imminent attack.

Charles Colson, "Just War in Iraq," *Christianity Today* 46, No. 13 (December 9, 2002): 72.

WHY ISIS MUST BE STOPPED

MATT REYNOLDS

Here's a chilling thought experiment that, given the arc of world events, might seem eerily like a peek into the not-so-distant future.

Imagine a community of Middle East Christians under assault from a ferocious, well-armed band of terrorists. The Christians live peaceably and faithfully, their presence stretching back centuries. The terrorists aim to destroy them or drive them out, and they have both the power and ruthlessness to prevail. Imagine, further, that the United States can halt the onslaught and restore harmony—but only by deploying military might. Should Uncle Sam send in the troops?

Now repeat the same thought experiment, but replace the besieged Christians with a community representing some other religious faith. Then ask yourself, once more, whether America should intervene to prevent genocide.

If the first scenario stirs you to demand boots on the ground, but the other doesn't, perhaps some soul-searching is in order. Why favor an aggressive national response only when Christians need protection?

Of course, few of us give voice to such blatant chauvinism. We're unlikely to tolerate a foreign policy governed by crude religious litmus tests. And yet, as Christians, the suffering of fellow believers tends to pierce our hearts more profoundly. We sympathize, often achingly, with the plight of non-Christians under persecution. But it's savagery against Christians that really gets our blood boiling.

It's important to keep this in mind as we encounter anti-Christian cruelty, with depressing regularity, in today's headlines. This summer, the world awoke to discover a jihadist army, styling itself the Islamic State (also known as ISIS) brutally seizing power across Iraq and Syria. In conquered territories, ISIS has proclaimed a new caliphate and introduced a draconian brand of Islamic law. Christians—along with dissenting Muslims and obscure religious minorities like the Yazidis— confront a terrifying choice: Leave home, convert to Islam, or die a martyr.

ISIS must be stopped. That much is certain. But how? By whom? To what extent? All are prudential questions that must be answered by those closest to the situation. Yet as we advance this case, we ought to refrain from making Christian suffering the clinching factor, as in *These monsters massacre Christians, and something has to be done.* Raise your hand if you've never entertained that thought. No need to scold yourself. Yet consider how it starts us down a problematic path.

Trouble is, the "something" needed to strangle ISIS is shaping up to be military force. President Obama ordered air strikes to help refugees escape the coming slaughter. It may turn out that nothing short of full-fledged assault will dislodge ISIS. Safeguarding American national security and averting humanitarian disaster may require wiping ISIS off the map.

But that's a far cry from wanting this particular enemy vanquished because—and *only* or *mainly* because—it oppresses Christians. The U.S. oath of enlistment requires soldiers to defend the Constitution against enemies, foreign and domestic. We might dream about heroic soldiers sweeping into town and stomping all over the bad guys. But they haven't signed up to stand between persecuted Christians and their persecutors.

Partiality toward Christians, however natural, shouldn't disproportionately influence American foreign policy judgments. We need to remember what the military is, and isn't, for.

A recent multifaith petition, spearheaded by the Catholic conservative Robert George, strikes a proper balance. The statement (endorsed by evangelicals, including Russell Moore, Eric Metaxas, and Jim Daly) calls for defeating ISIS, but without giving off the slightest whiff of faith-based special pleading.

It's not hard to envision a future of spiraling danger for Christians in the Middle East. And if the situation for Christians grows more precarious, the temptation to enlist American soldiers as avenging angels may intensify. Here's the sobering reality: As a global church, we will have to prepare ourselves to witness thousands of our brothers and sisters face extermination or exile, even as it lies within America's power to militarily save the day. That's a nightmarish thought, and it sounds cold-hearted even to suggest it. But even our own Messiah declined to summon angels to save his skin.

There's something natural and right about praying for justice to rain down and scorch the evil (look at the Psalms!). But let's not be selective about who counts as an enemy. Whenever any group, religious or not, finds itself at the dangerous end of rifles and swords, we are looking at the evil of injustice. And before the kingdom of God arrives, we are called to stop injustice wherever it assails the oppressed.

Maybe that means wielding military force against groups like ISIS, and maybe it doesn't. Either way, let's guard against the subtle temptation to desire one course of action when Christians are in the crosshairs, and another when they aren't.

Matt Reynolds, "Why ISIS Must Be Stopped," *Christianity Today* 58, No. 8 (October 2014): 30–31.

Chapter 4

DOMESTIC AFFAIRS

F oreign affairs may monopolize the attention of history books, possessing as they do a great deal more drama, but in people's day-to-day lives they are more likely to see the conflicts between domestic parties as the central theater of politics. In fact, as far as voters' ordinary experience goes, foreign affairs are seen as little more than a subset of domestic issues. This is particularly true if, as is often the case, the overall tenor of diplomatic and military policies remains in effect no matter which domestic faction is in power. It is there, after all, that people in democracies can see the impact of their actions in the makeup of legislative bodies. It is also there that party leaders spend the bulk of their time—and, not unimportantly, their money—to win the votes of their constituents and to diminish the role of their rivals.

From 1956 to 2016, *CT* offered a great deal of news coverage of domestic political concerns. For example, for many years the editors would include a list of the nascent Congress after each election. Not only would these lists include the name and district or state of the incoming or returning member, but denominational backgrounds were added so that readers could see the religious breakdown of their leaders.

Writers also commented on individual electoral races down through the years, but this was done normally only if the contest would have an effect on some issue of Christian morality or one of the candidates was known for having strong Christian faith. Beyond election campaigns, most other articles followed this same criterion of only mentioning a political dispute if it impinged on an element of Christian life or doctrine. For example, few if any pieces called attention to debates over the tax rate itself, but many highlighted debates of churches' tax-exempt status.

This means that while a myriad of subjects showed up in *CT*'s pages, certain issues took precedence over others. The civil rights movement and the abortion debate, especially, brought together the moral and political, and these two issues are the primary focus in the following articles. With these issues, the moral principles found in the Bible interacted with political reality in a manner that admitted little to no neutrality. In its discussions of race relations in the 1950s and 1960s, the magazine had to balance Southern tendencies, exemplified by executive editor L. Nelson Bell, and the Northern perspective of editor Carl F. H. Henry (this balancing act can be seen throughout this chapter, especially in the first two articles, which appeared in the same 1957 issue). But with abortion there was no such hesitation. From the late 1960s up to the present, *CT* has maintained a stalwart pro-life presence.

With both abortion and the civil rights movement, *CT* cut a countercultural path that sometimes, but not always, fit in with the Democrats or Republicans. The parties might go back and forth over this policy or that, but ultimately these questions are only so important as the moral basis behind them. In a way unlike tax rates or funding for various projects, these two concerns crystallized the political challenge for Christians in America.

One final note: the reading and writing of history often involves dealing with a great deal that is disagreeable. For the most part, the task of the historian entails looking at these things with clear-eyed objectivity, never flinching from the reality of human frailty. We can hardly gather a true understanding of events if we do not take them as they are. However, there comes a time now and then when the emotional power of certain things is so great that instead of offering clarity they bring cloudiness. Such is the case with the infamous term abbreviated in three articles below as "n----." At each point, its full spelling was found in the original article. While each use came in a piece condemning racism, the raw offensiveness of the word is such that it is best left to history, even if that means leaving it out of the history books.

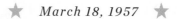 *March 18, 1957*

SEGREGATION AND THE KINGDOM OF GOD

E. EARLE ELLIS

R ace relations is probably the most important problem agitat-
ing the Christian conscience today. Secular integrationists
are calling upon the church to speak to the problem—assuming
that if it "spoke," it would call for the solution that the integrationists demand. As a matter of fact the church has spoken and
is speaking, but it does not speak with one voice. The cleavage is
particularly apparent if one avoids that un-Protestant confusion
of the voice of the clergy with the "voice of the church." Since the
Supreme Court decision of 1954, the issue has been focused in
terms of "segregation" versus "integration." Within this framework Christian integrationists champion their position as "the
Christian way" and dismiss the views of segregationists as naive
or prejudiced.

Most of the integrationist press treats the question as if all
segregationist thinking stemmed from emotional, ignorant or
ulterior motives. Religious periodicals, with some exceptions,
tend to identify integration with Christianity and segregation
with the forces of iniquity. This attitude is not just an oversimplification; it is a basic distortion of the issues. It identifies the
principle of segregation with certain evils in segregation-in-practice. It illogically leapfrogs from the proposition, "Integration

303

is concordant with Christian race relations," to the contention, "Integration is *necessary* for Christian race relations." Finally, it ignores the injustices present in integration-in-practice in the North, and the evil implicit in a consistent integrationist philosophy.

A SOUTHERN POINT OF VIEW

Few Southerners—certainly few Christians—will defend *in toto* segregation-in-practice in the South. Too often the color line has been viewed as horizontal rather than vertical; unchristian white men—like unchristian men everywhere—have used their racial status to bully or to prey upon the weaker group; and the slogan "separate but equal" has preserved the separate and forgotten the equal. The greatest sin of Christian segregationists has not been their individual relationship with Negroes but their indifference to chronic injustices within the dual social system. In the forties, Virginius Dabney and a number of other Southerners organized to correct some of these injustices within the segregation formula. Dabney cites the reason for their failure (*American Magazine*, August, 1956): "There was no cooperation from influential segments of Southern society. The result of such indifference was the removal of the Negro capital from Atlanta to New York and the shifting of Negro leadership from Southern moderates to Northern radicals."

This is not the whole story however. Raymond Moley has correctly identified the two salient facts in the segregated South over the past half-century—the great progress of the Negro and the great improvement in racial attitudes. Within the segregation pattern the South has opened the door to the professions for the Negro, in some ways surpassing integrationist areas. In each of several Southern states, for example, there are as many Negro school teachers (receiving "equal pay" and in some areas a higher average pay) as in thirty-one Northern and Western states combined (cf. Dabney); segregated Meharry and Howard universities have provided more Negro doctors than all of the integrated institutions of the North. For several decades preceding the Supreme Court decision, inequities had declined and the business and professional strata of Negro society had increasingly developed. "In the South they have segregation," replied a Mississippi Negro to his surprised Northern college professor, "but Southerners are kinder to Negroes than Northerners are." Segregation does not necessitate bad race relations, nor does integration guarantee good ones. On the contrary, the very opposite often appears to be true.

It is sometimes asserted that segregation almost always is associated with domination of and discrimination against the weaker group. It would be more accurate, however, to say that whenever diverse groups have been associated under a political unit, whether on an integrated or a segregated basis, the tendency has been to discriminate against the weaker. This is true of some "integrated" minority groups in Europe today—a problem that finds a "segregation" solution in the political realm through racial, rather than merely geographical, representation in parliament. On the other hand, eastern Canada is an example of segregation equitably administered. The French and the English have separate schools and churches, move in their own social circles and maintain distinct cultural divisions in an attitude of mutual respect.

It is not unnatural that the Christian in the North should look askance upon segregation. He can see no good reason for it (the "melting pot" philosophy worked for the Poles and the Germans, why not for the Southerner and the Negro?); he weighs it in terms of individual discriminations, e.g., the inferior Negro school (a complaint *passé* in many areas) or the poorer Negro residential

area; and he hears of it only in caricature. Emotional and sentimental factors are particularly strong where the problem can be
solved by a slogan. It is no secret that the integration sentiment
of most white Christians increases in direct proportion to their
distance from the Negro as a group factor in society.

The integrationist, viewing the problem as one of "personal"
exclusion, overlooks or denies the relevancy of treating it as a
group relationship. Christians in the South have a different reality
to face: There is *de facto* a biracial society with vast numbers of
each group; cultural, sociological and psychological differences
between the races are considerable. (Only a naive appraisal can
reduce the problem to one of "skin color.") Freedom of association, in the eyes of the South, is a liberty applicable to group as
well as individual relationships. The white South desires—and
holds it to be a right—to preserve its European racial and cultural
heritage; this cannot be done if integration is enforced in social
institutions, e.g., the schools. Intermarriage, whether in the 2nd
generation or the 10th, is a question which, in Alistair Cooke's
phrase, "only the intellectual, the superficial and the foreigner
far from the dilemma can afford to pooh-pooh" (*Manchester
Guardian Weekly*, May 24, 1956). The soothsayer may confidently
predict that this will not happen, or publicize as the "scientific"
view (as though scientists were agreed on the matter) that racial
differences are merely physical and environmental. The essential point is that the people who must live in the situation are
convinced, for reasons sufficient for them, that integration will
be destructive of their society, ultimately an evil rather than a
good. (Compare H. R. Sass, "Mixed Schools and Mixed Blood,"
The Atlantic, November, 1956.) And they are confident that, where
the white and black races live together in considerable numbers,
the concept of a dual society applying a principle of segregation in varying degrees according to the exigencies of particular

situations will, when directed by a Christian conscience, provide the more equitable and harmonious relationship.

The master-servant relationship is passing in the South, and some *modus vivendi* is desperately needed to replace it. Segregation has the potential to develop into a partnership of mutual respect; this partnership can never arise from a judicial force bill which is intolerable to one of the groups. Southerners often wonder whether integrationists are as interested in good race relations as in forcing a particular kind of race relations. The unfortunate fact is that ardent Christian integrationists, however conscientious, are one cause of the worsening race relations in the South today. Their moral superiority complex, their carica-ture of the segregationist as an unchristian bigot and their pious confession of the sins of people in other sections of the country have not been wholly edifying.

Segregation in America is, and should be, a fence not a wall, a division with many openings. In former years in the South the writer occasionally visited colored churches and enjoyed their fellowship in an atmosphere of Christian love; they on occasion visited his. At that time segregation was the norm, recognized and approved by both groups; yet it was no bar to friendship or fellow-ship in many areas. Then came the integrationist, a self-righteous harbinger of a "new world a-comin," pounding his pulpit drum and condemning all opposition to Gehenna. The outlines of his new world have come: and what is the cause of the growing resentment, fear, animosity and discord? Why, the segregationist, of course!

ACROSS THE OHIO

Whatever appeal integration has for Southern Negroes, it has been produced by the current identification of everything bad with segregation and everything good with integration. Even to the more sophisticated outside the South the word still casts a spell, but some of its luster no doubt has faded. They came north to the promised land, but they crossed the river to find it wasn't Jordan at all but only the Ohio. In the North Negroes are integrated—at the bottom. There are exceptions, of course, but by and large integration-in-practice is full of discriminations: A Negro student sometimes cannot fulfill his requirements because no integrated school will accept him for student teaching. In Negro sections business and professional services are largely in the hands of whites. There is no "separate but equal" formula to equalize facilities between "white" New Trier and Chicago's "black" south-side schools.

If the 90-year integration experiment in the North had produced a just and amicable relationship, it might be more attractive to the South. Actually, integration has most signally failed in just those areas which most nearly approximate—in population ratio—the Southern scene. The integrationist "blockbuster" approach is exemplified by Trumbull Park (Chicago) where Negroes were assigned to a white housing project. The result has been riot, race hatred and a 24-hour police guard for more than a year. In nearby Gary, Indiana, Andrew Means, a Negro contractor, using a segregationist approach, has built six Negro suburban-type communities. Race relations are good. Nevertheless, integrationists encounter a mental block at the suggestion that segregation has merit as a pattern-for-living in a multiracial society.

The Southerner can understand the sentimentalist, but the inconsistency of most integrationists is harder to comprehend. In the integrationist North, papers often censor local racial unrest (to prevent riot), then editorialize about *immoral* segregation in the South. When teaching Sunday School in Chicago's "black" south side, the writer failed to encounter any homes of Christian integrationists. They live in "white" suburbs, send their children to "white" schools, and then travel through Negro areas to their

editorial offices, professions and businesses where they expati-
ate against segregation. Sometimes they favor admitting a Negro
to their suburb if he is the "right kind" of Negro. A Christian
friend of the writer, quite integration-conscious, mentioned
having had Negro dinner guests. "Of course," he added, "they
were clean and educated—no one like Isaac (our janitor)." Is
this the fulfillment of New Testament ethics?

The point is not that the integrationist would defend
integration-in-practice in the North. But in condemning the
segregationist's failure to achieve a "separate and equal" society,
the integrationist fails to realize the implication of his own failure
to achieve a "mixed and equal" society. This failure hardly recom-
mends integration as "the solution" to racial discrimination and
animosity—a goal that both groups seek. If Southern Christian
leaders can do no better than to follow the integrationist approach
of their brothers to the North, the future is less than bright.

AND THE KINGDOM OF GOD

Both integrationists and segregationists are extremely eager to
quote God as on their side. However, the Scriptures most frequently used, the "curse of Ham" argument in Genesis and the
"one blood" argument in Acts, are irrelevant. The New Testament
does indeed picture all Christians as being united. In Christ there
is neither Jew nor Greek, male nor female, free nor slave, rich
nor poor, educated nor ignorant, clean nor dirty, black nor white
(cf. Gal. 3:28; Col. 3:11). But in New Testament Christianity this
is a unity in diversity, a unity which transcends differences and
works within them, but never a unity which ignores or denies
differences or necessarily seeks to erase them. The servant is no
less a servant, the master no less a master; the rich no less rich,
and the poor no less poor. The New Testament ethic is not "we
are the same, there is no difference; we are equal, therefore I love

you" but rather "we are not the same, we are not equal in many ways; but I love you and desire your good." The gospel was not primarily to change the pattern of society, but to bring to bear new motives and new attitudes within the pattern. It is true that Christianity effected changes in the pattern, but its approach was totally different from the integrationist's philosophy today.

Integration as a moral imperative has its roots in a secular view of the Kingdom of God in which the Kingdom is identified with the church and ultimately with the society of this world, and is to be brought in by social reforms. For the New Testament, however, whatever its manifestation within the Christian community is, the Kingdom of God is never to be identified with or find its consummation in a this-world society. (Compare T. W. Manson, *The Teaching of Jesus*, p. 134; E. Stauffer, *New Testament Theology*, p. 196.) Even within the church the differences between individuals and/or groups are not done away. Paul and Barnabas came to the conclusion that in certain circumstances their best unity lay in separation (Acts 15:36–46). Jewish and Gentile Christians differed in many practices, e.g., the observance of the Sabbath and other Old Testament laws (Rom. 14:5, 6; Acts 18:18; 21:23ff.), differences that ultimately resulted in "ecclesiastical" separation. Not only does the Apostle not view these differences as sinful, but he rather insists on the right of the groups to continue in them (Gal. 2:5; Rom. 14). In other words, the unity of Christians does not necessarily mean a physical "togetherness" or organizational conformity; the Kingdom in the church does not negate the church's relation to the social customs of the world and of the churches: The same Paul who said that there was neither male nor female in Christ also instructed women to be silent in church (cf. 1 Cor. 11:4; 14:34).

The creed of consistent integrationist Christians could be summed up in the phrase, "the right to belong"; and their heresy, "the refusal to belong." In their minds "togetherness" is a good, exclusiveness an evil. God—whatever else he is—is certainly "democratic"; segregation is "undemocratic" and therefore immoral.

Only when one applies the philosophy of integration consistently—thankfully most integrationists are not consistent—can he see its full implications. In Christ there is no rich nor poor; therefore, says the *economic* integrationist, we must integrate society through Christian socialism to eliminate evil class distinctions. It is wrong, cries the *political* integrationist, to discriminate against a man because of "an accident of birth"—birth in a foreign country; world government and world citizenship are the answers to this wrong. The *ecclesiastical* integrationist intones: denominations are evil *per se*, they divide us; we must fulfill Christ's prayer "that they may be one" by uniting in the "coming great church." Segregation is discrimination, concludes the *racial* integrationist, and "de-segregation" is its cure.

The argument for racial integration and the use of governmental force to implement it is a part of a pattern that is very evident in other areas of life. (And how often the voices in the argument vaguely remind one of voices heard at other times, on other issues.) It is a bad argument. Christian communism does not yield a good economic relationship; the "one church" organization does not give true Christian unity; cultural leveling does not produce a common bond of friendship; integration does not alleviate racial animosity and injustice. Further, it is an argument that is ethically anemic: in the name of equality it destroys the liberty of individuals and groups to live and develop in associations of their own preference; in the name of unity it points with undeviating insistence toward authoritarianism and conformity, eschewing the inherent sin root in human society with its inevitable consequence: power corrupts and total power corrupts totally.

If the Kingdom of God as a monolithic homogeneous structure is the goal of Christian ethics—if national, economic, cultural, racial, ecclesiastical distinctions are to be abolished as "immoral," then the integrationist argument is sound. But if the Kingdom of God is seen as intersecting—and yet above—a this-world framework, compatible with—and yet superseding—the many and varied distinctions in this present age; then segregation is, in principle, an equally valid answer. And in practice it is much more compatible with liberty. Christian integrationists are patently sincere in the path they are forging, but the road signs along that path sometimes remind one more of Aldous Huxley's *Brave New World* than of the New Testament's Kingdom of God.

E. Earle Ellis, "Segregation and the Kingdom of God," *Christianity Today* 1, No. 12 (March 18, 1957): 6–9.

THE CHURCH AND THE RACE PROBLEM

THE EDITORS

T he human predicament involves all the races in insecurity. Trouble and turmoil, hostility and hate, are wide as the human race, and not a matter merely of dramatic sectional clashes between the white man and the American Negro, or between Israeli and Arab. The real human predicament, of course, is mankind's condition in sin, and the universal need of redemption. A Christian view of the race problem must begin with this confession of wholesale racial rebellion and guilt. No man loves God and no man loves his neighbor as he ought. The fall has cheapened human worth; redemption restores man's dignity. Jesus' stress on the universal need of regeneration speaks to our own turbulent times: "Ye must be born again." The possibilities of fallen human nature are fancifully romanticized by those who expect a full solution of the race problem while they neglect this dimension of life.

Every man is somebody's neighbor, and God expects neighbor-love from every human being. Let no man think, because he has overcome some prevalent antipathy for Jew or Negro or some other victim of sectional feelings that merely on that account he has fulfilled the moral law. A white man may crusade for civil rights; he may sell his property to a buyer of another race; he may encourage social intermingling of all races—but he does not simply on this account fulfill the law of love. What passes for desegregation and even for integration, is often quite hollow alongside the biblical injunction of love for neighbor. The race problem dare not be detached, therefore, from the abiding requirement of Christian love.

It is a sad fact, however, that some circles recite these themes of the new birth and love of neighbor, yet do not actively promote the elimination of racial evils. They often fall below the lesser level of concern reflected by secular agencies that recognize race prejudice to be one of the ugly scars in American life.

Some observers today would add to Christian confession a pledge to desist from race prejudice as evidence of the genuineness of conversion. Why not a pledge against intoxicating liquors also? The liquor traffic is a serious social blight, blemishing every village in the land. And why not a pledge against driving in excess of the speed limit? Too many church folk, ministers included, leave their guardian angels ten or fifteen miles an hour behind them on the road.

The risk in all such proposals is in their tendency to shrivel the law of neighbor-love when Christian ethics is called on to sensitize in its fullness. Yet, while we do well to overlook such proposals, the Christian conscience had best face squarely the sins they aim to correct. For in each age and in every land the violation of Christian love falls into certain conspicuous patterns. And race discrimination is especially subtle. It is not externally measurable in the same way that sins of the flesh are: it cannot be gauged by jiggers or by speedometers. Race feeling is essentially a matter of false pride, an internal disposition to deny a fellow human's equal worth and one's own unworthiness also, before God. Nonetheless, it differs in degree, and not in kind, from other violations of the law of love for neighbor, which involves every area of life.

Evangelical and liberal churches alike are uncomfortable in the presence of the fact that segregation was not sharpened as an issue of social conscience in America through the preaching of the churches as firmly as through the secular ruling of the Supreme Court. The churches were not, of course, called on as churches to adjudicate all the delicate problems touching education and other spheres not directly answerable to church authority. But, as citizens, church members held a voice in civic affairs; if the Christian conscience was to find a mouthpiece, it was through them.

Christians are obliged to uphold the law of the land, unless they can show that law to be in conflict with Scripture. The Christian is called upon, therefore, not only to implement the spiritual rights of men, as equals in God's sight, but their legal rights as well.

There is little comfort for the churches in the added fact that secular agencies like the military program, telecasting and sporting events have contributed as dramatically to desegregation as have many churches. Developments in the military and in the worlds of television and sports are more widely publicized, of course, than the hushed and reverent atmosphere of the churches. In entertainment and recreation, moreover, special competitive considerations of talent are operative, involving only a small and strategic segment of the population. Integration, even on the sports level, is not achieved merely by the assignment of team positions without regard to color, gainful though it be to end racial bias in such assignments. Nor is "integrated entertainment" achieved—at least on the level of genuine love for neighbor—because Negro and white voices are blended in the latest musical jive, and some white crooner slips his undisciplined arm tightly around a Negro female guest on television. Such demonstrations can involve as much a perversion of propriety when the races are mixed as when they are not. Even when due credit is given the military, the theater and the arena for a measure of contribution, they have much to learn about a biblical concept of Christian love.

Nonetheless, churches in America surrendered something of their moral initiative in the life of the nation when they allowed other forces, in a partial and secular way, to implement the correction of one of the striking social wrongs. Granted we must not attach utopian expectations to the society of the redeemed in history; the church, at best, travels the road of sanctification in this life, not glorification. This present age has much to learn about the subtleties of original sin, even from theologians whose expositions do not always go to the depths of biblical theology. But, in our day, the church has more reason to fear a lack of moral insight and courage than an excessive moral achievement.

There are wrongs in the land, and the church had best be the church, and cry against them; there is no biblical mandate to preserve the shaggy status quo. Community tolerance of violence; forced segregation in public transportation; tactics of fear and intimidation; snobbishness that looks down upon Negro Christians virtually as inferior believers; the indifference to discrimination against the Negro in America even by some churches calling for missionaries to lift the life and culture of the dark-skinned natives of Africa—these factors suggest the deep need for soul-searching and repentance in the churches.

The church needs to recover the biblical point of view. The church itself was born in the glory of a multi-tongued and multi-colored Pentecost. It moved swiftly to make Christian brotherhood a reality in the experience of the inhabitants of Africa and Europe, no less than of Asia and the Near East. It did not preoccupy itself with the adoption of strategically worded resolutions at the top level of councils and conventions; it put Christian love to work at the local level. The early church unleashed a flood of kindness in a world of racial strife; the modern church has too often unleashed a flood of resolutions.

This same biblical point of view, moreover, will keep the churches from falling into unrealistic and faulty programs of action. For instance, one misguided Christian spokesman recently told young people that the biggest contribution a white girl can make to the advancement of Christianity in our generation is to marry a Negro. But if interracial wedlock best preserves the biblical concern for equal yoking, the essence of Christian marriage in the mid-twentieth century has deteriorated sadly. Nobody will prevent the clergy from giving their own children in marriage across racial lines, if such is their ideal, but many Christian leaders will remain unconvinced that a universally valid rule has been enunciated. The early church hardly made racial intermarriage the test of Christian love, nor dare we.

In its enthusiasm to do something vital, the church falls easy prey to secular and socializing programs. It has no mandate to legislate upon the world a program of legal requirements in the name of the church. Nor dare it disregard the existence of social rights in which the natural preferences of individuals may be expressed without compromising the legal or spiritual rights of others. Forced integration is as contrary to Christian principles as is forced segregation. The reliance on pressure rather than on persuasion has resulted in a marked increase of racial tensions in some areas. Christianity ideally moves upon the life of the community by spiritual means; the secular agencies, on the other hand, tend to resort to force, with the result that their achievements are continually endangered. Paul did not outlaw slavery legally, but he outlawed it spiritually; he sent Onesimus back

318 Domestic Affairs: The Civil Rights Movement

to Philemon as a brother in Christ. He knew that the church's weapons are spiritual, not carnal; that Christian progress is not revolutionary but regenerative. And a recovery of the imperative affectionate neighbor relations, and of the Holy Spirit as the dynamic of Christian living, is still the best—and the only durable—hope for a firm solution of the race problem.

While some churches seem determined to continue with a program excluding other races, and others are thrown into internal tensions between member and member, and member and minister, still others, without fanfare and headlines, have long welcomed all converts to Christ with equal dignity and rights as members of the body of Christ. Any church should be open to believers of any race. Forced segregation, however, involves the abrogation of a citizen's legal rights as well as his spiritual rights.

The church by a true example of the equality of all believers may rebuke the conscience of the world. The fellowship of believers still holds a power to vitalize the fellowship of the community at large. What has compromised this power is the secularization of the churches. Let the church be the church, and the sense of human brotherhood will be revived; the redeemed will find that their differences from each other pale alongside the fact of their unity in Christ, and that their differences from the unredeemed are less important than their common dignity and shame in Adam. The Christian is not without principles on which to base his personal relationships, and they are comprehended in the obligation of love for neighbor. A friendly smile, a kindly word, a courteous act, speak more eloquently than a press release.

A voluntary segregation, even of believers, can well be a Christian procedure. A church may be impoverished by the racial limitations of its membership and also impoverished through indifference to cultural ties. Churches in which integration is not practiced may be just as Christian as those where it is found.

The determining factor is exclusion or inclusion because of race. Are the Chinese congregations of New Orleans or Chicago or San Francisco unchristian because they prefer such an alignment? Are all-Negro or all-white churches necessarily monuments to racial prejudice? And may not the publicity of the integrated church reflect an emphasis on spiritual pride as much as the unintegrated church?

The churches in America are on the advance. The searching of soul is a good sign. Little can be gained by organizational pressures; more will be gained from mutual respect and forbearance. The long sweep of history not only shows the church and individual Christians on the side of justice; it shows the content of justice itself lifted and purified by the conscience of the church. In the long run, it will be so in America also even in matters of race. Let us hope this is a decade of decision and deed.

The Editors, "The Church and the Race Problem," *Christianity Today* 1, No. 12 (March 18, 1957): 20–22.

★ *September 30, 1957* ★

RACE RELATIONS AND CHRISTIAN DUTY

THE EDITORS

A merica is in the throes of great sociological change. Never has there been more need for Christian love and restraint. That the race issue has become political is to be deeply regretted. That the spiritual problem is ignored by some and stressed to the exclusion of sociological factors by others is equally regrettable.

In recent weeks incidents have arisen that should move every Christian with righteous indignation. The deliberate mutilation of a Negro in one city is one example; justice demands the severest penalty for those found guilty. Abuse accorded the few Negro boys and girls assigned to previously all-white schools by some young people in these schools has been a disgrace.

The unfortunate situation in Little Rock is eloquently appraised by a group of white and Negro ministers in that city expressing the Christian position in these words: "There is need for all to exercise constant and diligent prayer and a love which respects the dignity of all children of God and seeks equal justice for them. Because we have not walked in the way of the Lord we now find ourselves confused, disturbed and distressed. As Christian ministers we confess our own share in the corporate sin and guilt of our state and our own subjugation to the holy judgment of God. Our one hope in this hour of crisis lies not in our own ability to change ourselves, our people, or the social structure of which we are a part, but in the power and grace of God to bring order out of confusion, good out of evil and redemption beyond judgment."

In such situations (and they are not confined to the South) there is need for Christian love, sympathy and common sense. That the church should lead in Christian relations goes without saying. There are those who feel that she has been woefully slow in assuming her role of leadership in breaking down racial discrimination and injustice. In some instances the church has lacked courage in vindicating justice for all. But some leadership has shown more enthusiasm than good judgment, more zeal than understanding. Christian courtesy, love, humility and consideration form the only basis on which right race relations can be developed. There are vocal integrationists who themselves refuse to have social contacts with another race. There are segregationists whose personal dealings with those of another race put to shame some most ardently active on the other side. Each needs to learn from the other.

The Christian church should work for the elimination of every restriction, discrimination and humiliation aimed at people of any race. She should preach and exemplify love and compassion and consideration at all times. She should also refrain from confusing legal, spiritual, and sociological problems—for in so doing she is being neither Christian nor realistic.

The Editors, "Race Relations and Christian Duty," *Christianity Today* 1, No. 25 (September 30, 1957): 23.

★ *September 29, 1958* ★

CHRISTIANS AND THE CRISIS OF RACE

TIMOTHY L. SMITH

The renewal of the crisis over school integration in the South raises issues which go to the heart of the relations between the gospel, the church and the world. The Christian commitment to brotherhood and love is as much at stake as the central idea of democracy—the dignity of the individual.

The crisis makes us ask again some ancient questions. What is the role of the church of Christ in a democratic society? If it be granted that the gospel requires us to seek to have its truth applied to the social situation, are we to declare principles only, or programs for action? In any case, is it the organized church or individual Christians acting in their capacity as citizens who must bear this witness?

Such questions as these lie subordinate to another one whose significance the worldling often fails to see. It is this: can Christians speak or act unlovingly to gain the ends of brotherhood and love? Dare we compromise the means to reach the goals? Surely, our answer here is no.

THE SLAVERY CRISIS

All these issues resemble closely those which the slavery crisis raised among evangelical Christians a hundred years ago. Then, as now, an institution of long social and legal standing came to seem contrary to both God's law and democratic principle. Then, as now, churchmen debated whether the Christian witness against social evil was the task of the regenerate citizen or the believing community. The unity of both church and nation seem to be at stake. And the same law of love which condemned the Negro's bondage held Christian men back from direct action to strike away his chains.

The tensions of that crisis of long ago found resolution at last in the outbreak of a tragic civil war. In time, antislavery churchmen who had not wanted nor expected war came to see the bloody conflict as a work of divine judgment upon both North and South. Julia Ward Howe set this thought to unforgettable words and music in her famous "battle hymn." An awakened generation had learned at Fredericksburg and Chancellorsville a new conception of the Coming of the Lord. The wine of liberty was to flow blood-red from the sword of his wrath. Likewise Lincoln, in his Second Inaugural, reminded a sorrowing nation that the judgments of the Lord were true and righteous altogether.

What are evangelical Christians to do in the social crisis of our times, therefore, when they remember the involvement of their spiritual forbears—Charles G. Finney, William E. Boardman, Dwight L. Moody, and Gilbert Haven—with the conflict of that age?

The question comes with particular force when we realize that today's trouble arises from an evil expressly forbidden in God's Word, whereas slavery itself is not so condemned. The antislavery preachers had to establish the point that the Bible enjoined upon both masters and servants such commitment to personal respect, to brotherhood and mutual acceptance in the fellowship of the gospel, as to make slavery in the long course of Christian history unthinkable.

How, then, can today's Bible-believing Christian justify any permanent status for the racial injustices of our time? The essence of discrimination is a rejection of persons and a violence to the spirits of men which Christ and the Apostles clearly condemned. The Sermon on the Mount is very explicit at this point. Murder you have been taught to abhor, Jesus said. "But I say unto you, that whosoever is angry with his brother without a cause shall be in danger of the judgment: and whosoever shall say to his brother, *Raca* [of which a free translation might read, 'you n----'], shall be in danger of the council: but whosoever shall say, Thou fool, shall be in danger of hell fire."

Ought we not to ask ourselves in the light of these words what happens to the spirit of a sensitive Negro youth when he sees the sign "white only" over the cleaner drinking fountain, the more decent rest room, the more respectable tourist court and restaurant? Can we escape responsibility for the wounding of minds and hearts which goes on every day when bright young Negro couples try to escape the crowded colored districts of New York, Chicago and Detroit?

Is not the murder of the spirits of men which goes on every day, in my native Southland as well as in the North, a more literal contradiction of the Word of God than chattel slavery ever was?

To say this does not of course alter very much the roots of emotion and feeling which lie beneath every southerner's struggle with his conscience on this issue. This is especially true for someone reared among the small-farmer class of southern whites. Nor does seeing the reality of the evil resolve our dilemma concerning what we may do about it.

However, it is good to ask ourselves what courses of action or expression evangelical Christians, North and South, might follow in this crisis.

COURSES OF ACTION

Let us begin with first things. In whatever we say or do, we dare not violate the spirit of love and brotherhood into whose rich enjoyment we wish the Negro to be brought. The Kingdom of love cannot be enlarged through deeds of violence. For this great lesson's recent underlining we must be grateful to the colored population of Montgomery, Alabama.

A second mutual resolve seems open to us, namely, that we shall not allow ourselves to become partners in a conspiracy of silence. The editor of *The Arkansas Gazette* has said recently that the conflicts over the Supreme Court decision on school integration have turned the clock back 50 years, and undermined completely the freedom of "moderate" southerners to speak on this issue. If this be so, Christian men can have no business bowing to it. When in the history of Christ's church have men of piety had license to be silent in the face of evil?

There are ways in which we can speak lovingly. Agitation may not be the Christian's task, but intercession and witness ever are. In our public prayers, frequently in our sermons, in our Sunday School classes, and in the things we write and publish, we can find quiet but effective ways to say again and again that there is unfinished business at hand, that a great evil in our midst is not yet forsaken.

We must speak. Often enough for our hearers not to forget our concern and their duty. Lovingly enough for the world not to forget the crying compassion of a crucified Lord.

ABSOLUTIZING A PROGRAM

Yet a third common stand invites us. Ought we not to forswear putting the church of Christ in bondage to a particular program of reform? Confronted with the mystery of God's will and man's perverseness, can we presume to declare in Christ's name a specific solution to a social problem?

We can know the principles upon which the right answer may be based. We can believe that the gospel must judge in truth and love all solutions which fall short of those principles. As individuals, we can and must seek and support practical programs which we believe will accomplish ours and the Savior's ends. But the task of the Christian community is not agitation. We are commissioned to reach men's hearts with a saving gospel, and to prepare them for a better world.

The citizens of this country, and especially of the southern part, are the ones who must find the way to real progress toward a Christian and a democratic brotherhood. If they fail, and if the evangelical Christians within the citizen body contribute to that failure, the judgments of the Lord will again turn out to be true and righteous altogether. In any case, the church itself must not seek to force a program of reconciliation on unwilling men nor assume the moral responsibility which lies upon the nation as a whole.

THE CHRISTIAN FELLOWSHIP

One final suggestion to believing Christians seems worthwhile here. The regulation of the inner life and fellowship of the church is indeed the clear responsibility of the Christian community. The New Testament speaks very plainly about it, particularly on the point of respect of persons. Ought we not, then, prayerfully to consider the segregated condition of the church in the light of the Scriptures and a burning world? If we can not transcend it now must we not set our course toward a point where we can?

The writer is aware of the thousand and one problems which consideration of this problem calls up. Sometimes, it is true, the integration of congregations has turned out to be a way in which a company of Negro Christians, however unintentionally, have secured a building for their use at no cost to themselves. Moreover, as many will readily remember, the separated church was one of the chief desires of the enslaved Negroes, and one of their first and most permanent achievements after emancipation.

But the fact is that today the pressure to keep the church officially segregated is coming from the white people. In all too many cases, this pressure is part of the widespread campaign to prevent desegregation of the public schools. Wherever churches have gone further and promised the use of their buildings for schools organized solely to resist integration, they have brought shame to their fellow Christians.

It is no doubt true that only a small minority of Negroes actually wish to worship with other than their friends and fellows. However, the one who feels most keenly the rejection of closed pews, the one who senses when he cannot see the sign "white only" over the church doors, is the very person who most deeply needs the compassionate love of his white friends. The Negro preacher in his town may not be able to reach him at all, because of the wounds of conflict over race.

There was no segregated church in the first century. There was no segregated church in pre-Civil War America. Dare we commit ourselves for the long run now to an organization of church fellowship which requires men to be excluded from association with others in the house of God because of their skin?

What makes all these questions absorbing is their portent for the fate of both Christianity and democracy in the world beyond our borders. A hundred years ago, evangelical leaders believed that our nation's destiny was to nurture both Christianity and liberty for the benefit of the whole world. Then, as now, patriotism and piety flourished side by side. But its thrust was outward, rather than inward. The modern missionary movement was borne forward on its strength.

Again, today, human destiny hangs largely on the willingness and ability of America to remain a beacon of faith and liberty in a world of lawlessness and totalitarianism. Let judgment begin at the house of God. And the day may come, if Christ our Lord tarries, when the power of an awakened Christian conscience will stir the conscience of the nation and the world.

And so may we in that day see our children praying, with greater assurance than we now have, "Thy Kingdom come, thy will be done, in earth as it is in heaven."

Timothy L. Smith, "Christians and the Crisis of Race," *Christianity Today* 2, No. 25 (September 29, 1958): 6–8.

September 29, 1958

DESEGREGATION AND REGENERATION

THE EDITORS

T he problem of justice to the American Negro continues to be an acute one.

In secular circles the issues in debate pulsate between the poles of segregation and integration. Beyond doubt American conscience has been pricked repeatedly over the wrongness of race discrimination, disclosed most keenly in the bias that deprives the Negro of equal rights and thus implies his essential inferiority.

The reasons for pressures for swift solution are plain enough. Left to itself, the situation seemed to promise little in the way of improvement; the maintenance of "distance" between whites and blacks had gained sociocultural significance in the South. Whereas one might have expected Christian churches to lead the way to an era of improved relations, not a few were invoking the Bible, in circumvention of its emphasis on the equal dignity of men and on transcending racial distinctions in the body of Christ, to justify the status quo.

The months that have passed since the U.S. Supreme Court decision of 1954 have served only to emphasize the futility of forced solutions in the absence of high moral and spiritual conviction. Governor Faubus of Arkansas has questioned the high court's "authority." Others (too often implying that the mere passage of time will improve conditions) suggest that race relations are now worse than they were. More violence was predicted in Little Rock. Desertion of public schools for private schools has been promoted in some states to circumvent desegregation.

Perhaps the main occasion of rising tensions has been the drive for "integration," a fuzzy term that covers a multitude of ambiguities and ambitions. Many a proponent of desegregation turns a puzzled glance at integration. Does forced integration preclude voluntary segregation? What of interracial marriage? Do Negroes have the right to attend "white churches" to force a propaganda situation unfavorable to such churches merely because they have failed to endorse an integrationist program that appears to them too secular and political in spirit to hold promise of permanent and effective solution?

To evangelical churches the tensions that plague the human race require, for their solution, a reference to the indispensability of regeneration. They view the problem of racial antipathy as basically an acute aspect of the larger sin of lovelessness for one's neighbor. The church is obliged by the Great Commission to speak to unredeemed men only through the evangelistic and missionary summons. Philosophers of religion may argue that social problems are not wholly responsive to personal redemption, but the believing church knows that to turn elsewhere for a primary solution is to forsake the standpoint of apostolic Christianity, and to expect too much from legal compulsion and from unregenerate human nature.

One can well understand, therefore, a lack of enthusiasm for integration without regeneration. In the long run, the bent of human nature is such that, apart from spiritual renewal, human history turns out to be a variegated pattern of revolt against the living God.

Nonetheless, the church is obliged to proclaim a divinely revealed ethic of universal validity. She is not precluded from, nor can she be justified for failure to seek social justice for the Negro. The church has no license to make conversion a precondition of her support of right and decency in the world at large. If the church had taken a vigorous and courageous initiative in deploring the evils of segregation, even with a special eye on the Negro in her own fellowship, her hesitancy in approving some specific "program of integration" as the Christian solution would not give rise to misunderstanding.

As it is, secular agencies tend to equate a lack of ecclesiastical endorsement of their particular programs as approval of segregation—which is hardly fair to the conscience and intention of the churches. Moreover, ecclesiastical leaders professing to speak for organized religion add to the confusion when they publicize pressures on political leaders to display spiritual leadership by supporting integration. (Two major officials of United Presbyterian Church—Dr. Eugene Carson Blake and Dr. Theophilus M. Taylor—threw their weight for enforcing the Supreme Court desegregation decision "with troops and tanks if necessary," and the huge National Baptist Convention voiced the same sentiment.) Everyone will sympathize with the rebuke of any who seek to frustrate the law of the land when justice is at stake, but the weapons of Christian warfare are spiritual. It is curious that some ecumenical leaders condemned an American show of force in Lebanon while these leaders urged it at home.

Yet the churches themselves are to blame for much of the misunderstanding they have inherited, for it is a dividend yielded by their past silence. The evangelical churches glory in their heritage, the knowledge of the will of God communicated in changeless principles of morality. Now as never before, in the tensions and antagonisms of the race problem in America, they are given an opportunity to proclaim and to live those verities. If the churches have thus far failed to exert moral and spiritual leadership in facing this problem, the opportunity has not yet passed to exhibit to a democracy in trouble the dynamic virtue of brotherhood in Christ.

In a recent conference of Christian leaders in the South on the race problem, *Christianity Today*'s executive editor, Dr. L. Nelson Bell, prepared a statement on "The Race Issue and a Christian Principle" that commended itself spontaneously to the conferees. It follows:

1. Christians should recognize that there is no biblical basis or legal justification for segregation. Segregation, as enjoined in the Old Testament, had to do with religious separation while the New Testament lends no comfort to the idea of racial segregation within the Christian church. For these reasons it can be safely affirmed that segregation of races enforced by law is both un-Christian and un-American.

2. It can be demonstrated with equal cogency that forced integration of the races is sociologically impracticable and at the same time such forced alignments violate the right of personal choice.

3. The Christian concept of race may be expressed in the following way:

   a) God makes no distinction among men; all are alike the objects of his love, mercy and proffered redemptive work.

b) For this reason, all Christians are brothers in Christ, regardless of race or color.

c) The inescapable corollary to these truths is that church membership should be open to all without discrimination or restriction.

4. In the light of these basically Christian affirmations the church should implement them as follows:

a) All churches should be open to attendance and membership without reference to race or color.

b) Recognize that in so doing, in most areas and under normal conditions this will not result in an integrated church, since various races will prefer separate churches for social, economic, educational and many other reasons.

c) But, this opening of the doors of the churches will break down the man-made and sinful barrier which stems from prejudice and recognize the unquestioned Christian principle of man's uniform need of God's redemptive work in Christ, a need and a salvation which knows no distinction of race or color.

5. To aid in an honest and just solution of this problem on every level, the church should frankly recognize that racial differences, implying neither inferiority nor superiority in God's sight, are nevertheless actual differences. They usually express themselves in social preferences and alignments which are a

matter of personal choice, not related to either pride or prejudice. Because of this fact, and because there is no Christian principle involved, the church should neither foster nor force, in the name of Christianity, a social integration which may be neither desired nor desirable.

6. The church should concentrate greater energy on condemning those sinful attitudes of mind and heart where hate, prejudice and indifference continue to foster injustice and discrimination and in so doing show that these attitudes are sin.

7. The problem of the public schools constitutes a dilemma in many areas in the South which both the church and the courts of the land should recognize and admit. Because these schools are tax-supported, they are in name and in fact "public" schools. At the same time, because ratio of the races varies in different localities the problem also varies from the simple in some areas to the apparently insoluble at the present time in others. Those who live where only ten or fifteen percent of the population is of a minority race have no serious problem. Where that ratio is reversed the issue is one of the greatest magnitude and those who have to deal with it deserve the sympathetic concern and understanding of others. It must be recognized by both church and state that at this time, and under present conditions, the problem involves social, moral, hygienic, educational and other factors which admit no immediate or easy solution. The Supreme Court's phrase, "with all due haste," must be interpreted on the one hand

as requiring an honest effort to solve the problem, and on the other with reference to the leniency and consideration which existing conditions demand.

8. Finally, the church has a grave responsibility in this issue; a responsibility to proclaim love, tolerance and justice to all as the basic Christian virtues to be accepted in theory and practiced in fact. Basic to this concept is the urgent necessity of removing all barriers to spiritual fellowship in Christ, without at the same time attempting to force unnatural social relationships. The church has the responsibility of recognizing that more than spiritual issues are involved and that while freely admitting full spiritual and legal rights to all, there are, at the same time, social implications and considerations which involve the matter of personal choice, over which the church has no jurisdiction and into which it should not intrude in the name of Christianity.

The Editors, "Desegregation and Regeneration," *Christianity Today* 2, No. 25 (September 29, 1958): 20–21.

THE WHITE MAN'S DILEMMA

A sermon by the Rev. James L. Monroe, pastor,
Riverside Baptist Church, Miami, Florida.

Unashamedly and without apology I am a Southerner. Born in beautiful Alabama, January 4, 1920, I have always lived south of the Mason-Dixon line. My love for the South is inborn. My parents and my grandparents were poor, but God-fearing and hard-working people. They were not Southern aristocrats, but I am honored to be of their lineage—the lineage of farmers and mountaineers. I'm as Southern as grits and hush-puppies, as turnip greens and corn pone.

When God called me to preach as a youth of 18, I was willing to go anywhere. It was with relief, however, that I heard God's voice: "I want you to be my preacher in the Southern United States."

Like many of my fellow Southerners, I grew up with a guilty conscience. I do not know when it first dawned on me that something was wrong among my people of the South. Now it seems that I always knew it, but it took years of soul-searching and the chastening of God before I would confess it. Most often I was chastened through my own conscience; sometimes it would be by the word of Scripture, however, or at other times the voice of another with a conscience more troubled than my own.

I was taught a concept of freedom that declared all men were created equal. Yet I was taught that a great race of people were not equal to me. I was better than they because my skin was white and theirs was black. I was to remind them of their inferiority by never referring to them with the titles "Mr.," "Mrs.," or "Miss." Their first names only were sufficient even if they were my elders. I must relegate them to inferior status by maintaining a strict policy of segregation.

I lived in the Bible Belt and was taught to believe God's inspired Word from cover to cover. That Bible states in Galatians 3:28, "There is neither Jew nor Greek, there is neither bond nor free, ... for ye are all one in Christ Jesus." But this evidently was not to apply to the Negro. He might be my brother in Heaven, but never on earth. To be sure, I was taught to be good to the Negro. I must never take advantage of him. I must see that he heard the gospel.

When these inconsistencies first occurred to me, I was able to answer my conscience with the stock answers of white supremacy. After all, the Negro was just a few years out of the jungles. He could not expect first-class citizenship. He was dirty. He smelled. He was immoral. Besides, it was constitutional to provide him "separate but equal" facilities. The Supreme Court had said so in 1896. In addition, the Negro was satisfied with his segregated lot—except for maybe a few radicals. The most quoted Negro in the South was the one who allegedly said, "Boss man, I'd rather be a n---- on Saturday night than to be a white man all the rest of the week."

Then I began to see the system of "separate but equal" in operation. I saw the justice the Negro received in the courts. When a teenager I witnessed an accident. Since I was the only witness, my testimony completely absolved the Negro driver. Yet in a conference in my presence the white prosecutor and the white defense attorney agreed on a compromise fine of $100. And the judge accepted their agreement. There was no thought given to the possibility of his innocence. When I protested it was patiently explained to me that "we must be hard on these n----s to keep them under control." The Negro was controlled all right: he went to jail because he could not pay his fine.

I saw their so-called "equal" schools—modern schools for white children and one-room firetraps for Negro children. It was not unusual for the school board to spend $5 for each white child to $1 spent for each Negro child. I heard white men boast of black mistresses—men who would lynch a Negro man if he touched a white woman. I heard that the thing to be feared most of all if the Negro got out of hand was intermarriage and the pollution of white blood.

My "growing-up" years through college were spent in Birmingham. After seminary I returned for a three-and-a-half-year pastorate. This city has been called the capital of Jim Crowism and the most race-conscious city in the world. I saw there white supremacy in all its strength. Early in my ministry I served a small church in Cuba, Alabama, in Sumter County, where the Negroes formed 79 percent of the population. Race relations were far from ideal there, but the situation was superior to that in my home town, where police brutality, bombing of Negroes' homes, floggings, and mob violence were more commonplace than the good citizens liked to admit.

Voting rights were consistently denied many Negroes throughout the South. In a major city with over 100,000 Negroes of voting age, less than 5,000 were qualified to vote. Voter registration tests were set up so that the registrars could see that only a select few were able to pass.

Furthermore, I began to see what this prejudice was doing to the South. Men were poisoned with it so much that they could react only emotionally and not intelligently.

The time came when I could not accept sweeping generalizations about the Negro race. The Bible, sociology, and science
would not let me. Many had a troubled conscience, saw the evil
in the system, wanted something done about it. Yet few dared
speak. The price too often was to be ostracized, to be considered
a traitor to your race, to be called a "n---- lover." Some preachers
lost their pulpits for speaking out. The South discovered to the
further discomfort of its conscience that it really didn't believe
in freedom of speech.

No one has been caught in this dilemma any more tragically
than devout Christians of both races. There are sincere Christians
who love God and who mean to do his will, yet who differ dras-
tically in their opinions of what is right and wrong in this issue.
Some have "blind spots" which may obviously be wrong to
another person, but which are real and must be dealt with. Other
Christians with a moderate approach have been caught in a "conspiracy of silence." All too often the only voice heard has been that
of the extremists. We have tried to keep it out of the churches, but
only the churches have the answer. It is found in the gospel and
we must proclaim it. We must not keep silent any longer. Silence
could be fatal.

Let me confess two things. First, I am not free from racial
prejudice. It keeps cropping out in unexpected ways and places.
Second, I do not have all the answers to all racial problems. The
social structure of the South is complex, and it will take praying, planning, patience, and perseverance to work it all out. The
important thing is that we be willing to begin taking constructive
steps toward the solution.

Some center all their attack on segregation. Segregation has
been declared illegal by the Supreme Court. It is no longer legal
in public facilities. Segregation has absolutely no defense in the
Bible. However, this is not really the main issue before us. Other

areas of our nation have removed their segregation barriers and found that the problem remains. It is as if your house were on fire. The fire originated in the basement, but has now extended to the roof. It is not enough to put out the fire on the roof and leave the fire burning in the basement. Segregation is the fire on the roof. Racism is the fire in the basement. The house will be destroyed if all the fire is not put out, but the Christian may well focus his attention first on the source of the fire.

I do not know all the answers, but I am convinced that there is an answer, and that it can be found if Christian men, black and white, will search for it together.

As I first approached the Scriptures I had the feeling that I might find something to support the South's position. After all, many sincere Bible-believing Christians are staunch segregationists and believe firmly in white supremacy. Some base their beliefs on the "curse of Ham." I studied Genesis 9. I found not the slightest reference to the Negro. The curse was pronounced not by God, but by Noah awakening out of a drunken stupor, and not on Ham but on his son, Canaan. Canaan was not turned black, nor did he father the Negro race. Rather he was the progenitor of the Canaanites, who were not black. All this was obvious to the reader of the Scripture, and one could come to only one conclusion. Using this Scripture to justify calling one race of people inferior was totally unwarranted. Identifying the Negro race with the curse of Ham was a cruel hoax conceived in prejudice and perpetuated in ignorance. The Bible, as a matter of fact, does not mention the Negro race. It asks, "Can the Ethiopian change his skin ...?" (Jer. 13:23). In Acts 13:1 we have reference to "Simeon that was called Niger." "Niger" means "black," so we assume he was a Negro. If so, the church at Antioch was integrated, because he was either a prophet or a teacher there. Such references, however, give us no specific instructions. Such must be deduced from the great principles of the Bible.

The Bible teaches the common origin of man. God, the Creator, the Bible says, "made of one blood all nations of men for to dwell on all the face of the earth" (Acts 17:26). He placed Adam and Eve in the Garden of Eden, and from them all races have sprung. Man was created in God's image. Therefore, every man possesses infinite worth and should be treated with respect as a person.

When man sinned and was separated from God, a Savior was promised. Christ was the fulfillment. Those who experience his salvation become the children of God and brothers of each other. This spiritual relationship transcends race and all other considerations. Surely it would not be right for a Christian to show prejudice toward his brother. Rather he must love him. Jesus was most specific about that in 1 John 3:14: "We know that we have passed from death unto life, because we love the brethren. He that loveth not his brother abideth in death." Again Jesus said, "Thou shalt love thy neighbor as thyself." In view of the parable of the Good Samaritan that followed, surely no one today would seek to justify his white supremacist attitude by asking, "And who is my neighbor?" (Luke 10:25–37).

The Bible further teaches that God is no respecter of persons. ... Furthermore, the Bible teaches explicitly the equality of all men in Christ. Colossians 3:11 says, "Where there is neither Greek nor Jew, circumcision nor uncircumcision, Barbarian, Scythian, bond nor free: but Christ is all, and in all." Beneath the withering heat of Bible truth what faith I had left in white supremacy faded away. I was faced with a choice: accept Southern tradition or the Word of God. What else could a Christian do? ...

Nothing reached my heart more than the pleas of our missionaries around the world. I helped to send them out, and I felt a deep sense of responsibility to them. When they came home they told how stories of the Negroes' treatment in America were spread around the world, especially among other black people. People on the mission fields asked the missionaries if it were really true that there was segregation in America and if stories of racial discrimination were factual. Many lost confidence in the sincerity of the American citizen who had sent a missionary to him. The eyes of the world were focused on our treatment of minority groups. Missionary after missionary warned us that our attitudes were making their work less effective.

It seemed to me that if my prejudice would keep even one soul on our mission field from finding the Savior or add one ounce to the tremendous burdens already borne by our missionaries, it was a price too big to pay.

All over the world new independent nations are springing up. Many of these nations are predominantly of other races. In the past these people have looked to us with hope, for we were known as the champions of the oppressed. Now they are beginning to wonder if we really believe the ideals of freedom which we profess. The Communists have exploited the racial situation. J. Edgar Hoover says, "The controversy on integration has given the Communists a field day."

Communism is our most potent enemy. The Red wave moves on. Communists have made vigorous attempts to win the American Negro. The vast majority of American Negroes have rejected them vigorously. Both J. Edgar Hoover and the House Committee on Un-American Activities testify to the failure of Communism to reach any large segment of American Negroes.

In facing the question of what to do, let us acknowledge that much has been done already. The picture is vastly different from that of 25 years ago. In spite of the problems that remain, the lot of the American Negro is better by far than that of his colored brethren elsewhere in the world. His standard of living is rising; he attends free public schools, is voting in larger numbers, and has freedom of worship and many other privileges denied to his fellows in some nations.

There is much the Negro must do for himself. I would challenge those organizations working for Negro rights to remember that privilege demands equal responsibility. A demand for rights without acceptance of that responsibility can only result in chaos.

But let us recognize there is much we as white Christians can do. I have tried in this message to describe what has taken place in my own experience. This was no sudden change, nor did it take place recently. Much of what I have said has been said in part in other messages. I preach it now most of all to awaken your conscience, to commit you to the proposition that Christ has the answer to the racial problem, and that we as Christians must find it and proclaim it.

You must decide what you will do about it, but as a Christian I remind you that Jesus Christ has the right to control your attitudes and your conduct. Seek his guidance and do not be afraid to do as he commands. "And whatsoever ye do, do it heartily, as to the Lord, and not unto men; knowing that of the Lord ye shall receive the reward of the inheritance: for ye serve the Lord Christ" (Col. 3:23, 24).

James L. Monroe, "The White Man's Dilemma," *Christianity Today* 7, No. 2 (October 26, 1962): 71–73.

TRAGEDY IN RETROSPECT

THE EDITORS

A fter the nation-wide expression of shock and compassion and the anguished question of why the Birmingham outrage had to happen, this tragedy still speaks. How good if we could sweep it under the rug of an anesthetized conscience! How we should like to believe that four little children had not been killed at Sunday school, more than a score had not been injured, two youths had not been shot dead in the streets, and two teenage boys had not been charged with first-degree murder! But it did happen, and it will go down as one of the worst crimes in our history.

What does this crime say beyond the immediate tragedy? Surely it speaks to us all, North and South, white and Negro, of the sin of racial hatred. One must always refer with reverent caution to God's acts. Yet it may well be that He allowed the tragedy to happen to reveal what lies beneath racial hatred. It may well be that it happened in God's sovereign will that "sin [the sin of racial hatred] might appear sin" and be unmasked for all to see the deadly evil behind the prejudice from which few are wholly free.

The tragedy says another thing. It reminds us that the Christian fortitude and the restraint exhibited by the parents of the victims and by the Negro leaders of Birmingham should cause every Christian to reexamine his heart.

The racial problem will never be solved by violence. It must be solved within the context of Christian love and patience, sanctified common sense, and respect for law fairly administered and willingly obeyed.

The Birmingham tragedy was a grave handicap to the solution of the problem of race; it is a stain upon our national record. We should like to forget it or ignore it. But we cannot. We must take to heart what it says.

The Editors, "Tragedy in Retrospect," *Christianity Today* 8, No. 1 (October 11, 1963): 28.

FLOOD TIDE IN SELMA

THE EDITORS

A ll citizens of good will must feel a sense of outrage at the brutality of the Alabama State Police at Selma. The use of tear gas against unarmed men and women, the attack upon them with clubs, whips, and ropes, the scores of casualties seem like an episode out of Nazi Germany rather than news from an American city. The spectacle was disgraceful and deplorable. It cannot but sicken every American who cherishes his freedom.

The issue at Selma goes to the root of democracy. It is a constitutional matter. What the Negroes were dramatizing in their "Freedom Walk" was the Fifteenth Amendment to the Constitution: "The right of the citizen of the United States to vote shall not be denied or abridged by the United States or by any State on account of race, color, or previous condition of servitude." For ninety-five years this right has for multitudes of Negro citizens been abridged and even denied. What is in question in Selma is whether a nation will act consistently with its constitutional guarantees to its citizenry. And because consistency with national commitment to liberty is indissolubly linked with justice, the question is one of morality. As such it cuts deeply into the conscience of the great majority of Americans. It probes the very heart of respect for law and order. It underlines the difference between lip service to liberty and justice and their actual administration to all alike.

Every tide must turn. It may be that Selma, Alabama, will stand in history as one of the places where the tide turned for justice to Negro citizens. Paradoxically, the blows they received may prove a crucial strike for freedom. Surely the answer to the question "What will be the end of such disgraceful scenes?" is in sight. The Governor Wallaces of our nation must realize that they can no longer frustrate and abridge the Constitution. The concept of first-class citizenship for just one race must go. Only thus can Americans and their children pledge with clear consciences their "allegiance to the flag of the United States of America and to the Republic for which it stands, one Nation under God, indivisible, with liberty and justice for all."

One hopeful aspect of the Selma situation should not be overlooked. It is the demonstration in this unhappy city by a little group of white residents of Alabama. Small though the group was, its action showed that within the state there are white citizens willing to stand publicly with the Negroes in their struggle for justice and freedom. Moreover, the clergymen from northern cities who flew to Selma to join the second march chose the right moment. To be sure, it would have been better had white Alabama clergymen stepped into the places they occupied and better still if hundreds of white laymen had rallied to the ranks and led the way. Yet this response from the North was existential identification with the rightness of the Negro cause at a time when police brutality compounded the evils of a sad record of racial discrimination. Tragic evidence of the cost of that identification came not in any march to Montgomery but on the downtown streets of Selma, where the Rev. James J. Reeb was fatally clubbed in an attack by a group of white men.

The Editors, "Flood Tide in Selma," *Christianity Today* 9, No. 13 (March 26, 1965): 27–28.

A CORDIAL WELCOME— IF YOU'RE WHITE

THE EDITORS

Outside the First Presbyterian Church in Sumter, South Carolina, there is a sign that says, "We extend a cordial welcome to you." Several weeks ago two black students at Sumter's Morris College made the mistake of taking that welcome seriously. As they attempted to enter the sanctuary, the way was blocked by some of the members of the congregation, one of whom reportedly said, "No n----s can come in here."

The black students, well dressed and carrying Bibles, then tried to force their way into the church, only to be arrested on a charge of disorderly conduct, fined $100, and sentenced to thirty days in jail. One church member denied that entry was refused because of race; he explained that they were kept out because "their participation would have created an emotional disturbance." However, one senses that the fear of an "emotional disturbance" was not totally unrelated to the fact that the two students happened to have black skin. The students, both ministers' sons, were released on an appeals bond and were later admitted to services at the church.

This incident brings to mind a similar well-publicized happening at Macon, Georgia's Tattnall Square Baptist Church in

September, 1966. A black Mercer University student was physically prohibited from entering the church for worship. A special touch of irony in this situation was that the student was an African who had been led to Christ by missionaries sent out by Tattnall Square Church! Subsequently the three ministers of the church who took their stand against this unchristian act were dismissed from their jobs. In the recently published book *Ashes for Breakfast* (Judson), Thomas J. Holmes, the ousted senior minister, records the whole dismal story.

These two scenes speak for themselves—and they say that there are those within the church who harbor in their hearts attitudes that are totally foreign to the Christ they claim to follow and to the Scriptures they claim to believe. In many churches the barrier of race has been broken down, and this is honoring to God. But as incidents like these—and the attitudes that lurk behind them—are allowed to continue, the gospel of Christ is blasphemed.

The Editors, "A Cordial Welcome—If You're White," *Christianity Today* 14, No. 11 (February 27, 1970): 28.

RACE AND ECONOMICS

FRANCIS A. SCHAEFFER

I f I were writing my early books again (for example, *The God Who Is There* and *The Church at the End of the Twentieth Century*), I would make one change.

I would continue to emphasize that previously in the Northern European culture (including the United States) the controlling consensus was Christian, and that this is now changed and we live in a post-Christian world. However, in doing this I would point out that previously, when the Christian consensus was the controlling factor, certain things were definitely sub-Christian.

Christians of all people should have opposed any form of racism. We know from the Bible that all men have a unity because we have a common origin—we had a common ancestor. The "Christian" slave-owner should have known he was dealing with his own kind, and not only because when he had sexual intercourse with his female slave she produced a child, which would not have happened had he performed bestiality with one of his animals; he should have heard the message of a common ancestor not only taught but applied in a practical way in the Sunday-morning sermon. This applies to slavery, but it applies equally to any oppression or feeling of superiority on the basis of race.

Liberal theologians do not believe in the historicity of a common ancestor, and the orthodox, conservatives, or evangelicals all too often did not courageously preach the practical conclusion of the fact of a common ancestor. The evangelical taught the doctrine of loving one's neighbor as oneself but failed to apply the lesson in the context in which Christ taught it, namely, in the setting of race—the Jew and the Samaritan. This lack discredits the Christian consensus and dishonors Christ.

The second point, no less wrong and destructive, is the lack of emphasis on the proper use of accumulated wealth. In a world of fallen, sinful men, the use of wealth has always been a problem that the true Christian should face, but it came to a point of special intensity with the Industrial Revolution and the rise of capitalism. Happily we can look back to some orthodox Christians, especially in England, who as a part of the preaching of the gospel saw, preached, and stood for the proper use of accumulated wealth. But, to our shame, the majority of the church, when it was providing the consensus, was silent. Christians failed to see that a failure to preach and act upon a compassionate use of accumulated wealth not only caused the church to lose credibility with the working man but was actually a betrayal of a very important part of the biblical message. This fault was not only a thing of yesterday; it is often still with us in evangelical circles.

The Bible does clearly teach the right of property, but in both the Old Testament and the New Testament it puts a tremendous stress on the compassionate use of that property.

If at each place where the employer was a Bible-believing Christian the world could see that less profit was being taken so that the workers would have appreciably more than the "going rate" of pay, the gospel would have been better proclaimed throughout the whole world than if the profits were the same as the world took and then large endowments were given to Christian schools, missions, and other projects. This is not to minimize the centrality of preaching the gospel to the whole world, nor to minimize missions; it is to say that the other is also a way to proclaim the good news.

Unhappily, at our moment of history, in almost each place where true Christians are now speaking in this area, the tendency is to minimize missions and the preaching of the gospel and/or to move over to some degree to the left. On the left, the solution is thought to be the state's becoming stronger in economic matters. But this is not the answer. Yes, the industrial complex is a threat, but why should Christians think that if modern men with their presuppositions use these lesser monolithic monsters to oppress, these same men (or others with the same presuppositions) would do otherwise with the greater monolithic monster of a bloated state?

The answer is where it should have been always, and especially since the Industrial Revolution: namely, in calling for a compassionate use of wealth by others, and especially by the practice of a compassionate use of wealth wherever true Christians are.

We must say we are sorry for the defectiveness of the preaching and the practice in these two areas, and we must make the proper emphasis concerning these an integral part of our evangelicalism.

Francis A. Schaeffer, "Race and Economics," *Christianity Today* 18, No. 7 (January 4, 1974): 18–19.

★ *September 22, 1966* ★

ABORTION AT ISSUE

JEROME F. POLITZER

The abortion trial of nine San Francisco Bay area doctors this fall will highlight a controversy with complicated religious and political overtones that has been smoldering for some time in the nation's most populous state.

The major issue: Should a doctor perform an abortion when there is a high probability the baby will be deformed? Episcopalians and many other Protestants are lining up on the "yes" side. Roman Catholics and Missouri Synod Lutherans are by and large in opposition.

The present furor began May 20 when the State Board of Medical Examiners filed charges of illegal abortion against Dr. John Shively, obstetrics chief at St. Luke's Hospital (Episcopal), and Dr. Seymour Smith of non-sectarian St. Francis Hospital. Since then, seven other highly reputable Bay area doctors have been charged.

They are accused of arranging, approving, and performing abortions illegal under the present California law, which permits only those "therapeutic abortions" deemed necessary to save the life of a mother in critical condition.

State prosecution by Attorney General Thomas Lynch, a Roman Catholic now running for re-election, was provoked by recent candor of the medical profession in admitting that some women are aborted for reasons other than life-saving.

Doctors largely favor a more liberal law that would permit abortions if mental health is endangered by continued pregnancy, if pregnancy resulted from rape or incest, for girls under 16, or if there is a substantial risk that the child will be born with serious physical or mental defects.

Hearings last year on the Beilenson Bill to liberalize abortion laws brought to light the increasing number of therapeutic abortions performed by doctors on women who, while pregnant, had contracted German measles in the epidemic that broke out in California a year ago. The disease causes deformed babies in many cases. That bill died in committee, but the current furor should help a new version in the next legislative session.

Delegates to the March convention of the California Medical Association gave overwhelming approval to a resolution supporting a new law "taking into consideration the health of both the mother and the product of conception." They added that a new law should provide proper control of abortions through established medical staffs or medical society committees.

Those supporting the nine men accused of unprofessional conduct rest their case on a liberal interpretation of the present law and on growing public acceptance of abortion for reasons other than life-saving.

"The public wants this," said Dr. Edmund Overstreet of the University of California Hospital. "A vast majority of physicians want it. Only a small, organized, die-hard group opposes liberalizing the law."

His opinion is bolstered by a survey made last year by San Francisco State College. It found 79 percent of "representative adults" polled favored abortions for women who had German measles in early pregnancy. About 72 percent favored abortions for women psychologically upset by their pregnancies; 83 percent favored abortions for victims of rape or incest.

The major target of medical anger expressed all over the state is Dr. James V. McNulty, a member of the state medical board and a leading Roman Catholic figure in Los Angeles. McNulty vehemently opposes any law changes.

Last March, as the medical association appealed for liberalization, McNulty threatened the state's doctors with a state board crackdown if they persisted in interpreting the present statute loosely.

Several doctors under investigation charge McNulty seeks to push the views of a small minority and thereby dictate an essential aspect of medical practice to a majority of the state's physicians. They feel McNulty not only has appointed himself a watchdog for his church's point of view, but also is piqued at the medical association's determination to push for reform of the law.

McNulty's defenders point out that the Board of Medical Examiners does not make or interpret the laws. Its legal responsibility is to see that the laws are enforced, and only open and repeated violations caused the board (unanimously) to bring the charges.

"Those who want to change the law have lost the consciousness of life as God's creation," says Monsignor Timothy O'Brien, director of health and hospitals for the Roman Catholic Archdiocese of San Francisco. Mainstream Roman Catholic thinking regards life as beginning at the moment of conception; therefore, any interference with the process of pregnancy is regarded as the unlawful taking of life.

The Northern California Conference of Ministers of the Lutheran Church—Missouri Synod agrees. Conference public relations director Arnim Polster, a Daly City pastor, said "human life does begin at conception, rather than birth. To kill that life is murder."

Polster approves of abortion following rape or incest, because in these cases pregnancy is imposed contrary to consent. But he believes abortion because of the possibility of deformity is a starting point toward euthanasia—the taking of the life of weak, deformed, or suffering persons after birth.

Episcopal Bishop James A. Pike appointed a priest to work for a new abortion law full-time and declared abortions to prevent deformed babies are a "commendable form of civil disobedience." He advocates such massive, open disobedience of the law that the attorney general and medical board would be deterred from applying the statutory penalty—revocation of license—to so many practitioners.

Joseph L. Zem, administrator of St. Luke's Hospital, emphasized that the accused doctors were not trying to test the law or engage in civil disobedience. Rather, they were acting under the conviction that the present law permits abortions for women whose mental health is seriously threatened. He said the abortions were performed with the approval of the hospital committee on abortions, and that the police department was notified of each operation.

The attorney general's hearings against the nine doctors have been held up pending a Supreme Court ruling on a technicality, which is not expected before next month. That would conveniently put the trial after the November elections. Governor Pat Brown, a Roman Catholic seeking re-election against movie star Ronald Reagan, is maintaining silence on the volatile abortion question.

Jerome F. Politzer, "Abortion at Issue," *Christianity Today* 10, No. 23 (September 22, 1966): 51–53.

ABORTION AND THE COURT

THE EDITORS

Writing to Christians in Rome about the spiritual condition of the pagan world, Paul diagnosed it in this way: "Although they knew God, they did not honor him as God or give thanks to him, but they became futile in their thinking, and their senseless minds were darkened. Claiming to be wise, they became fools. ... Since they did not see fit to acknowledge God, God gave them up to a base mind and to improper conduct" (Rom. 1:21, 22, 28).[1] Not only the thinking but often the laws of men, and even the decisions of religious councils, can conflict with the laws of God. That is why Peter and John, called before the Sanhedrin, declared that they must obey God rather than men (Acts 4:19).

In a sweeping decision January 22, the United States Supreme Court overthrew the abortion statutes of Texas, indeed, of all the states that protect the right of an unborn infant to life before, at the earliest, the seventh month of pregnancy. The Court explicitly allows states to create some safeguards for unborn infants regarded as "viable," but in view of the present decision, it

---

1. RSV.

appears doubtful that unborn infants now enjoy any protection prior to the instant of birth anywhere in the United States. Until new state laws acceptable to the Court are passed—at best a long, drawn-out process—it would appear impossible to punish abortions performed at any stage.

This decision runs counter not merely to the moral teachings of Christianity through the ages but also to the moral sense of the American people, as expressed in the now vacated abortion laws of almost all states, including 1972 laws in Massachusetts, New York, and Pennsylvania, and recently clearly reaffirmed by statewide referendums in two states (Michigan and North Dakota). We would not normally expect the Court to consider the teachings of Christianity and paganism before rendering a decision on the *constitutionality* of a law, but in this case it has chosen to do so, and the results are enlightening: it has clearly decided for paganism, and against Christianity, and this in disregard even of democratic sentiment, which in this case appears to follow Christian tradition and to reject permissive abortion legislation.

The Court notes that "ancient religion" did not bar abortion (*Roe et al. v. Wade*, No. 70–18 [1973], VI, 1; by "ancient religion," it clearly means paganism, since Judaism and Christianity *did* bar abortion). It rejects the "apparent rigidity" of the Hippocratic Oath ("I will give no deadly medicine to anyone if asked, nor suggest any such counsel; and in like manner I will not give to a woman a pessary to produce abortion") on the grounds that it did not really represent the consensus of pagan thinking, though pagan in origin, but owed its universal acceptance to popularity resulting from "the emerging teachings of Christianity" (*ibid.*, VI, 2). To these, the High Court unambiguously prefers "ancient religion," that is, the common paganism of the pre-Christian Roman Empire. Against the official teaching of the Roman Catholic Church that the "life begins at conception" (curious language on the part of the Court, for no one denies that the fetus is human, or that it is alive; the Court apparently means *personal* life), the Court presents "new embryological data that purport to indicate that conception is a 'process' over time, rather than an event, and ... new medical techniques such as menstrual extractions, the 'morning-after' pill, implantation of embryos, artificial insemination, and even artificial wombs" (*ibid.*, IX, B). It is hard to understand how the contention that conception is a "process" of at most a few days' duration is relevant to the possible rights of the fetus at three or six months, and even harder to comprehend the logic that holds that "new medical techniques" for destroying or preserving the embryo "pose problems" for the view that it was alive before being subjected to those techniques.

Pleading "the established medical fact" that "until the end of the first trimester, mortality in abortion [of course the reference is to *maternal* mortality—fetal mortality is 100 percent] is less than that in normal childbirth [nine maternal deaths per 100,000 abortions vs. twenty-five per 100,000 live births, a differential of 0.016 percent, of course not counting the 100,000 fetal mortalities]" (*ibid.*, X), the Court decreed that a state may not regulate abortion at all during the first three months, and during the second, only to protect the health of the mother. After "viability," defined as "about six months," when the fetus "presumably has the capability of meaningful life outside the mother's womb," then, "if the State is interested in protecting fetal life ... it may go *so far* [emphasis added: since abortion is 100 percent fatal to the fetus, it is hard to see the value of "protection" that goes less far] as to proscribe abortion during that period, except when it is necessary to preserve the life or health of the mother" (*ibid.*). Since health is explicitly defined to include "mental health," a very flexible concept, this concession to the protection of the fetus from seven to nine months will, in practice, mean little.

The Court based its abortion decision on the right of privacy, and that without empirical or logical justification. "This right of privacy ... is broad enough to encompass a woman's decision whether or not to terminate her pregnancy," Justice Blackmun wrote in delivering the opinion of the Court. But the right of privacy is not absolute, and, much more important, no abortion decision can ever be by any stretch of the imagination a purely private matter. The fetus, if not a full-fledged human being, is at least a being owing his existence as much to father as to mother, and is therefore an individual distinct from both. Curiously, fathers are scarcely mentioned in the fifty-one-page majority opinion! The decision would appear to contradict itself when it insists that the "private" abortion decision must be made in conjunction with a physician and/or in line with some kind of medical judgment.

In his concurring opinion, Chief Justice Burger fatuously comments, "I do not read the Court's holding today as having the sweeping consequences attributed to it by the dissenting justices [White and Rehnquist]." The New York state tally stood in 1971 at a ratio of 927 abortions for 1,000 live births; now that abortion has become allowable nationwide, the ratio will presumably change, but the experience of nations with easy abortion suggests that it may very well remain as high as one abortion for every two live births, or even higher. What would the Chief Justice consider sweeping? Mandatory abortion for all those falling into a certain class? Infanticide? Mass extermination of undesirables? Make no mistake: the logic of the high court could be used with like—in some cases with greater—force to justify infanticide for unwanted or undesirable infants; the expression, "capability of meaningful life" could cover a multitude of evils and will, unless this development is stopped now.

In his dissent, Justice White sums up the situation and the Court's action:

The common claim before us is that for any one of such
reasons [he cites convenience, family planning, economics, dislike of children, the embarrassment of illegitimacy,
and others], or for no reason at all, and without asserting or claiming any threat to life or health, any woman
is entitled to an abortion at her request if she is able to
find a medical doctor willing to undertake the procedure.
The Court for the most part sustains this position: during
the period prior to the time the fetus becomes viable, the
Constitution of the United States values the convenience,
whim or caprice of the putative mother more than the life
or potential life of the fetus.

In arriving at this position, the majority of the Supreme Court
has explicitly rejected Christian moral teaching and approved
the attitude of what it calls "ancient religion" and the standards
of pagan Greek and Roman law, which, as the Court notes in
self-justification, "afforded little protection to the unborn" (*ibid.*,
VI, 1). It is not necessary to read between the lines for the spiritual significance of this decision, for the Court has made it crys-
tal clear.

In view of this, Justice Rehnquist's dissenting observation
that the Court is engaging in "judicial legislation" may seem
almost insignificant. Nevertheless, we must ask what remains of
the democratic process and the principle of local initiative when
not only long-standing older laws but the most recent state laws
and even the will of the people expressed in state-wide referendums are swept from the board in a single Court ruling, when
the people and their representatives are prohibited forever—or
at least until the Constitution is amended—from implementing
a higher regard for the life of the unborn than that exhibited by
seven supreme judges.

Having previously seen fit to ban the formal, admittedly superficial, and possibly hypocritical acknowledgment of God that used to take place in public-school prayers and Bible readings, the Court has now repudiated the Old Testament's standards on capital punishment as cruel and without utility, and has rejected the almost universal consensus of Christian moral teachers through the centuries on abortion. Its latest decision reveals a callous utilitarianism about children in the womb that harmonizes little with the extreme delicacy of its conscience regarding the imposition of capital punishment.

Christians can be grateful that the Court has not yet made the "right" to abortion an obligation. It is still possible for us to consult the will of God in this matter rather than the laws of the state. The present decision makes it abundantly clear that we are obliged to seek his will and not to be guided only by public law. We should recognize the accumulating evidence that public policy is beginning to display what Paul called "a base mind and improper conduct," and for similar reasons. Will the time come when this nation "under God" is distinguishable from those that are aggressively atheistic only by our currently greater material affluence? Christians should accustom themselves to the thought that the American state no longer supports, in any meaningful sense, the laws of God, and prepare themselves spiritually for the prospect that it may one day formally repudiate them and turn against those who seek to live by them.

The Editors, "Abortion and the Court," *Christianity Today* 17, No. 10 (February 16, 1973): 32–33.

DECISION '76: WHAT STAND ON ABORTION?

C atholic bishops across the United States will take a page from the revivalist's book next month, and in the process they may learn just how big an issue abortion will be for Catholic voters in November. Every parishioner at mass October 3 (just a month before the presidential election) will be asked to sign a decision card renewing his commitment to the sanctity of life. The cards will be collected at the exits, and diocesan pro-life coordinators will then tally the results and report them to the bishops' Washington headquarters.

The unprecedented decision-card procedure, officially called a "bicentennial reaffirmation," is just one indicator of the role being played by religion in this year's presidential politics. Abortion is only one of the "religious issues" in the campaign, and Jews, liberal Protestants, and evangelicals are just as involved as the Catholics, but so far, it has been the issue receiving the most attention. Democratic nominee Jimmy Carter has been working since his party's convention to try to undo the damage his platform writers did when they inserted a plank opposing an anti-abortion constitutional amendment.

The former Georgia governor sought a conference with Catholic hierarchy leaders, and the bishops finally granted a meeting with their executive committee on August 31. Among those present was New York's Cardinal Terence Cooke, chairman of national pro-life activities. After the one-hour session in Washington, Archbishop Joseph L. Bernardin of Cincinnati, president of the bishops' conference, announced, "[Carter] did not change his position. At this time he will not commit himself to supporting an amendment. We therefore continue to be disappointed with the governor's position."

There was no photograph of the candidate and the bishops in a happy meeting. The pictures in the papers the next day were of Carter and one of the nation's most popular Catholic politicians, Senator Edward Kennedy, who had just promised to campaign for the former governor. Before the day was over, Carter was telling reporters in New York, "I've never said I would actively oppose every possible constitutional amendment that was proposed on the subject of abortion."

President Gerald Ford, the Republican nominee, meanwhile was trying to conserve any support generated by his party's platform plank favoring an anti-abortion amendment. He invited the same group of bishops to meet with him at the White House ten days after their meeting with his opponent. They accepted, but their agenda was sure to include discussion of current government procedures (which they believe encourage abortions) as well as other issues.

While Catholic leaders were in the spotlight on the abortion question, evangelicals who share their concerns were watching from the sidelines. Even though the media have been full of speculation about the political power of evangelicals (estimated to number upward from 40 million), neither candidate is known to have sought an audience with any group of evangelical leaders on moral issues. The anti-abortion Christian Action Council sought conferences with both candidates, but as of early this month the only commitment was for a meeting with a Ford aide.

Pro-abortion forces were heard from immediately, however, when Carter sounded as if he was softening his position. The Religious Coalition for Abortion Rights, representing twenty-four Protestant, Jewish, and unofficial ad hoc Catholic organizations, asked the Democrat for a meeting on the issue.

Rabbi Richard Sternberger, chairman of RCAR, declared, "Any kind of amendment is unacceptable to those of us in the religious community who support the law of the land [a reference to the 1973 Supreme Court decision legalizing abortion]. No constitutional amendment can avoid causing injustices, no matter how framed and with how many exceptions. Any amendment would violate constitutional rights to exercise one's freedom of religion and rights of privacy."

Also raising questions about Carter's stand on a moral issue was Guy Charles, the Arlington, Virginia, ex-gay director of Liberation, a Christian ministry to homosexuals. Gay activists have claimed that Carter agreed to sign an executive order assuring homosexuals of equal-rights protection and also to favor criminal-code amendments. Charles said repeated attempts to get a statement from the governor have been fruitless.

Carter was also dogged by the discovery of a preface he wrote for a 1972 book, *Women in Need.* In his page and a half he does not actually state a position on abortion, but he lists it as one of the methods of birth control deserving consideration by lawmakers and other community leaders.

Also discovered by campaign-year sleuths was a 1973 proclamation in which Carter, as governor of Georgia, hailed the Reverend Sun Myung Moon as one who "has dedicated his life to increasing worldwide understanding of hope and unity under

God." At the time, Moon was relatively unknown in the American press. A Carter campaign spokesman had no immediate comment about either the Charles or Moon issues.

Anonymous, "Decision '76: What Stand on Abortion?" *Christianity Today* 20, No. 25 (September 24, 1976): 54.

IS EVERY LIFE WORTH LIVING?

THE EDITORS

A senior English pediatrician, charged with the attempted murder of a three-day-old baby born with Down's Syndrome (Mongolism), was acquitted by a unanimous jury verdict after an 18-day trial. The verdict prompted applause and cries of "Thank God!" from the public gallery.

Not everyone, however, was happy about making God party to such a decision. The essential facts were not in dispute. Last July in the Derby city hospital, John Pearson's life ended after three days. His mother had rejected him at birth because of his affliction. He had been given dihydrocodeine, an analgesic (sensation-killing) drug, on the instructions of Dr. Leonard Arthur, a highly qualified and experienced physician. The effect of the drug, with accompanying pneumonia, had reportedly caused his death.

A national newspaper estimated that 300 severely handicapped British babies a year are left to die without treatment that would prolong their lives. American figures for infanticide (that is the word we have always used for "uncivilized" people who carried on this practice) are proportionately much larger.

The British trial raised a nest of wide-ranging issues of deep concern to all evangelicals. Sir Douglas Black, president of the

Royal College of Physicians, defended the doctor's action and hoped there would be no McCarthy-style witch hunt in the medical profession. Former medical professor and eminent pediatrician Hobert Zachary, on the other hand, commented: "If you sedate a new-born baby so heavily that it does not feed, it will die from starvation; and that is as positive a way of killing it as if you cut its throat."

Evangelicals recognize there is no simple answer to the dilemma faced by Dr. Arthur and the parents of the deformed baby. They understand the anguish felt by doctors when confronted by such appalling and irreversible deformities. The burden placed on society and especially on parents can be excruciating. For both the newly born and the terminally ill, therefore, evangelicals tacitly accept the dictum of Arthur Hugh Clough:

> Thou shalt not kill; but needs't not strive
> Officiously to keep alive.

In response to the murder trial concerning the Pearson baby, Anglican Bishop John Habgood argued that we must take all "ordinary" means to support life; but there is a limit. An example of "extraordinary" means—means beyond that limit—would be "a long series of operations when his chance of survival to live a decent life is minimal."

Cardinal Basil Hume, however, asserted that it is morally wrong to end or shorten life, whether by action or neglect. "If people have a basic right to life," he declared, "then they have also a basic right to all the normal things, including simple nourishment, which are necessary to sustain that life."

Two recent trends, however, make evangelicals profoundly uneasy. First, they are disturbed by the rapid shift away from extraordinary measures to preserve life to ordinary measures, to no measures at all, to positive action to destroy unwanted human life. No doubt what constitutes extraordinary measures will vary from culture to culture. We can appreciate the fact of inevitable differences of opinion about the boundary between extraordinary and ordinary. But there is a wide and easily discernible gap between a long series of involved operations that have little or no possibility of success, and the deliberate administration of a drug that will cause starvation. Clearly the latter falls under the command, "Thou shalt not commit murder."

A second cause of evangelical unease relates to the increasing, and increasingly more trivial, grounds for "mercy killing": the effect of "defective" children on a marriage, the cost of keeping them alive, the psychological damage to brothers and sisters, the quality of life of the disabled or of the parents of the disabled. More and more, human life may be terminated when convenient. The sacredness of human life becomes a myth of the past.

WHY EVANGELICALS OPPOSE ABORTION

Mercy killing and abortion are closely related. Just as evangelicals have resisted mercy killing, so do they stand against abortion—and for the same reason. Here again they recognize that the issue is not always simple. Most of them will permit an abortion to save the life of the mother. Many will add an exception in case of rape: the rights of the mother must be considered, too. In such a case they may question if a mother must be forced to sustain at great personal cost a life that has been forced on her. A few evangelicals are loath even to condemn a mother who chooses at an early stage to abort a fetus after the testing of the amniotic fluid shows that the child would be radically incapable of functioning as a live baby.

But in spite of hesitation on this or that exception, evangelicals are clear on the central issue: they are opposed to abortions.

Those who favor easy abortion cannot understand this. They do not object to evangelicals refusing to abort their offspring. They may deem evangelicals stupid and misguided or even inconsiderate of others—of the handicapped offspring or society that will have to stand the burden.

Usually, however, they will agree that evangelicals have a right to choose for themselves. They grant us liberty. But why, they ask (always in puzzlement and sometimes in outrage), must you impose your standard on me? Why do you seek to destroy everyone else's freedom? You do what you want, but stay out of my affairs. Let me at least have the freedom to choose as you do.

WHY LAWS AGAINST ABORTION ARE NECESSARY

Episcopal Bishop George Hunt even argues that it is basically unchristian to "legislate" anyone's moral standards for others. Religious people, he asserts, must "affirm the necessity for maintaining the human freedom without which moral and ethical decisions cannot be made," and they may not use the government to coerce a minority into particular obedience to their precepts. "I am convinced that each of us has a God-given responsibility to exercise that freedom we have been given by Him by struggling with moral and ethical choices." He adds, "If we allow someone else to legislate a moral posture for us, we have given up our God-given duty to make responsible choices."

But the good bishop has the matter all mixed up. Evangelicals do not seek to legislate moral convictions. They agree that moral character is built through exercising "our God-given duty to make moral decisions." We do not put in jail those who think it is right to steal, but those who actually steal property from another.

Why, then, are evangelicals so adamant on this point? They do not oppose abortion simply because they believe the Bible prohibits abortions. To be sure, the Bible seems abundantly clear on this matter—thou shall not murder; and evangelicals, by definition, settle ethical decisions on the basis of biblical teaching. But the Bible teaches many things, and evangelicals are not trying to make every biblical teaching into the law of the land.

Biblical teaching about abortion, however, touches on a matter basic to the structure of society as a whole. To take a human life made in the image of God is to take what belongs to God. All society has a stake in the preservation of human life, including the rights of the unborn child.

The evangelical is not indifferent to the rights and freedom of a mother who considers an abortion. But the freedom of one person always ends where the freedom of the next person begins. The freedom to take the life of an unborn child is not, therefore, simply a private matter: it is the concern of all. The evangelical seeks to protect the unborn child's freedom to live. Society has the special duty to protect the freedom of those who cannot protect themselves.

Beyond defending the freedom to live, most evangelicals believe it is right to make laws against abortions for a second reason. They hold that the welfare of humankind depends on the value we set on human life. Evangelicals oppose abortions out of a basic regard for humankind. They wish to protect society against a policy that would deny the importance of human life and lead people to take it cheaply.

No doubt abortions spring from mixed motives. But the will to abort invariably involves an attitude toward life. Abortions are accepted because life is cheap: if it is inconvenient to bear a child to full term, destroy it; if the child will not be what we would desire, kill it. Most abortions take place because humans do not choose to be inconvenienced. Or to be deprived. Or to permit a handicapped child to live. And this, so evangelicals affirm, is a dangerous attitude that society for its own protection does not dare permit a person to act upon. Society has the duty to protect itself against actions that would destroy it. Human life is sacred, since every man, woman, and child is made in God's image.

Along with freedom of thought, freedom of speech and press, freedom of religion, and freedom to pursue one's own calling, freedom to live is a fundamental right of mankind. For its own good, society must stand against any attempt to destroy this fundamental human right to life, and protect it at every possible point.

The Editors, "Is Every Life Worth Living?" *Christianity Today* 26, No. 6 (March 19, 1982): 12–13.

UP IN SMOKE

STEVEN BAER

B raving temperatures indistinguishable from those that gave inaugural parade planners cold feet a day earlier, at least 70,000 undaunted prolife protesters made their annual January 22 descent on Washington and the Supreme Court. They came to mark the twelfth year since the Court declared a constitutional right to abortion—a year of escalating violence at abortion clinics and "family planning" centers.

Episodes of violence were and are justly condemned. But to understand the perpetrators and why the term "terrorism" is generally misapplied to their acts, one must also clearly understand the routine violence that occurs daily within abortion clinic walls.

A $500 million-a-year abortion industry has sprung up around *Roe v. Wade*—an industry exponentially more violent than any of the attacks to date on its facilities. By seven weeks gestation, about the time most women know they are pregnant, the fetal heart has been beating for a month, and the brain is emitting brain waves. The fetus has a delicate face, and hands are already emblazoned with unique fingerprint patterns. By the end of the first trimester, during which 85 percent of America's 1.5 million annual abortions occur, the fetus is sexually differentiated, her major organ systems are functioning, and ultrasonography reveals that she can suck her thumb and swim almost as freely as a fish within her dark, amniotic confines.

But this is no phylogenetic throwback to the Devonian age—as some abortion rhetoric based on debunked ontogenic theories once suggested. Neither is the fetus a "mere blob," "mass of tissue," or simple "product of conception." For all who have eyes to see, the infant's form is undeniably, unmistakably human.

And to watch her die, as I did in a recent viewing of a suction curettage abortion via ultrasonography, is a numbing experience. It happens nearly 4,000 times a day in this country, and prudence has not restrained its practitioners from pressing to the limit the expansive legal parameters drawn by the Supreme Court. By 1980, according to the Centers for Disease Control, at least 50,000 abortions annually were occurring in the *fifth and sixth months* of gestation.

Most empathic Americans represented by Washington's pro-life marchers express their opposition to abortion's brutality by supporting the efforts of their movement's lobbyists, political action committees, and courtroom activists. Focusing on the *two* lives involved each time a pregnant woman enters an abortion clinic, many attempt to dissuade through sidewalk counseling and offerings of housing and help from a growing network of crisis pregnancy centers. Increasing numbers are picketing abortion clinics and the homes of those who operate them. And on the fringes of a movement frustrated for more than a decade by governmental recalcitrance and 16 million abortion deaths, some are building bombs.

To call them terrorists, at least in most cases, is overbroad. Dictionaries define terrorism as efforts calculated to inspire fear. Yet as abortion-rights leaders admit, the clinic assailants have apparently gone to great lengths to ensure that no one is hurt by their actions. Such circumspection runs counter to terrorism's aims. The obvious *primary* aim of these individuals is not to intimidate abortionists or their often troubled clientele, but to save concrete, individual lives. For this group, letters to Congress and the editor are not enough; the most helpless members of their communities are dying daily with state sanction, and they cannot tolerate it. For them, destroying the local clinic and its suction aspirator with a firebomb simply means no unborn babies will be killed there the next day. It is as justifiable, they would likely say, as destroying a Dachau or an Auschwitz.

Such thinking is, however, shortsighted. It ignores the fact that the totalitarian system that gave rise to Dachau and Auschwitz provided no institutional means for dissenting citizens to alter its violently unjust policies. The American system does provide such means, however slow the processes of change through them may be.

For prolifers to resort to violence before exhausting the alternatives—including nonviolent civil disobedience of the sort seen in the civil rights movement preceding this one, and lately made chic by proabortion congressmen like Senator Lowell Weicker in the siege of South Africa's embassy—is to jeopardize both the cause and the nation. The moment someone the whole country recognizes as human dies in an abortion clinic blast, the battle lines may be drawn irrevocably.

Those on the violent fringe of the movement must realize that America's constitutional democracy and rule of law, even when it has dehumanized, is too precious a system to put at risk. Those who defend the Supreme Court's radical decision of taking human rights from the unborn must realize the need for reform. There are millions of lives at stake, on both sides of the womb.

Steven Baer is executive director of the
United Republican Fund of Illinois.

Steven Baer, "Up in Smoke," *Christianity Today* 29, No. 7 (April 19, 1985): 19–20.

ABORTION CLINIC OBSOLESCENCE

CHARLES COLSON

This is a time of tragic irony for the right-to-life movement— for at the same time prolife activists are courageously escalating their fight for life, events and technology are conspiring to render such efforts moot.

Let me explain.

Last fall Operation Rescue hit the streets and television screens of America. During the last weekend in October, 2,212 prolife supporters were arrested for blocking access to abortion clinics in 32 cities, bringing to 7,000 the number of prolife arrests since the Democratic convention last July.

Why this sudden intensification of prolife commitment? This new willingness to sacrifice?

Some of the urgency may well come from desperation. After all the promises of the Reagan years, prolife forces have few victories to show for all their efforts. Few expect that George Bush will manage to get much of the social agenda that Ronald Reagan could not. Civil disobedience, for some, may vent years of frustration.

But from what I have seen of Operation Rescue, this is not the whole story. Their antiabortion sit-ins are not publicity stunts.

They are attempts to save lives based on clear-cut beliefs. Christy Anne Collins, a prolife leader in the Washington area, has been jailed several times. As she describes her motivation, "The fact of the matter is, God said it's a crime to shed innocent blood. I think we have to stop the killing. If we believe that abortion is murder, and I do, then I think we have to act like it is murder and try to stop it."

Some Christian leaders have argued that Operation Rescue shows disrespect for the law. But to say that a law may never be violated under any circumstances is a form of extremism more disturbing than anything done by prolife activists. Certainly one could justly break a "no trespassing" law to save a child drowning in a lake; Operation Rescue, I believe, is the moral equivalent. Placing the value of a just law against trespassing above the attempted rescue of innocent lives is an inversion of Christian priorities.

It is a sad commentary that we live in a nation that puts such rescuers in jail. They are the most unlikely of prisoners. They are often intensely religious, both Protestant and Catholic. They have a deep respect for the law, though they value life more. They are nonviolent, but they are not easily intimidated.

These are, in short, the best of citizens—people who would be valued by any government under normal circumstances. But they populate our jails. It is a telling question: what kind of society would force its best citizens to violate the law as a matter of conscience?

But just as these principled protesters were indicting a calloused American conscience, events were taking place an ocean away that may soon render their protests impotent altogether.

On October 28, a day that saw a number of Operation Rescue arrests, the French government ordered a pharmaceutical company to resume distribution of RU-486—the abortion pill. Under pressure from prolife groups, the company had earlier withdrawn it; but France's Socialist government ordered the drug back on the market, asserting that it was "the moral property of women."

The pill, in effect, causes an early miscarriage. It means that a home abortion could eventually be as close as two tablets and a glass of water. It means fast, effective relief—like Alka-Seltzer or Tylenol.

Certainly there are things that can and should be done to restrict the availability of RU-486 in the U.S. Experiments with the drug are already being conducted here, though it will be several years before it could be approved by the Food and Drug Administration. Prolife groups must make it clear to American politicians, health officials, and businessmen that this drug must not be legalized.

But the drug is already in use in China and Thailand. Populous Third World countries have made it clear they will be customers. Because it replaces surgery, the drug could easily be used on women who have little or no access to medical care.

And if RU-486 is used this widely, it would be impossible to prevent the creation of a black market. American demand would be high. Columnist Ellen Goodman comments, "Even if the opposition manages a legal ban, the abortion pill will become available. These pills are called in the trade 'bathtub' drugs; they are easy to make. ... Anyone who believes that we could control their importation hasn't checked the cocaine business recently."

Faye Wattleton, president of Planned Parenthood, gloats that "the right-to-life movement has seen its last gasp. If these drugs get to the market, the fight is finally all over."

What response is left to us?

Of course we must fight for legal restrictions. But the effect of any law is bound to be limited, given the size of demand and the extent of legal distribution.

And of course we must continue to protest. But abortion clinics in the future may well be necessary only for the few. How do you intervene to save a life when an abortion is as near as the medicine cabinet?

What RU-486 will eventually mean, I fear, is a dramatic shift in the rules of the abortion battle. It will mean that our fight against abortion will no longer focus on the clinic, the dumpster, the Supreme Court steps. It will be relational and educational: Christians persuasively pressing the point among their peers that a life conceived is precious to God and must not be poisoned by a pill. The struggle will no longer be focused on legislatures and suction machines, but on people and the individual values they hold, the values that create their choices. What it means is changing the hearts and minds of a self-centered, callous generation.

That is a challenge perhaps even more daunting than the threat of a prison cell.

Charles Colson, "Abortion Clinic Obsolescence," *Christianity Today* 33, No. 2 (February 3, 1989): 72.

★ *August 17, 1992* ★

ESTRANGED BEDFELLOWS

Are evangelicals abandoning the Democratic
party, or is it abandoning them?

KIM A. LAWTON

Representative Tony Hall of Ohio has a ready reply when
fellow evangelicals ask how he can be a Christian and
remain a Democrat. "The last time I read it, Jesus came riding into
Jerusalem on a donkey, not an elephant," he says with a wry smile.
The answer may be lighthearted, but Hall admits that the question,
which he hears often, really annoys him. A seven-term Democratic
representative, Hall says his party offers many views that should
resonate with evangelicals. "The Democrats have always had the
reputation of being for the downtrodden and the oppressed, the
widow and the orphan, the powerless and the hungry."

In past years, most evangelicals agreed with Hall. In fact, the
majority of evangelical Christians in the United States were registered Democrats, though in recent elections many had been
voting Republican, earning the nickname "Reagan Democrats."

However, a new survey suggests that evangelicals are now
officially moving away from Democratic roots and into the
Republican party. According to a recently released study by the
University of Akron's Ray C. Bliss Institute of Applied Politics,
47 percent of all white evangelicals now identify themselves as

Republicans, while 34 percent identify with the Democrats, and 18 percent consider themselves either independents or third party. (The survey, which questioned 4,000 Americans, was conducted this past spring, before the Supreme Court's controversial abortion ruling and before Ross Perot suspended his unofficial run for president.)

"White evangelical Protestants have gone from being a group being wooed by the GOP to being one that looks like it has been won by the GOP," says James Guth, a codirector of the study (*CT*, July 20, 1992, p. 43). The new statistics contrast sharply with a similar survey in 1960, when only 32 percent of evangelicals regarded themselves as Republicans, while 60 percent were Democrats, and 8 percent were independent or third party. "There has been a very dramatic change," says Bliss Institute director John Green.

DEEP FRUSTRATION

Last month, as the Clinton-Gore ticket was officially launched, evangelical Democrats expressed hope that their party may reach out to those Christians who have felt alienated. At the same time, many admitted they were not optimistic about that prospect. "There is a deep level of frustration for evangelicals and many Catholics [within the party]," says former Democratic state legislator Stephen Monsma, now a political science professor at Pepperdine University. According to Monsma, Democratic leadership has been insensitive to those holding traditional views on issues such as abortion, homosexual rights, pornography, and the family. That attitude, he says, is pushing people out of the party.

Such was the case for Dave Medema, executive director of JustLife, a Christian political action committee that promotes a "consistent prolife ethic" on abortion, the military, and economic justice questions. Medema believes the Democrats' "general drift away from socially conservative values" has estranged many evangelicals like himself.

Abortion, he says, has become a lightning rod for that drift. As a representative of JustLife, Medema has attended many Democratic functions over the years. Increasingly, he found that his prolife stand made him a pariah. "It was a question of tolerance," he says. "If basic moral questions couldn't even be asked, and if societal moral issues couldn't be connected to individual ones, then it was a pretty hard place to be."

Finally in 1990, Medema switched his personal affiliation to the Republicans. He admits it is not a perfect match but says that the Republicans at least are willing to discuss issues that concern him. "I haven't changed over the years. I haven't become more conservative," he says. "[The Democratic party] left me."

ABORTION INTOLERANCE

In his opening invocation at the Democratic convention in New York City last month, Rep. Floyd Flake (D-N.Y.) prayed for a new model of democracy, "one that is tolerant of differences of ideas and opinions." But prolife delegates to the convention say their views were met with more hostility than ever before. The abortion issue, which the Democrats avoided in 1988, was wholeheartedly embraced in 1992. This year's platform contains a lengthy paragraph affirming *Roe v. Wade*: "Democrats stand behind the right of every woman to choose consistent with *Roe v. Wade*, regardless of ability to pay, and support a national law to protect that right."

On the night the platform was adopted, the Democratic National Committee (DNC) sponsored a "choice rally" on the convention floor, complete with 15,000 placards that read "Prochoice, Pro-Clinton," patriotic band music, and a rousing "Choice, Choice" crowd chant. The National Organization for

Women contributed thousands of "Keep Abortion Legal" signs, and the president of the National Abortion Rights Action League, Kate Michelman, was called on stage to take a bow.

At the same time, prolifers say they were gagged, DNC and Clinton campaign officials denied repeated requests by Pennsylvania's Democratic governor, Robert Casey, to speak in opposition to the party's abortion plank, even though they allowed five Republican women to speak in favor of Clinton. The National Right to Life Committee was forced to scramble for a meeting place when the DNC instructed a New York hotel to cancel the group's reservation for a press conference room. And ten uncommitted prolife delegates from Minnesota who cast their presidential votes for Casey reported being pushed and shoved, jeered, and spat upon by some of their fellow delegates.

"My grandparents told me the Democratic Party was where everyone had a voice," says Ann Maloney, one of the ten. "This is not the party of my grandparents."

Another Minnesota delegate, Grant Colstrom, who describes himself as a born-again Christian active in union politics, says he was saddened by the prominence that both abortion rights and homosexual rights were given at the convention. But he adds he is equally saddened by the void created by Christians leaving the party. "I love Jesus Christ, and I love this party," he says, asserting that he is in the battle for the long haul.

Congressman Hall, a convention delegate himself, acknowledges that the party's stands on several issues, particularly abortion, frustrate and disappoint him. But he, like Colstrom, remains committed to the party. Hall believes the Democrats still offer the best programs to help the poor and the hungry. He is pleased they have been pushing a key project of his, welfare reform, and says Gov. Clinton's theme of "putting people first" should continue that tradition.

FAMILY VALUES

Also encouraging, according to Hall, is the new focus within the party on "family values." An entire section of the new platform is devoted to "strengthening the family," and much of the language is a departure from past Democratic ideas. "Governments don't raise children, people do," the platform says. "People who bring children into this world have a responsibility to care for them and give them values, motivation, and discipline."

The nation's most prominent evangelical Democrat, former president Jimmy Carter, told *CT* that it is the Democrats, not the Republicans, who hold the high moral ground on family values. "It's easy to talk about television programs and things of that kind, but as far as any substantive programs that would give families the motivation to stay together and live a peaceful and productive life, to live in decent homes, and to have good health care, very little has been done."

Concern for the environment is another issue that can draw evangelicals back to the Democratic party, says Dordt College professor Richard Hodgson, a Democratic delegate in 1988. "Frankly, I believe that as evangelicals begin to wake up, they will see that they are being duped by the Republican Party, which on a national level is ... closing its eyes to social justice and environmental issues," he says.

Many Democrats believe the Clinton-Gore ticket represents their party's strongest chance in a decade to win back disenfranchised evangelicals. Both men are Southern Baptists with strong church-attendance records. They both referred to Scripture during their acceptance speeches, possibly signaling a new effort to reach out to Christians. However, Clinton and Gore have also come out firmly in favor of abortion rights, a position that turns away many evangelicals.

Hall urges evangelical Democrats not to become "too one-issue" and leave, but rather to stay and work for change within the system. Minnesota delegate Colstrom optimistically agrees. "I'd really like to see the Judeo-Christian Democrats come back," he says. "We can take this party back."

Kim A. Lawton, "Estranged Bedfellows," *Christianity Today* 36, No. 9 (August 17, 1992): 40–42.

★ *August 12, 1996* ★

OUR SELECTIVE RAGE

A pro-life ethic means more than being anti-abortion.

RON SIDER

Inconsistency marks our major political options. As a consequence, Christians seeking a biblically balanced political agenda find it difficult to find a political home. President Clinton champions the "right" to abortion and then leads the campaign against smoking out of respect for the lives of the 400,000 people who die annually from cigarette-caused cancer. Sen. Jesse Helms leads the pro-life forces against abortion and then lobbies for tobacco subsidies.

Many of the members of Congress who receive a 100 percent score (and thus the Friends of the Family Award) on the Christian Coalition's Congressional Scorecard also receive large donations from the tobacco and liquor PACs. One also has to wonder why the Christian Coalition's Congressional Scorecard considers eliminating environmental and safety regulations as "pro-family" votes. Surely God cares about the family and the poor, the unborn and creation.

So often the Christian Right has rightly championed the family and the sanctity of human life but neglected to work for equal opportunities for the poor, uncritically endorsed American nationalism, ignored concern for God's creation, and neglected the struggle against racism. Equally one-sided has been a Christian Left that rightly promoted justice, peace, and the integrity of creation but largely forgot about the importance of the family and sexual integrity, and failed to defend the most vulnerable of all—the unborn and the very old.

The result is that many evangelical Christians find it increasingly difficult to feel at home within the current political landscape. Evangelicals who seek to be good stewards of the environment find some of their strongest allies to be folks who think mandatory parental notification for teenagers contemplating an abortion is oppressive. Meanwhile, activists who seek the legal protection of the unborn find themselves keeping company with elements on the Right who think the United Nations is part of an international conspiracy designed to usher in a demonic New World Order.

This can all be sloughed off with the rationalization that "politics makes strange bedfellows." But there is a deeper problem. In this polarized environment, the voices of those are effectively muted whose Christian convictions lead them to support the legal protection of the unborn and who want to protect endangered species, who oppose legalizing homosexual marriages and favor restrictions on the tobacco industry.

This is not to say that the failure to protect endangered species or regulate the tobacco industry is morally equivalent to the current regime of abortion on demand. But it is unbiblical for pro-life Christians to overlook the sanctity of life of those who die unnecessarily because of tobacco, war, pollution, or starvation.

WHAT CAN BE DONE?

Evidence demonstrates that the current popular political options fail to represent a large segment of American Christians. Lyman A. Kellstedt at Wheaton College and Corwin E. Smidt at Calvin

College have studied evangelical political attitudes more extensively than anyone else in the last ten years. They point out that
although evangelicals now overwhelmingly vote Republican (78
percent in 1994), only 39 percent of all evangelicals feel "close or
very close" to the Religious Right.

The secular media sometimes seem to suggest that evangelicals care only about the family, the unborn, and biblical sexual
norms. But the Kellstedt/Smidt team discovered in a 1992 nationwide poll that a majority of evangelical voters favor tough environmental regulations (54.7 percent), comprehensive health
insurance (54.9 percent), and vigorous efforts to ease hunger
and poverty (53.8 percent).

Most black Christians want government to continue to battle
against racism and poverty, but most also strongly oppose homosexual practice; research indicates that over the last 20 years,
blacks have consistently demonstrated a lower approval rating
for abortion than whites. A similar pattern exists in the Hispanic
community: in one survey, 71 percent agreed that all human life
should be protected, including the unborn.

Other Christian groups do not easily line up with current partisan options. Instead, they support a consistently pro-life Christian
agenda. Evangelical Anabaptists have long sought to preserve the
sanctity of human life whether the issue was starvation, abortion,
war, capital punishment, or euthanasia; and theologically evangelical Christians in mainline Protestant churches are dissatis-
fied with their denominational leadership and are also looking
for the kind of balance represented by a consistent ethic of life.

We should not neglect Catholics as potential partners as well
as models. For more than a decade the American Catholic bishops
have officially supported a consistent ethic of life. Their public
policy efforts are pro-life and pro-family, yet they are deeply concerned with the poor, peacemaking, and caring for creation.

Evangelicals, African American and Hispanic Christians, and Catholics constitute a substantial number of American voters. Is it too much to hope that in the next two decades these groups could discover new ways to work together to shape American culture and public policy in a biblically balanced way?

Together we could hammer out strategies (both cultural and political) that would help us recover sexual integrity and empower the poor, respect the sanctity of human life, support the dignity and equality of women and racial minorities, affirm heterosexual marriage as the societal norm without scapegoating homosexuals for the decline of the family, restrain evil and work for peace, and strengthen the family and renew the creation.

Several caveats are in order: our efforts at political engagement need to be informed by a biblical perspective on God's mission in the world, not by the platforms of partisan politics. Some of the problems with which we need to struggle do not, ultimately, have political solutions; political means do not resolve what, at heart, are moral and spiritual problems. Further, if judgment begins with the household of God, then renewal must start there also. The church cannot expect of the body politic what it does not demonstrate itself.

Nevertheless, a new coalition of evangelicals, African American and Hispanic Christians, the historic peace churches, mainline Protestants, and Catholics could contribute substantially to the renewal of our society in the next two decades—if we could agree to cooperate and develop a biblically balanced consistent ethic of life. If we do not, we will have ourselves to blame for our persistently frustrating options, and the immoral, inconsistent society they reflect.

Ron Sider, "Our Selective Rage," *Christianity Today* 40, No. 9 (August 12, 1996): 14–15.

★ *December 6, 1999* ★

THE ABORTION DEBATE IS OVER

FREDERICA MATHEWES-GREEN

The twenty-seventh anniversary of *Roe v. Wade* is coming up and I have some bad news. The abortion debate is over.

For a couple of decades it was the hot topic, the subject of television debates, and flash point of political campaigns. Many a punditorial brow furrowed over "this difficult, controversial choice."

Then the public got bored and saw only two possible positions: thoughtful, regretful pro-choice and hysterical, prudish pro-life. Pro-lifers, the average person thought, did not realize life is tough and women deserve compassion. Never mind that pro-lifers began establishing free care centers to support pregnant women eight years *before* the *Roe* ruling.

Then the outrageous assassinations of abortion workers began. Peaceful pro-lifers were presumed guilty by association, and any residual feeling that fair play guaranteed them a hearing evaporated. While 15 or 20 years ago abortion opponents might be seen as reasonable-but-wrong, after these shootings they became dangerous kooks. In fact, pro-lifers were accused of pushing murderers off the deep end by using terms like "killing unborn babies." Just as pro-lifers were about to lose their right

to free speech—rendering the unstable few even more explosive—
the debate ground to a halt. The curtain was rung down and the
"sensitive, difficult question" escorted offstage.

It's been said that the American political attention span
is two weeks long, so logging over 20 years is something of an
achievement. During that time the movement acquitted itself
well. In the early years there was a mistaken overemphasis on the
rights of the unborn, based on the erroneous presumption that
the average person would oppose abortion upon realizing that
the life in the womb was a baby. When ultrasonography made
this obvious, Americans still preferred to keep abortion available.
They were uneasy about it, but wanted to keep the procedure
legal, as pro-choice leader Kate Michelman said, for only three
reasons: rape, incest, and "my situation."

This isn't a logical position. Either an unborn child has a right
to life and abortion is an appalling injustice, or it is the equivalent of a root canal. Yet it's where public opinion settled, and pro-
lifers saw that they had overestimated the average American's
allegiance to logic. In the last decade or so pro-lifers have also
realized the folly of dividing baby from mother and treating them
as combatants. This played into pro-choice rhetoric of antago-
nism and struggle, a setting in which might makes right. Of the
two—mother and baby—only one was empowered to enforce
her choice, so pro-life language picturing them as opponents
backfired. A more holistic pro-life approach, summarized as
"Love Them Both," makes more sense, and in recent years support for pregnant women has bloomed and professionalized to
an impressive degree.

The abortion debate is over. The pro-life *cause* is not. Christians have opposed abortion since the first-century Christian
code, the Didache, specified: "Thou shalt not kill a child by

abortion." Valuing the unborn and newborn, women, slaves, and the disabled were distinctive ways early Christians challenged their prevailing culture.

What about our current culture? We can grow numb, but abortion is one of those monumental issues of justice that comes along once in a lifetime. It is violence against children, a hideous act of poisoning or dismembering tiny bodies, then dumping them in a landfill or garbage disposal. Over 37 million children have died this way. We must respond, and as always this means giving practical help—building support services for pregnancy and adoption, as previous generations built leprosariums, hospices, and hospitals. It also means working patiently for legal justice, since the minimum purpose of law is to protect the weak from violence. To our great-grandchildren it will be obvious that this was the civil-rights challenge of our time, and we will be judged for our response. If we are not moved when people kill children, nothing will ever move us.

I also have some good news: the abortion debate is reemerging transformed. This moment of silence may have been necessary for hardened hearts to hear the whisper of conscience. Pro-choice leaders mourn that disapproval of abortion is rising while their own troops are graying. The average member of the National Abortion and Reproductive Rights Action League is 55, while college freshmen have dropped their support for legalized abortion from 65 percent to 51 percent since 1990. A 1996 poll found those most likely to agree that "abortion is the same thing as murdering a child"—a stunning 56 percent—are between the ages of 18 and 29. No wonder young people oppose abortion. Anyone younger than 27 could have been killed this way. A third of their generation was.

People longed to be in the pro-choice in crowd and avoid pro-life stigma, and to keep abortion handy. Yet deep inside they knew it was wrong, and a rising generation appears ready to tell us so. Columnist Paul Greenberg put it best: "Some questions will not be answered till they are answered right." That right answer gets clearer every day.

Frederica Mathewes-Green, "The Abortion Debate Is Over," *Christianity Today* 43, No. 14 (December 6, 1999): 86–88.

CHANGING HEARTS AND LAWS

Our recommendations for President Bush
and the 107th Congress.

THE EDITORS

As 100,000 prolife activists marched in Washington during the 28th anniversary of *Roe v. Wade*, President Bush delivered on a crucial campaign pledge. With the stroke of a presidential pen on his first day on the job, Bush blocked use of federal funds for abortion counseling overseas. Though the president's executive order focuses on abortion practices in other countries, his move puts the debate over abortion policy back on the national agenda.

The editors of *Christianity Today* recently ranked our selections for the leading priorities for the incoming Bush administration and the new Congress. Hands down, prolife initiatives topped our list. The prolife movement holds out hope for passage of a federal ban on partial-birth abortion and the Born-Alive Infant Protection Act. These two measures will be important steps toward restoring our national commitment to unborn human life. A federal ban on partial-birth abortion would end the gruesome practice of ending a third-trimester pregnancy by removing a fetus feet-first and then destroying the skull cavity.

The born-alive bill would provide more humane care for mortally ill newborns and babies who survive a botched abortion.

What about overturning *Roe v. Wade*, the 1973 Supreme Court decision that granted women the right to abortion? Though the First Lady doesn't think it should be overturned, President Bush is not ruling out support for a legal challenge to *Roe*. "We'll just have to see," he told reporters. Bush appropriately makes the point that it's premature to comment fully on overturning *Roe* since there is no case before the high court that has the potential to undo this historic wrong.

Even if overturning *Roe* is not in the near future, prolife Christians must not sit on their hands. Vicki Thorn, founder and director of Milwaukee's Project Rachel, has worked in the prolife movement for 30 years. For the last 14 years, she has focused her efforts on post-abortion trauma counseling, which is now a nationwide movement. While she favors prolife legislation, Thorn told Catholic News Service, "It's not about changing the law. It's about changing the country."

Profound change in American culture is already underway. Christians must do their part to steer the culture even more in a direction that fully values all human life. President Bush and members of Congress who support the prolife cause should persevere in making a compelling and public case for new prolife legislation. If our values change, so will our public laws.

OTHER IMPORTANT CONCERNS

Here are the five other key areas *CT* editors think worthy of focus for the president and Congress:

Education reform: In many inner cities, 68 percent of low-income 4th-graders cannot read at a basic level, despite $120 billion in federal spending since 1965 to improve the educational achievements of poor children, according to the Heritage Foundation. Failing schools must be fixed or replaced by private or semi-public alternatives. Well-designed school-choice programs should be expanded without delay, or another generation of undereducated, poor kids will grow up with limited access to opportunity.

Religious freedom: A 2000 survey by the Center for Religious Freedom indicates that 75 percent of the world (more than 4 billion people) does not enjoy broad religious freedom. Conditions for Christians and other minority faiths in China, India, and Sudan have grown worse during the past five years. Both Congress and the Bush administration must keep the public's attention on widely violated international standards as well as enforce provisions in the 1998 International Religious Freedom Act, even if it becomes necessary to restrict trade.

Faith-based initiatives: In Norfolk, Virginia, the Department of Social Services (DSS) awarded a $45,000 contract in 1998 to the Norfolk Interfaith Partnership to provide welfare-to-work mentoring services. Under this program, permitted by the 1996 welfare reform law, volunteer mentors (recruited from Norfolk churches) meet regularly with DSS clients for their first six months in a new job. The vision for such programs is to move needy individuals from dependence to interdependence within their communities. President Bush's creation of the White House Office of Faith-Based and Community Initiatives in late January is a praiseworthy first step in helping other effective faith-based groups to blossom.

Racial tensions: In separate cases in January, two white supremacists pleaded guilty to fomenting racial hatred. One was caught in a cross-burning incident in South Carolina. The other was convicted of shooting at a Jewish center near Los Angeles.

African Americans, only 8 percent of whom voted for Bush, are looking for clear signs that the new president will help them in their quest for racial justice and equality. President Bush has made an admirable beginning with appointment of African Americans to key posts. The president must continue to make such key political appointments as well as build stronger relationships with African-American leaders.

The marriage tax: Most married couples pay more in federal income taxes than they would as singles. Efforts to end this so-called marriage tax have failed, but it's time to try again. This tax policy has unintentionally created a disincentive for marriage. One legislative measure that has real merit would double the standard deduction for married couples and make other adjustments in tax brackets to minimize the marriage tax.

To be sure, other items demand attention, but success in these six areas would make for an effective and fresh start for Congress and the president.

The Editors, "Changing Hearts and Laws," *Christianity Today* 45, No. 4 (March 5, 2001): 38–39.

THE POWER OF PRO-LIFE WOMEN

It's time to harness "feminine authority"
to protect the unborn.

KATELYN BEATY

The videos are hard to refute, and much harder to stomach. Conversations recorded and released by the Center for Medical Progress have dealt a hefty blow to Planned Parenthood's public image. While the reversal of *Roe v. Wade* seems a distant legal mirage, the videos have powerfully reminded us what abortion *is:* it is always the death of an unborn person, whose body parts can be crushed and extracted and exchanged for money.

Planned Parenthood has responded tepidly, apologizing for the "tone" used by its medical director. The activists behind the videos have slated several more for release. As the videos continue to stir public debate, we can expect to hear a common refrain: If you care about women, you will support their right to choose an abortion. You are either for women's well-being and empowerment, or you are pro-life.

This is a false dichotomy—one that women in particular need to dismantle.

The dichotomy is reinforced by lobbyists, media, and tone-deaf politicians alike. In 2012, pro-choice advocates warned of a "war on women," arguing that male politicians can't create policies that involve women's bodies. Meanwhile, Todd Akin's "legitimate rape" comment and Richard Mourdock's statement that rape is God's plan reinforced that, if there wasn't a war, there was serious lack of compassion toward women. Throughout 2016, Planned Parenthood will assuredly argue that Hillary Clinton—whom they awarded for her "unwavering support of women's health and rights"—"gets" women like other candidates can't.

But on the level of hearts and minds, politicians don't have the last word. Charmaine Yoest, president of Americans United for Life, and Carol Tobias, president of National Right to Life, are shaping pro-life federal and state legislation. Lila Rose and Abby Johnson are younger activists exposing the brutalities of the abortion industry. Together, they show that you can understand women's experience from the inside out, and still believe that women deserve better than abortion. As Yoest told *CT*, "One big reason I'm in this movement is that I'm offended by the idea that abortion is foundational to women's power."

These and other leaders remind us that to be pro-women *is* to be pro-life. The first U.S. feminists knew this instinctively. Elizabeth Cady Stanton, Susan B. Anthony, and others understood that partners and doctors often coerce women into abortions; that abortion can compound women's shame over an unplanned pregnancy; and that it often entails a grief as deep and scarring as a child's death outside the body. When pro-choice advocates ignore these realities, they fail women and undermine their well-being.

"The abortion movement essentially tells women that they are weak, that they cannot handle an unintended pregnancy," Abby Johnson told *CT*. A former Planned Parenthood director, Johnson believes young women are ready for a new women's movement: one that says "women are strong enough to face whatever comes our way, including unintended pregnancy," she says. Indeed, millennials are more likely to identify as pro-life than previous generations. And one of the biggest pro-life groups comprises college students; under Kristan Hawkins's leadership, Students for Life of America has tripled in size since 2006 to 900 campus groups.

When it comes to advancing a pro-life ethic, Christians have many resources at our disposal. We can appeal to moral reasoning, that unborn persons have a fundamental right to live. We can appeal to spiritual authority, that every major religion views abortion as killing of the innocent. We can point to astounding research that shows unborn babies are, physically speaking, tiny humans. But in a postmodern culture in which personal experience is given much authority, women can make a powerful contribution to the pro-life movement.

Abortion is not a "women's issue"; rather, it is a human issue that affects women uniquely. Congressman Henry Hyde, drafter of the Hyde Amendment (which restricts certain federal funds from being used to perform abortions), understood this well. In debates with pro-choice Democrats in the 1990s, he was accused of speaking on something he knew nothing about. So he turned to Marjorie Dannenfelser, now president of the Susan B. Anthony List, and said, "We've got to have women doing this." Hyde supported the pro-life nonprofit in its early years.

"When men speak, people can hear the intellectual argument," said Dannenfelser, "but they want to hear if there is female support for the position." As the 2016 election approaches, may more people hear that support loud and clear.

Katelyn Beaty, "The Power of Pro-Life Women," *Christianity Today* 59, No. 7 (September 2015): 25–26.

Chapter 5

GOD AND COUNTRY

C hurch and state issues are arguably the most important ones for understanding the Christian's place in politics. The relationship between our place in the pews and in the voting booth unites all manner of questions: What is the relationship of the state to the church? Of the individual to the nation? Of the state to society? Of political leaders to our heavenly Ruler? This is, in a manner of speaking, the heart of the problem.

Few public temptations are so great to evangelical Christians as the urge to unite our political goals with our biblical faith. Granted, we tend to do it in different ways, but this is one sin to which few can claim immunity. Conservatives veer toward an idolatry of the nation, where America becomes a substitute Israel, destined by God for immortal glory. Progressives shun this error but slide toward an idolatry of the state, where the government's role is to make incarnate the kingdom of God. The expression differs, but the reality of the compromise involved is the same. It is fair to say that pieces in *CT* were as liable to each of these errors as anyone else, but the writers were normally successful in their attempts to be aware of this trap and avoid it.

Another aspect to these issues is the danger posed by the state to the church. This was a running concern in *CT* articles from the start. As noted in the introduction to chapter 1, one of the earliest examples of this concern (and the strangest to contemporary minds) was the perceived growing power of the Roman Catholic Church in the discussion of John F. Kennedy's presidential candidacy. As time went on, this fear shifted first to the external threat of Communism and then to more domesticated rivals like secular humanism. In more recent days, the concern has erupted once more with the rise of progressive sexual ideologies threatening to lump the historic evangelical Christian sex ethic with America's segregationist past.

Straddling the gap between these two concerns stands the attempt by Christians to find their places as citizens of a pluralistic republic, fully aware of their fealty to a higher citizenship yet striving to live as fully engaged Americans. Many *CT* contributors looked back with pride upon the Bible's influence on the democratic development of the United States, looking to history as an inspiration for the future and as a requiem for what once was. Others spoke more proactively with an emphasis on the way that only Christianity can provide a sufficient moral and philosophical basis for a long-lived democratic society. Finding the balance between these concerns is the end of the matter for faith and politics.

WORSHIP IN THE LIFE OF THE NATION

EDWARD L. R. ELSON

A merica today is a nation at worship. Under many forms and in a variety of practices, the people of the United States are bowing before the Eternal God. Men and women, boys and girls everywhere go to church, say their prayers, participate in the offices of praise and thanksgiving in this period of national spiritual renewal. Once more at this season of the year we are being summoned by the president to observe our only national religious day—a Day of Thanksgiving.

All of this is as it should be. America began with men on their knees, has been strengthened and sustained as it has kept close to God, and Americans—when most truly themselves—have been people of faith and prayer.

THE REFORMATION AND 1776

The United States was born at a pinnacle in the progressive emancipation of the mind and spirit of man. Although many streams in the historical process flowed to the confluence of time on July 4, 1776, the most significant stream was the floodtide of the Protestant Reformation. And the dominating influence at our origin was the Calvinian theology and the way of life it fostered.

God was the sovereign ruler of a moral universe before whom all nations and all men would finally be judged. A man was a man in his full stature only as he acknowledged the majesty and holiness of the Creator and humbly yielded himself to the divine will and purpose in life. Our forebears were committed to the elemental Christian virtues of chastity, sobriety, frugality, and the disciplined will. God, in the most vivid sense, was the source of our national life. And this life can be sustained only at its main source. That is why the worship and knowledge of God are so important.

LIFE NOURISHED BY WORSHIP

From the very beginning to this Thanksgiving Day in 1956, we have been a people whose life has been undergirded by faith in God and nourished by worship of the Almighty. In this faith our institutions were created, our culture promoted, our philanthropic endeavors initiated, our liberties secured and freedom for men everywhere promoted. Men accustomed to freedom in their approach to God, as they were accustomed in the dissenters' paradise—the American Colonies—insisted upon freedom in the public expression of their ideas and the ordering of their lives. Men could be trusted with their own destiny so long as they lived in obedience to a higher authority—the authority of God. The soul of man in this new world would be most free, most trustworthy when captive only to God.

America has become great and strong not simply by vast natural resources made secure from all enemies by wide oceans and friendly neighbors. Other nations have had all that and for longer periods. America has become great and strong principally because of a creative spirit emanating from her religious faith, chiefly and dominantly evangelical Christian faith. In some, this faith has been intimate and personal. In others, it has been a way of life derived from the social atmosphere and psychological climate produced chiefly by evangelical piety.

GOD AND OUR SURVIVAL

The United States is so completely the child of a great religious heritage that the worship of God is essential to its survival in the purity of its pristine character. The worship of God is not an option in our life, but an indispensable requisite for our very existence. Allow worship to languish and we begin to deteriorate. I am not now concerned with the technical liturgical concepts of worship, although I believe that a true Protestant liturgy is the only sure protection against shallow, insipid and unrewarding worship. I am here desperately concerned that there *be* worship, that men *go* to church, enter into its life and in concert with other men give testimony to the glory of God in our common life.

NO FULLY CHRISTIAN NATION

In the absolute sense and on the perfectionist basis there is no such thing as a "Christian nation." In terms of the higher order of the Kingdom of God, no political entity, in this imperfect world, is thoroughly Christian. But some nations embody more Christian principles than other nations. Some nations are more hospitable to Christian truth than others. And some nations are more thoroughly responsive than others to Christian motivations and to doing the will of God. Christian ideas, ideals and culture flourish to a greater extent in some nations than in others. And such nations, in God's time, become less obstructed conductors of the Christian evangel and more direct conveyors of God's truth to the world.

When America is most faithful to its origin, to its truest self and to its God, it is that kind of nation.

In humility and fullness of dedication, it may well be that in this epoch when America carries such a heavy international responsibility, God can use her as an instrument of His purposes on the earth. Should that be true, as I believe it is true, the leaders and the people of this land must keep close to God, seek to discover His will and resolutely perform this providentially bestowed role of world leader.

A NATION UNDER GOD

A nation under God is a nation under His authority, under His power, and under His judgment.

If a nation is to be a "nation under God," it must be a worshipping nation. Genuine worship is the offering of one's self to God. For the Christian, it is accepting the gift of a new life in God through Jesus Christ, which is the result of repentance and faith. God is not to be used but to be served.

THE EXPLOITATION OF RELIGION

Much is being said these days in religious circles about the "exploitation" of religion as a weapon of ideological conflict. In the highest sense, pure religion is not to be "exploited" for anything except God's purposes. God is to be worshipped and served for God's sake. Righteousness is to be sought for righteousness' sake. Nothing in Jesus' teaching is more emphatic than that. But is it not true that a nation spiritually weak in our kind of world is also ideologically vulnerable? It therefore follows that a people constantly strengthened and renewed by the worship of God is better equipped for an age of sharp ideological warfare. When God is sought for God's sake, and righteousness is served for righteousness' sake, the nation becomes a citadel of strength for free men.

MORAL SAG AND REVIVAL

In the decade since World War II, American life has been characterized on the one hand by a moral sag and cultural deterioration, and on the other hand by a moral resurgence and a spiritual awakening. Both are real and both arise out of the vast and variegated life that is America. Both the negative and the positive derive from a dynamism inherent in the cultural soil of the New World. The presence of the former does not invalidate the latter. That we are living in a period of great religious revival of continental proportions is too clear to need documentation. The evidence is all about us. It is too cumulative and too impressive to be ignored or minimized. We ought not to mistake motion for power, religious activity for religious renewal. But, allowing for all the exaggeration, the excesses, the sentimentality and the superficiality which appear in every age, the truth remains that there has rarely been a period in our national life when the movement of God's spirit has been so manifestly real as today.

AMERICAN CHRISTIANITY

We have an American way of doing things, an American way of expressing ourselves and the American manifestation of religious vitality. This may be mystifying, even an enigma to foreigners, but it is *our* way. Our own church statesmen have always contended that in our missionary outreach, we should seek ultimately to make the Christian faith indigenous in the lands to which the gospel is carried. But when we have such a vigorous indigenous American expression of Christianity, some of the same articulate churchmen lament the "nationalization of religion," and the "domestication of the church." Paradoxically, to some folk Christianity is good when expressed in some distant cultural pattern but when it appears under American patterns and forms it appears somehow corrupted. At best it seems to them synthetic or artificial. Indeed, we need always to refine the accent of the gospel in our nation, and we need to purify the expression of Christian piety among our people. And we must ever be submissive to the searching judgment of God. But we need not be, and we are not called upon to be, something other than Christians in the rich soil of freedom we call America.

SPIRITUALITY IN WASHINGTON

Our nation's capital has become a dramatic focal symbol of a people at worship. Washington shares with the entire nation the drive and force of the contemporary revival. The way of Christian faith and the life of prayer are the norm for most of the leaders of our government. This return to the ways of the Spirit crosses all party lines and penetrates all religious groupings. In Washington it is transparently genuine.

Most of the persons who hold public office today are men who believe in and worship God, who seek to discover His will and who in the stewardship of their offices attempt to do God's will. After a decade of intimate association with leaders of national life on all levels, through three presidential administrations, it is my judgment that by and large, the men whom we send to the highest offices of the land make the Christian evangel and the reign of Christ's spirit as relevant and as meaningful in their lives as do men anywhere in the land.

POLITICS AS DIVINE VOCATION

For generations the church has encouraged Christian laymen to enter politics as an expression of the Christian vocation. We have spent our years persuading Christian men to perform public service. Many have been willing to do this.

Today, when such men come to Washington, enter into the life of the church, attend services, read their Bible, teach Sunday School classes, hold church offices and go to prayer meetings, there are some religious analysts who seem to think this is all hypocritical and sneer at it as "piety along the Potomac." Religion is good, they imply, for the barber and the baker, for the banker and the butcher, for the teacher and the tool maker, but when it appears in Washington in a politician, a diplomat or a military leader, there is something sinister and suspect about it. This is what the new cynicism suggests—a sneer is substituted for sagacity.

Can there be any more effective way of discouraging devout churchmen from seeking public office, or preventing good men already in office from worshipping God, than to impugn their motives?

At this moment of history, when we must be great and strong spiritually, it is no service to the nation and no real contribution to the cause of Christ to indict as insincere those who witness to the truths of God and to our historic faith from high places, or to debunk as something "phony" the widespread revival of religion in our land. By all means, let there be precise evaluation, profound judgment, real prophetic insight. That is the way of correction and growth. But let it all be in the spirit of love, in a constructive and not corruptive mood. The ecclesiastical tent must be big enough for all sincere Christians. In this hour, we need a solidarity of religious witness. We need a nation which is a bastion of spiritual power if we are to be adequate for this age.

It was only from a position of moral eminence and authentic spiritual elevation that the president of the United States was able to make his audacious proposals at Geneva. The whole concept was wrought in prayer. It was that which gave lasting meaning to that historic gathering. And it will ever be so.

Americans simply must honor, worship and serve God as He has been revealed in Jesus Christ, our Lord. For the most part, our ideals are Christian ideals, our standards Christian standards, our goals Christian goals, our motivations Christian motivations. Under whatever form or denominational auspices, let us thank God for every American who today says out of a sincere heart, "I was glad when they said unto me, let us go into the house of the Lord."

> *Edward L. R. Elson is minister of the National Presbyterian Church in Washington, D.C. President Eisenhower and other leaders high in the echelons of government are found in its pews. Dr. Elson has published* One Moment with God *and* America's Spiritual Recovery.

Edward L. R. Elson, "Worship in the Life of the Nation," *Christianity Today* 1, No. 3 (November 12, 1956): 10–12.

GOVERNMENT SERVICE AS A CHRISTIAN VOCATION

THE EDITORS

O ne of history's greatest philosophers, Plato, voiced the verdict that democracy cannot survive. The interest and trust of the Western world in popular government have been encouraged for a century and a half by the American form of government, a republic within a democracy. Since World War I, however, faith in the democracies has waned. Fears are deepening that, apart from a vigorous rededication to spiritual and moral values, even the American form of democracy must decline and decay.

One can therefore sympathize with all efforts to infuse American governmental life with Christian principles. The past history of the West attests that the Christian religion supplied a new moral earnestness and excellence and furnished a spiritual framework that unified the masses in their devotion to the right. American state affairs in colonial and revolutionary times were Christian in temper at least, and the concern for separation of church and state arose within this disposition. The loss of Christian principle and perspective in recent generations, however, has produced a withering sense of religious and ethical priorities. Today the attempt to temper national affairs with Christian principles is resisted by secular forces hostile to supernatural

religion and ethics and is resisted also by some agencies spiritually and morally aggressive yet fearful of ecclesiastical dominance
in state affairs by a single voice like the Church of Rome.

The Roman Church, at any rate, has a specific philosophy of
political action. Its militant concern for religious government
gains sympathy from the drift of the Communist world to irre-
ligious government. Pressures behind the Iron Curtain drive
Christians out of government leadership. Soviet disregard of justice and moral law, with its enthronement of deception and the lie,
has pricked the Free World's conscience. Can Christians, whatever their communion, be blamed—ought they not indeed to be
lauded—for seeking to inspirit American politics with Christian
leadership?

Roman Catholicism encourages political service, and imple-
ments such encouragement. It sponsors a training program for
government leadership in which the Edmund A. Walsh School
of Foreign Service at Georgetown University plays a leading role.
Admittedly, somewhat less than half of Georgetown's graduates
are Roman Catholic; about one-fifth are Jewish. But the cur-
riculum reflects the viewpoint of the Vatican. From the halls of
Georgetown, Roman Catholic alumni in significant numbers find
their way into diplomatic service.

Roman political gains in the United States are increasingly
evident. In the state of Rhode Island, Catholics have a majority,
52 percent of the population, and only one Protestant now holds
state office there. Increasing Catholic strength in Congress is
clear. This year for the first time Catholics number second in the
religious census of Congress, outnumbering Baptists, and nar-
rowing the lead of Methodists. One Washington news correspondent thinks it "almost inevitable" that within five or ten years
Catholic congressmen will take the lead, and that, once they gain
control, that lead will be irreversible. Catholic maneuvering for a

presidential or vice-presidential candidate has been an obvious phase of recent party conventions. Catholic policy includes the objective of a U.S. ambassador to the Vatican, preferably Roman Catholic. In Roman Catholic lands like Latin America, where a disproportionate number of Catholic consuls represent the American government, visas for incoming Protestant missionaries have frequently been opposed as disruptive of the unity of those lands. The Catholic program of encouraging government careers and of equipping candidates for those careers with a specific philosophy of government is politically efficient.

This way of stating things, however, is reactionary, for it tends to an anti-Catholic mood. In a democracy, after all, no citizen is less a citizen because of the religion he espouses. Catholic forces are not alone in a religious political vision for America. Across the years, Protestant ministers' sons have found their way in significant numbers into State Department service, some inspired in past decades by the untenable "social gospel" vision of a Christianized government. Protestant lay leaders are conspicuous in Cabinet and congressional posts; Secretary of State John Foster Dulles, Director of National Security Harold Stassen, Congressman Walter Judd are three of a great many. In the Department of Agriculture, Mormons reportedly have been in full harvest in recent years. Methodist leaders, determined to translate church influence into political life, are projecting their own costly school of foreign service in the District of Columbia.

Roman Catholic citizens have seized opportunities that other American religious groups have neglected, and for this they ought rather to be envied than blamed. It would be sheer prejudice to exclude an American citizen from public office because his private worship and witness fall into some particular religious communion. The real concern, however, is Rome's official philosophy of politics. The Roman Catholic conception is that every government (the United States included) is the temporal arm of the Roman Church. History is too clearly written to ignore the fact that Rome utilizes the democratic framework to subordinate national interests to the totalitarian religious and political goals of the Vatican. It would doubtless be uncharitable to suspect every Catholic in politics of being an agent of the Vatican's foreign policy. But the only way to determine whether a candidate does or does not share the official view of the hierarchy that the State is the temporal arm of the Vatican is to press for a personal statement.

Evangelical Christianity is apprehensive about direct church influence in politics, whether that influence be Catholic or Protestant. The minister and church in politics threaten the principle of separation of church and state by entangling the church in government, and reviving the ogre of the medieval church-state.

Yet evangelicals have been spurred to a new look at the political arena. The major motivations for this growing interest in government are two: a reaction to the growing power of Romanism, and the evidence that political neglect abandons this area of life to secularism. The slogan "the best politics is no politics" breeds inferior politics. Politics has its seamy side, as someone has remarked, because so few Christians are in it.

What evangelical Christianity lacks today is a philosophy of Christian social action which sets political responsibility and activity in a consistent and compelling frame of thought and action. Good politicians are not only men of high principle and moral courage, but men of political insight and consistency. Evangelical interest in politics lacks the motive drive of a full-orbed outline of social duty. For that reason evangelical action tends to be needlessly reactionary, to be stirred to activity only on grave issues, to be one-sidedly competitive as a parallel effort.

Its creative contribution and dynamic are impeded through this lack. There is the danger of enlistment only in short-term programs, of premature commitment to excessive positions, of effort wasted in programs of enthusiasm. Whoever has moved in evangelical circles during the recent decades has sensed their interest in headlines more than in study commissions in social ethics.

What is needed today, as a background for virile evangelical political action, is a renewed interest in the study of comprehensive principles of Christian social ethics governing the whole of life and culture. It will take more than salvage and patchwork to arrest the decline of democracy today.

The Editors, "Government Service as a Christian Vocation," *Christianity Today* 1, No. 19 (June 24, 1957): 22–23.

IS AMERICA LOSING HER CULTURAL DISTINCTIVES?

S. RICHEY KAMM

"American civilization has not merely changed its inspiration and its character but its epoch as well." Thus André Siegfried, one of the leading French humanists, describes the cultural revolution in the United States. For him "the epoch of the pioneer has been replaced by the epoch of the machine" (André Siegfried, *Nations Have Souls*, G. P. Putnam's Sons, 1952, pp. 170–171). Siegfried has emphasized the obvious. He has brought into focus the everywhere-apparent emphasis upon material values—the trend toward "bigness"—the decline of the significance of the individual.

THE VISION OF LIFE

Latent in his analysis is the thought that culture is not made up alone of what we see. It may also be found in what we dream. Culture, in the sense of life's habits—one's way of doing things from day to day—may vary greatly from land to land, from community to community, and even from family to family. But the real question to be fathomed is this: What is the vision of life that a people carry about in their heads? Do they think of themselves as playing a part in a dramatic conflict with forces unseen, or are they cogs, bars, endless belts in an ordered mechanized existence?

The distinctiveness of American culture lies in its "myth"—its vision of life. This picture of life is highly dramatic. It conceives of man as an individual, discrete, intelligent, purposive, active. He is part of the society yet separate from it. He possesses capacities that are comparable to his fellows but always manifests a singular uniqueness in their demonstration. He is limited by his companions, yet is not bound by them. He is buffeted by circumstances yet never defeated. He is the servant of nature and likewise its master. He is a "free" man and not a slave. He knows life in the sense of destiny and purpose.

Such a vision of life is unique. The source of its singularity is to be found in its inspiration. This is hardly in the presence of "free land" in America nor in the abundance of the natural resources of the region to which men came. Neither was it imbibed from the changing climate of this north temperate region. Rather, it is to be discovered in the religious symbolisms of the men and women who laid the cultural foundations of American society.

PURITAN INFLUENCE

The early vision of life in America was strongly influenced by the Puritan. His "cultural myth" was biblically inspired. Living in a day when church and state placed great emphasis upon the principle of order and unity, the Puritan protested against the cultural dominance of these external forms. He raised his voice against this tendency to uniformity in life and boldly asserted that man was no longer to be cast in the time-honored mold of his culture. Man was to be a "free" personality who would rise dominant over his culture. The basis for such a vision? It was to be found in the biblical view of God's redemptive work for man, and in the realization of the individual reality of this experience by an act of individual faith. Alan Simpson's recent study, *Puritanism in Old and New England* (University of Chicago Press, 1955), has again brought to light the importance of this vision in the life of early Puritanism. From it came the dynamic which drove men to oppose the church, the crown, and every semblance of regimentation until men were made free.

The real basis of the Puritan protest has great meaning for our present predicament. What the Puritan saw was this: that man tends to project the cultural form of the present into the future by codifying it as natural law and by employing the organized forces of society to sustain it. This made man the creature of his culture, rather than the creator. It further tended to divorce him from the real source of cultural inspiration, namely, God, and to deprive every cultural form of its real meaning and intent. In opposition to this tendency the Puritan asserted again and again that God, alone, was lord of the conscience. This meant that man must be free to follow the dictates of his own conscience in matters of law and government as well as in religious practices and in ethics. It gave man a basis upon which to assert the value of the individual over against the values of the group. It is the source of the spirit of individualism in American culture. As such, it is most important to consider in approaching the cultural transition of our times.

A PEOPLE OF LIP SERVICE

America's cultural problem today is the problem of a people who give lip service to a set of cultural distinctives—forms of expression, standards of life, visions of reality—which are cut off from their real essence. The transition has been slow and gradual. The concept of liberty, once grounded in the belief that man must be free for the worship of God in every phase of life, is now confused with a man's right to express himself or some vague assumption that the public welfare will be advanced by a scarcity of legal limitation. The concept of equality, which founds its inspiration in the biblical view of man's creation by an eternal God and man's universal state of sin or rebellion against God, is now confounded with weights and measures of economic privilege or physical capacity. The concept of private property which was conceived as a gift or trust from God and, hence, subject to limited political control, is now viewed either as the sole bulwark against arbitrary political power (that is, a very poor substitute for God), or it is viewed as a mere matter of social convenience. The institution of the family, which was once looked upon as of divine ordination and, therefore, not subject to man's tinkering, is now often accepted as a product of an evolving set of social relationships. The state, once conceived as an instrument of God's justice is now decried as the instrument of man's inhumanity to man.

How may we retain our cultural distinctiveness? The answer lies in our readiness to abandon our prophets of monism and our willingness to return to a view of culture which accepts the various orders of inspiration—the spiritual, the intellectual, the material—and place them in their proper relationship to one another in the reinterpretation of American life.

THE LOSS OF BALANCE

Cultural history in America exhibits an alarming tendency to lose that sense of balance in orders of values that is so essential to a healthful cultural life. Beginning with a vital cultural vision gleaned from the Bible and interpreted in the forms of the evangelical Christian tradition it soon began to lose its distinctiveness. Seventeenth-century Puritanism with its wholesome balance of supernaturalism, rationalism, and observationalism, sat down to converse with its snake in the garden and lost its freedom to an incipient intellectualism. Roger Williams detected the transition in Massachusetts Bay and was driven into exile for his protests. It all came about in a manner quite common to men who desire to preserve a revolution through the deification of new forms of expression. In its effort to preserve the vision of the individual God-man relationship through a personal experience of saving faith, Puritanism created its own "golden chain of being"—the concept of "covenant"—to connect the transcendent with the imminent and thus to give order to this new vision of life. The concept of "covenant" viewed all of life on this earth as related to God through the Living Word, Jesus Christ, and through the inspired word, the Scriptures. These somewhat mystical forms had to be translated into concepts intellectually prehensible. Then followed the "federal theology," the elaborate explanation of the meaning of the "covenant" concept. It brought to American culture a vision of life which has never been transcended. In it the individual was most important. All institutions were divinely ordained, but man had a coordinate responsibility for their projection and maintenance. He was given a sense of responsibility and a vision of destiny that linked him with the Eternal. But tragedy became imminent when the son of the Puritan began to worship this theological formulation which often smacked more of Plato in its manner of expression than of its biblical typology. The idea of "covenant" which was basically an idea of personal relationship and order, was reduced to a principle of uniformity, a law. The result was manifest in the eighteenth-century preaching of New England which emphasized the rationality rather than the personal aspect of God's dealing with men. To put it theologically, the "covenant of grace," whereby God extended salvation to his elect, was by-passed for the "covenant of works"—the rational explanation of God's dealings with men as part of the whole order of nature. Man thereby lost his identity as a person; he became known only as part of a rationally conceived order of life. Man was no longer dominant over culture but had surrendered his spiritual and intellectual powers to its control. With the passing of the "covenant of grace" there was little justification for change.

SHIFT OF SOVEREIGNS

It was against this transition in American culture that Jonathan Edwards thundered in the middle of the eighteenth century. Edwards was concerned that America should assert the supremacy of the will as over against the domination of the intellect. He was determined that the sovereignty of God should be restored to American culture in opposition to both the intellectualist and the romanticists. In spite of his valiant efforts eighteenth-century rationalism in the form of Deism wrought significant alterations in the American cultural myth. God, the Creator, still remained as the author of all order and truth. But the "golden chain of being," the mediator between God and man, was no longer Christ and the Scriptures. It was Nature, conceived in the ordered vision of Newton's *Principia*. The scientific experiments of Franklin and the writings of Jefferson and his friends tended to reinforce, yes, even to deify this concept. There had been brought back into American culture the principle of uniformity under the guise of science.

It was in the light of such a vision that Jefferson stated the basic principles of the American creed. These great ideas of equality, rights, and happiness were traced to "Nature's God," not the God of nature. In so grounding them Jefferson laid the basis for our cultural confusion. The modern conflict with atheistic materialism has demonstrated that there can be no "scientific" justification for such concepts. Man cannot look upon them as intellectual abstractions alone; they must be accepted as divine imperatives that are essentially spiritual in nature and can be understood only in the light of a Divine Creator who is also a Divine Redeemer. This is what Jefferson left out. Since then we have been trying to shore up the foundations of our cultural forms with new types of scientifically drawn intellectual abstractions only to discover that they are insufficient.

DISTINCTIVES IN PERIL

From the vantage point of the mid-twentieth century it is now possible to see quite clearly what happened to American culture in the nineteenth. Transcendentalism sought to perpetuate a basis of uniformity in the cultural myth that was not dependent upon human experience. God, in Emerson's concept of the "Over-Soul," would transcend finiteness and thus give stability to culture. But there was something lacking, the sense of tragedy, the presence of sin. The vision became optimistically rigid. There was no deviation from the path of progress in the pattern of change. This vision served to strengthen the American vision of destiny and to awaken the social conscience to the enormities of human slavery. But the dynamic of action for the reform movement which followed sprang from the vision of God and man which burst upon the American scene in the Finney revivals.

Simultaneously, another movement sought to restore the concept of grace, of needed change, in the American cultural myth. Having rejected the vision of revelational grace which moved the Puritan Jonathan Edwards, and Charles G. Finney to clamor for reform, the new prophet sought inspiration from the scientific doctrines of change which were then emerging. The evolutionary view of life—dialectical, survivalistic, or emergent—became the inspiration for the American dream. God became imminent in the very motion of matter. In fact, there was no need for any transcendent God or any absolute; all that was necessary was the ability to determine the trend of the motion. This would provide the oracle for man's action, the vision for his dream.

It is quite obvious that this tendency to monize our cultural inspiration does violence to the basic constructs of knowledge itself. Long ago the Greeks laid it down that all knowledge deals with origins (being), behavior (becoming), and ends (telesis). Our latest cultural inspiration has been drawn from behavior, alone. We have tried to explain both origins and ends in terms of behavior. We have lost the sense of balance and completeness which comes when one recognizes that both origins and ends are to be interpreted in terms of revelational truth. This places our absolutes where they belong—in God. It saves us from the error of confusing our ideas about God with absolutes, that is, it places rational truth in its proper place—namely, as one form of under-standing. Likewise, it helps us to recognize that the knowledge derived from experience is meaningful only as it demonstrates in a non-deductive manner the realities of the absolute.

The American cultural myth is a rich one because of its basic inspiration derived from the person of God. It is sound when rational truth is brought into conformity with this "heavenly vision." It is real when it permits man to experiment and to learn more of life through the realm of experience. This balance of the spiritual, the intellectual, the experiential, is the genius of American culture. When we lose this balance and endeavor to project either the principle of order, rationality, or the principle of change, experience, as the basis of our culture, we lose the proper foundation for any sound cultural system. We then become slaves either to the "god" of our intellectual abstractions, or of our observational generalizations. We can know freedom in our culture only as a free God is posited as its base. Without this assumption America will continue to lose her cultural distinctives.

> *S. Richey Kamm is Chairman of the Division of History and Social Science at Wheaton College in Illinois. He holds the A.B. degree from Greenville College, A.M. from University of Michigan, and Ph.D. from University of Pennsylvania, and in 1952 was awarded the LL.D. degree by Seattle Pacific College.*

S. Richey Kamm, "Is America Losing Her Cultural Distinctives?" *Christianity Today* 1, No. 20 (July 8, 1957): 2–5.

February 17, 1958 ★

AMERICA'S FUTURE: CAN WE SALVAGE THE REPUBLIC?

CARL F. H. HENRY

Has America, like Rome of old, crossed its Rubicon? Some observers say yes. They have begun charting the republic's decline and impending fall. Apart from any threat of sudden international war, they insist, America is tottering on the brink of tragedy. A decisive turn in national thought and life assertedly has placed the United States beyond redemption; the only hope that now remains is for emergency rescue and ailing survival.

THE SENSE OF DOOM

Pronouncing judgment on America is no longer an exclusive franchise of a few weeping Jeremiahs. Nor is it peculiar to evangelists constantly reminding the nation of its spiritual decline, its neglect of a great Christian heritage, its whoring after false gods of money and ease. Many pulpiteers are indeed swift to show that despite America's religiosity no sweeping repentance and faith, no decisive change of heart and life, places social forces in our great cities conspicuously in the service of the living God. Billy Graham readily admits this even of New York City. Religious analysts are finding America spiritually and morally second-rate.

While indisposed to talk much about the one true God, students of American culture likewise decry the idols of the masses. Determination of the right by mere majority opinion, and an infatuation with popular approval, have inseminated a cheap and artificial sense of values into modern life and thought. Broadway measures worth by length of run. On television or on radio, Nielsen and Hooper ratings and audience polls determine contract renewals. What is popular is right, not to mention "good" business. Thus the god of conformity snares individuals into group thinking, and loyalty only to society. Detachment of responsibility from the will of God has led to a vanishing sense of responsibility. American culture has accordingly become mediocre.

Scientists no less than religionists are doom-conscious. Pointing to Soviet superiority in the satellite sphere, they question America's capacity to reverse the balances of strategy to overtake and outdistance the Soviet program. They decry our loss of scientific leadership. By late 1959, they warn, the United States will be less than 15 minutes from 75 Russian ICBMs capable of wiping out the Strategic Air Command's existing bases.

A similar verdict of retrogression attaches to still another sphere, our traditions of government. In the disregard of inherited values that hinder controls and centralized power, and in the subtle restriction of individual freedoms, some students of political science see the nation drifting toward the whirlpool of a secret totalitarianism (while congratulating itself for having avoided the Soviet variety). In this matter of controls, former editor of *The Washington Post* Felix Morley is not alone in his conviction that "the Rubicon has already been crossed; nobody can any longer think escape from this trap an easy matter." Adventure on the collectivistic toboggan slide both explains and evidences America's demotion to a second-rate republic.

Leaders in economics report similar disturbances. Soaring costs of government, the temptation to accept inflation as a way of life, the control of credit for political purposes, national prosperity geared to the federal budget (especially to growing defense expenditures, perhaps leading ultimately to a vested interest in regard for other world powers as a military threat), the endless spiral of punitive taxation (personal income taxes estimated at $32.5 billion for 1956 alone)—to many economists these tendencies disclose America's permanent surrender to the squeeze of socializing forces. Since it is politically unfeasible for either major party to repudiate this centralizing trend, the process may never be reversed but only modified "here" and "there." Some warning voices like Frank Chodorov's once mounted soapboxes as young radicals to espouse socialism. Today these same political theorists recognize the symptoms of cancerous collectivism in our national life and lament a blind economic policy. They warn us that America has already taken the decisive collectivistic turn. Not only Big Labor but Big Business also often seeks its own special privilege above the principles of freedom. Free enterprise is now so frequently pushed to secondary importance that the populace is no longer shocked nor chagrined. A controlled economy meanwhile nourishes the worship of mammon. The multitude tolerates and approves, and even demands and clamors for this household god, while the almighty state perpetuates the existence of the idol. The masses have thus enlarged socialistic concession through leaders endorsing the tawdry popular values and thereby perpetuating their personal power and office. Leaders, the masses and the "privileged groups" alike, therefore, have all sown the wind. Obscured by the resultant whirlwind is the heritage that once made America unique among the nations of the world. Both the visibility and the vision of the nation are impaired.

THE CLOUDED VISION

The extraordinary origin of the American republic the Founding Fathers ascribed to divine providence. To them the United States represented the major political effort in human history to limit the powers of the state and to guard human freedoms under God from the encroachment of tyrants. As clearly set forth in the American Constitution, establishment of a federal government with powers restricted, divided into separate branches, balanced by states' rights, dependent on the consent of the governed, envisioned the preservation of specific human rights and values.

The basic and sustaining principle of these values and freedoms—that government is limited—is directly antithetical to that by which the U.S.S.R. abolishes individual rights (viz., that all power is concentrated in the state). One constitutional provision that dramatically enforces limited government is separation of church and state, which boldly contradicts the long European traditions of the church-state and the state church. This disjunction was both to limit political power and guard human rights, and also to protect the nation against a monopoly of political interests by one sectarian tradition. Separation of church and state did not aim to isolate spiritual from political concerns so churches lost significance in political affairs; least of all did it aim to subordinate the spiritual to the political order. There was no desire to weaken the role of the churches in the life of the nation; rather, restricted state power was intended to support and strengthen those spiritual priorities through which a nation remains virile and noble.

In this debate between limited government and state absolutism, the position of Christian conscience is obvious. In Romans 13 Paul delineates the Judeo-Christian view: political authority derives from God and is answerable to God. Likewise, man's obedience to the state is under God. Man bears inalienable rights by creation, the Declaration of Independence insists, and these the state is to preserve, not to destroy nor to curtail. The Bible asserts that the state must not frustrate the obedience man owes to God; it gives no quarter to the doctrine of the omnipotent state. The Old Testament prohibited even kings from seizing the private property of the people (1 Kings 21).

Skepticism over absolute values underlies the Soviet thesis that human rights are relative. Marxist evolutionary philosophy forces modern culture to choose between supernaturalism and naturalism; human dignity and human degradation; absolute truth and values and state-determined and imposed opinion and ideals. Totalitarianism compels its citizens to comply with whatever the state defines as right and good. Skepticism over changeless values creates the void into which the state rushes to propound temporary values with absolute rigor.

If all values are unfixed and ever-changing, political leaders in a democracy no less than in a totalitarian state may assert and enforce personal expediency in the name of principle. Majority opinion is not inconsistent with self-government, but self-government becomes impossible in the absence of values. If human preference alone determines policy, political theory simply vacillates with the changing tides of prevailing opinion.

THE LOSS OF FREEDOMS

In the present century Marxian Communism has whetted the world's lust for power and state controls. During the past 25 years the cancerous philosophy of state power, civilian controls, transient values and principles, has so penetrated even America's heritage and life that suddenly the United States appears incurably riddled with disease.

The federal government's encroachment into many areas of American life shows up especially in affairs once considered the responsibility of the Christian churches. Education, for example, was long the concern and duty of the family and of the churches. (Few people any longer realize that much of the impetus for mass education rests ultimately on the biblical conviction that every person must be reached with a core of information vital to his temporal and eternal happiness.) But during the past century has come the rise of mass public education. Influenced in our generation by the naturalistic and relativistic philosophy of John Dewey, educational administrators have by and large nurtured socialistic tendencies, including the growing clamor for federal support of public schools. Like education, charity and welfare also were once the concern of the churches. (The effective alleviation of human suffering owes more to the biblical view of God than twentieth-century humanism allows us to remember.) The state has assumed increasing direction of these responsibilities, too. On the domestic scene, social security and unemployment insurance have won their way; socialized medicine now waits in line as a hopeful government project.

More could be said to illustrate the government's assumption of responsibilities once belonging to the churches. But equally striking is the fact that in the aforementioned areas of enlarging state power, as well as of civilian controls not directly involving Christian traditions, the churches have shown little resistance. How far the Christian conscience had lost its sense of heritage in some of these matters, e.g., education, is evident from the official statement on *The Church and the Public Schools* approved by the General Assembly of the Presbyterian Church in the U.S.A. in 1957. This report not only throws the weight of Christian approval behind the public schools as such; it also throws the weight of Presbyterian influence against private schools. This is exactly what could have been expected from a committee dominated (as it was) by public schoolmen, but it hardly represents one's expectations from the Presbyterian conscience. Such surrender of responsibility could hardly augur resistance against additional inroads of the state.

If America has crossed the Rubicon; if the nation's heritage is now beyond preservation; if the drift to the power-state and to a controlled society cannot be stayed, communist penetration from the outside is not alone to blame. Equal judgment falls upon the churches for indifference and ineffectiveness in the hour of America's greatest trial. Amid the world's subtle conflict between political and spiritual loyalties, the churches sin by their silence. Today not Nero but the churches fiddle while Rome burns. The churches have even approved leaders who support socializing and collectivistic trends in the name of the Christian community, and have permitted them without protest to speak for Christian conscience.

WHEN THE CHURCHES FAILED

What explains this deadly lassitude of the churches? In America's tragic transition from limited government to the power-state where is the churches' repellent force?

1. Pre-empting the right to speak for all Protestant churches in politico-economic affairs, the National Council of Churches (formerly the Federal Council) has tended in its social pronouncements to support collectivism and controls in national life. In two respects the NCC has failed to undergird the tradition of limited government and human liberties; its social declarations, bold and specific, veered to the left, while its theological affirmations were nebulous and obscure, since NCC's inclusive policy subdued doctrinal issues for the sake of peaceful ecclesiastical co-existence. While neglecting a Christian theology of government and freedom, the massive voice of American Protestantism approved socializing tendencies in American life. The entrenched leadership even violated the conscience of its own constituency

by often pledging that conscience without its consent. Sensing its repressive force and fearing its coercive and punitive power, local member churches and ministers seldom protested such organizational commitments; ministers hesitated to contradict the official statements. The Protestant churches themselves thus became vulnerable to the fetters of ecclesiastical control.

2. Although some independent agencies publicized official resolutions of protest against the National Council's collectivistic pronouncements, they offered little guidance in positive Christian social ethics. Inside or outside the preaching ministry, they seldom faced the matter of God and government, faith and freedom, with active concern. While NCC spokesmen abetted the pressure for controls, most evangelical pulpits lacked a careful recital of man's rights and duties under God.

3. Though becoming increasingly amoral, the state preened itself with morality and many trappings of religion. Some politicians espoused the indispensability of religion in national life even while they voted for more socialistic controls. They shaped plaudits "appropriate to the constituencies," which not only approved special interest but basically revealed political expedience. Certainly, to doubt unduly the sincere churchly interests of many government leaders is unwarranted. One of *Christianity Today*'s contributing editors, Dr. Edward L. R. Elson, properly insists that piety must not be suspect simply because it dwells by the Potomac. Whenever the state speaks with a sacred voice, however, it requires special scrutiny. In its beginnings even the German Nazi movement attracted many people by "spiritual qualities" that obscured its evils. In recent decades, one American president on re-election eve made political use of the Episcopal Prayer Book. Examination of public speeches discloses American politicians to be more gifted with complimentary references to Deity than with sustained expositions of the theology

of politics. Labor, business and government all become more inclined to locate a religious justification for their objectives. Labor uses its Religion in Labor Movement to propagandize its legislative goals; management and labor resort to clergymen to propagandize their positions. This tendency of big government, big labor and big business to "use" religion in support of their programs is a reflex of America's growing religiosity that calls for careful scrutiny. Rather than being flattered by it, the churches need to challenge it. Behold the terrors of Communism, tolerating only as much "freedom" for the churches as serves the tyrant's whim!

MISGUIDED SOCIAL ACTION

Leaders who endorse specific social measures in the name of the church may think thereby to make "the gospel relevant to our times." Usually they only embarrass the church. There are many reasons for this:

1. For every churchman who endorses a particular organization and its program (cf. the forthcoming AFL-CIO propaganda effort for the closed shop, as against "right to work" laws), there is another to oppose it. The public soon wonders if the church does not know her own mind, or whether she is a propaganda agency for whatever social movement best exploits her endorsement. The competing and conflicting proclamations of ecclesiastical leaders not only lessen the church's stature in the eyes of the outside world, but also confuse the membership within the churches themselves.

2. Such pronouncements tend to be divisive. Often "social action" declarations by ecumenical and denominational leaders agitate their constituencies. Admission is long overdue that such statements were often ill-advised and represented only the personal opinion of certain individuals and pressure groups.

3. Such proclamations frequently do not express the thinking of the local churches and therefore ought not to be issued in
their name by the top echelon. An element of pressure shadows
the church member's affiliation with organizations professing to
speak "for so many denominations" or for "so many millions of
Protestants." A movement that not only propagandizes the views
of certain leaders, but catapults those convictions into prominence by exaggerating their known support, becomes a vehi-
cle of misrepresentation rather than of truth. Mr. Leonard Read,
president of the Foundation for Economic Education, recently
criticized both clergy and laity who do not protest social action
pronouncements that misrepresent their convictions. Mr. Read
suggests that the minister who disagrees with ecumenical social
policies but feels obliged to "stay in" and "straighten things out"
should apply that logic to the Communist party. The best way
to "straighten things out," he contends, is to decline support. Mr.
Read further contends that membership in organizations which
repeatedly violate politico-economic views of their constituencies [theological and economic views of most American churchgoers are considered far to the right of ecumenical leadership]
weakens the very personality of the members. Integrity requires
an individual to represent his convictions accurately to those
about him. Each unprotested misrepresentation of one's beliefs,
each unprotested identification with groups that do not express
one's convictions, weakens and finally destroys an individual's
character. Mr. Read warns that personal integrity always suffers
when loyalty to a group takes precedence over loyalty to the truth.

WHAT CAN BE DONE?

What is the churches' responsibility when a nation's decline is
concealed by a proud front of military power, of scientific genius,
of commercial efficiency and is undetected by the self-satisfied

masses in pursuit of luxury or pleasure? The Christian community is not without biblical guidance in this matter. In apostolic times many conditions in the old Roman Empire were not far different from ours. In treating social ethics in his epistle to the Romans, Paul writes the believers: "You know what hour it is. ... The night is far gone. ... It is full time now for you to wake from sleep" (13:11ff., RSV).

Christianity neither deifies nor humanizes the state. Romans 13 no more means the God-state (the state is God) than Revelation 13 means the Beast-state (the state is inherently demonic). Human government is divinely willed to preserve justice and to restrain evil in a sinful society. Government may indeed deteriorate, overwhelmed by the very injustice and wickedness it ought to restrain. The Book of Revelation warns that government most readily becomes a Beast-state when it thinks itself the God-state. It then arrogates to itself the right to control every phase of human experience and to require the worship of itself.

Romans 13 speaks not only of the powers of the state, but refers as well to Christian social responsibility. Paul declares that the state is to be supported by taxes, by honor and by good works in general. More than this, he obligates Christian conscience to social fulfillment of the Commandments in a spirit of love. "Render ... to all their dues. ... Owe no man anything, but to love one another: for he that loveth another hath fulfilled the law. For this, Thou shalt not commit adultery ... kill ... steal ... bear false witness ... covet; and if there be any other commandment, it is briefly comprehended in this saying, namely, Thou shalt love thy neighbor as thyself" (13:7–9).

LIMITS OF THE STATE

The first conclusion to be drawn is that the state, deriving its authority from God, cannot require of its citizens anything that violates the revealed commandments; since the power is ordained for the good of the people, passive obedience is not required when it ceases to be good. The second is that the Christian citizen by obedient fulfillment of these commandments in the spirit of love exhibits the highest patriotism.

The Scriptures here provide another equally important guideline. That is the directness with which the Apostle proceeds to the governing principles of revealed morality to fix Christian social responsibility. The Bible contains tenets that define love of God and love of neighbor in greater detail than the Ten Commandments. Biblical ethics asserts, for example, such specific rules as to pray for rulers, and to pay one's taxes. But one thing characterizes biblical social ethics: it nowhere endorses specific contemporary movements and organizations in such a way as to throw the sanction of Christianity behind them. Rather, it states the great social concerns of revealed religion in terms of divinely disclosed ethical principles that must determine and motivate social responsibility and action. It does not even condemn slavery, though it states the principles that sounded the death knell of that evil.

RULE OF CHRISTIAN ACTION

This norm for Christian social responsibility guards the church from two errors so frequently committed by modern ecclesiastical spokesmen. First, it exhibits Christian duty as performance of the revealed will of God. This deters the churches from social action of merely humanitarian and humanistic nature. (One major turning point in recent American life was prominence of "the welfare of man" as the dominant social goal. Under the umbrella of this cliché, and detached from any of the priorities of revealed religion, the masses gave life a purely materialistic interpretation. Furthermore, many political leaders successfully proclaimed the solution of all problems [international relations, unemployment, education] to be simply the spending of more money.)

To frame Christian social action primarily in terms of revealed principles of social morality protects the church from a second error, that of indiscriminately approving or disapproving specific movements and organizations and even individuals in the name of authentic Christian action.

In this time of confused principles in national life the church surrenders moral leadership by supporting isms and temporary movements, instead of conspicuously exhibiting the divinely revealed principles of social ethics that define human liberty and human duty. Besides the primary duty of evangelizing a lost society, the church is responsible for upholding the will of God in social life, expressed in biblically revealed principles and values. To endorse particular movements and specific activities in isolation from this primary social orientation cuts the church adrift from her moorings. Although presuming to represent God and church, her spokesmen become insensitive to those revealed verities, and even support movements and positions whose attachment to those principles is often obscure and sometimes nonexistent. Certainly the church must be specific, must not confine social interests to platitudes. The revealed principles of right, however, are never platitudinous; nor is the absolute less absolute because it is neglected and scorned. Revealed principles may illuminate contemporary movements and actions by the pulpit's use of illustration and example. Always, however, the revealed will of God must predominate and must be the gauge for everything else. Who then dare validate the church's permanent endorsement of a movement? (The church is on the side of the worker rather than of the idler, but is she therefore eternally committed to AFL-CIO? The church is on the side of the poor and oppressed, but is she therefore committed to a program of government subsidy and a welfare state?)

In the decline of the American republic the church will count for little in a rear guard action for national survival unless she returns to the great realities of divine revelation and unless her social message centers in personal regeneration and in fidelity to revealed morality.

BETRAYING A HERITAGE

Today influential men are selling the nation's birthright on every hand. In an official decision in 1955 even a member of the Supreme Court endorsed the denial of absolutes. The church did little to challenge this assertion of relativity, a theory quite in keeping with the Soviet philosophy of political expedience. In fact, the church today harbors a theory of knowledge that engenders skepticism over the very existence of revealed truth and principles of right. Neo-orthodox theology has not reversed the modernistic trend that considers revelation as inexpressible in words and propositions.

But absolutes do not cease to be absolutes, imperatives do not cease to be imperatives, because of failure to recognize them as such. Biblical theology and ethics give little credence to the modern notion that God does not articulate permanent principles. Unless the church accepts her biblical heritage and enunciates the great ethical principles that sustain our tradition of freedom, her own liberties may vanish together with those of the nation she fails. There may not always be a U.S.A., but there will always be a church. As the believers in Russia can eloquently testify, however, the church sometimes is chained and imprisoned not alone for her courage to affirm the superiority of spiritual over limited political loyalties, but as penalty also for her silent and unprotesting subjection to the power-state.

Carl F. H. Henry, "America's Future: Can We Salvage the Republic?" *Christianity Today* 2, No. 11 (March 3, 1958): 3–7.

★ *March 29, 1963* ★

THE ROLE OF RELIGION IN CIVIC LIFE

THE EDITORS

The nation now awaits the Supreme Court's ruling on Bible reading and recitation of the Lord's Prayer in the public schools. The verdict may not be given until June (controversial decisions often are not announced until just before the Court's adjournment). Like other recent decisions, the ruling is likely to reflect not the nation's past character and traditions but rather the growing pluralism of American society. In defining the kind of nation the United States shall be, the Supreme Court more and more conforms its pronouncements to the temper of the times rather than to the heritage of the past.

A number of American theologians, ironically enough, are promoting a secular non-theistic view of the state due to a misunderstanding of the nature and content of divine revelation. This misunderstanding is a baneful fruit of Karl Barth's theology, which denies the reality of any general revelation and considers all divine disclosure to be saving revelation. The proper emphasis that all divine disclosure is revelation of the Logos (be it the redemptive revelation of the incarnate Logos or the general revelation of the cosmic Logos) is distorted to mean that all revelation is Christocentric and hence always redemptive or saving.

On the basis of this error these theologians oppose all religious affirmation in civic life and in the public schools; these they consider to be either necessarily sectarian acknowledgments and therefore contradictory to church-state separation, or meaningless incantation.

This theological misconception underlies some of the support given the controversial study on "Relations Between Church and State" which will come before the General Assembly of the United Presbyterian Church in the U.S.A. in May, and for which some denominational leaders now predict endorsement despite the wide flurry of earlier hostility. In properly opposing the disturbing American trend toward "multiple establishment" in national life, the report commits the egregious error of promoting an objectionably secular state which in its public functions will tend to act as if there were no God.

There is, of course, the constant danger that theistic affirmations under civic auspices will become either a meaningless routine, or the uncritical pronouncement of a divine benediction upon national policy, or an opportunity for sectarian exploitation. There are those, too, who oppose religious elements in civic life simply on anti-Catholic grounds: what if the Methodist chaplain of the Senate or the Presbyterian chaplain of the House of Representatives in another decade were to be a Roman Catholic priest? It is always pertinent to ask how much of our program springs from genuine church-state concerns, and how much from sectarian bias that is dignified with the motive of pluralistic sensitivity.

The far greater danger, however, is the possibility that through its neglect of civic recognition government may lose also its sense of civic obligation to the transcendent God and to objective justice.

Voluntary prayer by congressmen and by citizens is not only highly desirable, but is indispensable if the nation is not to sag into the gutters of expedience. But the plea for voluntary religion does not demand a conformity of public institutions to secularism. The contention that the United States might well dispense with the rule that requires each legislative day to begin with prayer, as long as prayer is pursued individually on a voluntary basis, deserves penetrating scrutiny. What are the implications of "free exercise" of religion in civic life and in public schools? Is it possible that negation by the Supreme Court may constitute an unjustifiable "free exercise"? Is not the tradition of religious devotion in public life which the founders approved and encouraged alongside their repudiation of religious establishment a sounder guide to the distinctive character of the United States than the pressures for obliteration brought by some expositors of a pluralistic society? The concept of a pluralistic society itself is susceptible of varied definitions, and ought not be summarily equated with the ambitions of atheistic crusaders who renounce unchanging morality and objective justice.

It is true, of course, that theistic emphasis in national life opens a door to inter-religious cooperation that is not specifically Christian. A possibility even arises thereby among the higher religions for an inter-faith ethos working for world peace. Wherever religion recognizes something beyond mere national interest it poses a problem for the totalitarian state; every recognition of an eternal order of morality and justice is therefore to be welcomed. This kind of cooperation need not necessarily lead to religious syncretism, since the promotion of justice is not the only dialogue in which Christianity must engage, particularly if it is true to its claim of being the religion of redemptive revelation.

Among church leaders there is growing interest in an inter-faith congress to promote world peace. More than twenty Protestant, Jewish, and Catholic leaders outlined such ambitions recently to Secretary of State Dean Rusk. Dr. Dana McLean

Greeley, president of the Unitarian Universalist Association, asserts the effort springs from a conviction that "the various religious bodies should not lag behind the nations in a coopera- tive or concerted effort" but insists it has "no ready-made answer and no ideological axe to grind." The effort could be worthwhile if it really promotes justice as the foundation of peace. But if it reflects the mood of "peace-at-any-price," propagandists inevi- tably will exploit it for partisan ends.

The founders of our nation guarded against the dangers of religious establishment, whose perils we are prone to overlook. At the same time, by their emphasis on the supernatural source and sanction of man's inalienable rights they guarded also against the dangers of naturalism. To erase this theistic affirmation and recognition from the nation's civic life and public schools leads just as surely to national chaos as does the path of religious estab- lishment, be it pluralistic or otherwise.

The Editors, "The Role of Religion in Civic Life," *Christianity Today* 7, No. 13 (March 29, 1963): 21–22.

★ *December 18, 1964* ★

WE'RE STILL ONE NATION UNDER GOD

THE EDITORS

What the Supreme Court did not do last month may indicate what it will do in the future. Its refusal to hear an appeal that sought to eliminate the phrase "under God" in the pledge of allegiance to the United States flag may be a hint that the court is not minded to decide all spiritual claims in public life in terms of absolute negation. This should allay some of the apprehension that many felt after the court struck down Bible reading and prescribed prayers in the public schools. Its recent decision not to adjudicate formally the appeal against the pledge of allegiance may indicate the approach the court will take to cases now pending, or said to be pending, on opening prayer in House and Senate, chaplains in Congress, chapels and chaplains in the military, naval, and air force academies, and the taking of an oath of office by public officials.

By refusing to hear the appeal, the Supreme Court in effect left intact the pledge with its acknowledgment of "one nation under God." We believe the court acted wisely in allowing the recognition of God to remain in the pledge of allegiance to the flag. We also believe that it will continue to act wisely if in the cases pending it refuses to move in the direction of a nation that acts in its public life as if God were non-existent. Had the court decided against the phrase "under God" in the official flag salute adopted by Congress in 1954, its position would have rendered impossible any consistent defense of the mention of God in public ceremonies or even on coins.

When the Supreme Court decides not to hear an appeal, it merely announces its decision, giving no reasons and putting nothing down in writing. This leaves the American people to find their own reasons for agreeing or disagreeing with the court's action. The reasons given by those who uphold the action often confuse the basic issue.

Thus *The Washington Post*, for example, agreed editorially with the court and then went on to infer the reasons for the court's action. The *Post* contended that the flag pledge that we are "one nation under God" is "in no sense an act of worship" and for that matter "not a religious observance." "Consequently," the *Post* declared, "it has nothing to do with ... the separation of church and state." In this approach, the reasons given in defense of the court are more transparently weak than those given by the appellant to the court for an opposite decision. Admittedly, saying the pledge is not praying or engaging in a formal act of worship; but it is a religious act, and no mere verbalism can hide this from parents who know better and who appealed to the Supreme Court because it is a religious act. No acceptable definition of separation of church and state can be achieved if one holds that only formal religious acts are religious acts.

Similarly, James E. Allen, Jr., New York State Commissioner of Education, defended the inclusion of "under God" by asserting that it is not, in view of the nation's history, an "essentially religious exercise." But if the public assertion that this country is one nation under God is not essentially religious, what is it?

As was said, the court gave no reasons for last month's decision. But when it rendered its prayer decision in 1963, Justice William J. Brennan referred to the pledge of allegiance: "The reference to Divinity in the revised pledge of allegiance, for example, may merely recognize the historical fact that our Nation was believed to have been founded 'under God.' " Even if we ignore the fact that "under God" was added in 1954, the argument is transparently weak. He who recites the pledge is not merely reciting a historical fact. He is declaring his allegiance to his flag and country, and the words "under God" are as much a part of his declaration as anything else contained in the pledge. Should not he who pledges his loyalty mean all of what he says?

The Supreme Court's decision to leave the official allegiance pledge alone comports with our national history and with the intent of the framers of the First Amendment, who never intended an absolute detachment of the nation from recognition of the Deity in public life. The First Amendment excludes preferential sectarian treatment—for atheists no less than for theists of whatever kind. It protects the plurality of religious denominations from government control, and it protects government from the control of any group that would impose its own concept of religious pluralism or monism on public life. The Supreme Court, to its credit, realized that the best way to perpetuate this heritage is to let things remain as they stand.

The Editors, "We're Still One Nation Under God," *Christianity Today* 9, No. 6 (December 18, 1964): 26–27.

★ *March 4, 1983* ★

WHEN SHOULD CHRISTIANS STAND AGAINST THE LAW?

The rising tide of civil disobedience highlights
different approaches Christians are taking.

KENNETH S. KANTZER
AND PAUL FROMER

Should a Christian ever deliberately disobey the law in America? Randall J. Hekman and Everett G. Sileven have recently answered, "Yes," and are paying a price for it.

They do not object to distinguishing between private and official spheres of authority. They agree that Paul authorized both. Individually we are to love our enemies and not act vengefully toward them (Rom. 12:19–20), yet the state has a God-given right to "bear the sword," and to use force to restrain evil (Rom. 13:4). Both men accept the difference between personal ethics (refusing to take the law privately into our own hands) and the ethics of politics (the duty of society to restrict evildoers and to punish their evildoing). Some things that might be wrong for us if we acted personally, might be right for a policeman who officially represented his government and acted legally.

But though Hekman and Sileven accept this distinction, they have still run afoul of the law. The two cases, however, do not have equal merit.

THE CASE OF JUDGE RANDALL J. HEKMAN

Hekman is a highly regarded probate judge in Grand Rapids, Michigan. As befits his office, he has a solid reputation as a man of law and order. He is also a committed evangelical who not only loves his country, but also seeks to obey Christ and live by Scripture. Last November a 13-year-old girl five months pregnant came before his court, demanding her legal right to abort because she did not want her child. Judge Hekman refused her petition.

Ten years ago he would have been found guilty of a crime if he had so much as given her encouragement. But in 1973 the United States Supreme Court ruled that all state laws making abortion a crime were unconstitutional. The Supreme Court transformed what was formerly a crime into a sacred right protected by the Constitution. And it also thrust upon trial judges the responsibility of protecting this right, requiring them when necessary to order the death of the unborn child.

As a result Judge Hekman himself must now appear before the Michigan Judicial Tenure Commission because of a complaint filed by NOW (the National Organization for Women). The commission has the authority to relieve him of his duties as judge, and he awaits its decision.

He defends his disobedience to the law: "The idea of judges putting themselves above the law should be repugnant to all citizens. ... [But what if] a judge is required by law to order Jewish people to concentration camps or gas chambers because the law says that Jews are nonpersons? What if a judge, sitting on a case involving a runaway slave, disagrees with the Supreme Court's 1856 decision in which black slaves were ruled to be nothing more than chattels?

"Can the judges in these cases escape moral culpability either by obeying the law and saying they were 'just following orders,' or by disqualifying themselves so that other judges without their scruples can issue the unjust decrees?" Judge Hekman believes that, if a judge deliberately gives the case to another judge, he remains "a knowing and willing part of the ultimate injustice."

It is Hekman's conviction that such cases demand disobedience to the law in order that we may be obedient to Christ and the Scripture. Judge Hekman asks us to draw a parallel between a judge asked to order the killing of an unborn child, and one who is asked to order the execution of an innocent man. "When faced with this issue, a judge should courageously do what is ultimately right," he says, by resisting the action requested. "When a judge is faced with the option of doing that which is ultimately just versus that which is merely legal, he ought to choose the just—and be willing to suffer, if need be, the consequences of doing so."

DIVINELY APPROVED
CIVIL DISOBEDIENCE

The Bible gives many examples of those who chose to obey God at the cost of breaking the law. Moses' parents are cited in the biblical Hall of Fame for their disobedience to the Egyptian government when they hid their baby (compare Heb. 11:13 with Ex. 1:15ff.). The apostles, commanded not to preach the gospel, deliberately chose to disobey the law at great risk to their lives. Their defense was simply, "We must obey God rather than men" (Acts 5:29). Daniel and his friends refused to bow before the statue of Nebuchadnezzar, and God miraculously delivered them from the furnace (Dan. 3). Later Daniel violated the law by choosing to pray to God, and God saved him from the royal lions (Dan. 6).

THE CASE OF
PASTOR SILEVEN

But not all cases are so clear-cut. Everett G. Sileven, pastor of the Faith Baptist Church in Louisville, Nebraska, spent months in jail because, for conscience's sake, he refused to secure a license for his church's elementary school from the authorities of the state of Nebraska. He proved the depth of his conviction by going to jail for what he believed was right. He chose to obey God rather than men. We admire him for his sincere endeavor to live by biblical principles, and we are grateful for a Christian pastor with the courage of his convictions.

Yet we seriously question the wisdom of his decision. He argues that the church stands under the lordship of Christ only and not at all under the government. Therefore, he believes, government has no right to demand licensure of a church school or the teachers it employs; when it attempts to do so it infringes on the rights of the church and on the lordship of Christ.

GOD HAS GIVEN RIGHTS
TO GOVERNMENTS, TOO

Pastor Sileven, of course, is correct in saying that the church is under the authority of Jesus Christ and owes its complete obedience to him. But the government also has rights. God himself holds it responsible for protecting its citizens and providing for their welfare in appropriate ways. Therefore, in any church, but particularly in a church that operates an elementary school, we have a case of overlapping jurisdiction. It is the duty of government to protect the church from theft or from fire (so we have police patrols), or other dangers caused by badly designed structures (so we have building codes). Governments often license ministers to perform marriages so that records may be properly preserved. In the case of a school, government is properly concerned that all children should receive at least a minimum of general education. No parent has the right to keep his child in absolute ignorance. It is imperative, therefore, that we recognize government's divinely ordained duty in such areas. Dangers can arise from the abuse of these duties, but this does not negate their validity as ordained by God and deserving of our support.

WHEN TO STAND AGAINST GOVERNMENT

Where, then, should the church draw the line against governmental control? The answer emerges as we study out the legitimate sphere in which church and state each operates. Christ alone is head of the church. Its sphere concerns worship, instruction in the Scripture, evangelism and church growth, discipline, and ministry to its membership. If the state dictates what doctrine must be taught or not taught, or prescribes a way of life contrary to Scripture, or refuses to allow either free communication of the gospel or the nurturing of Christian life within the church, then the government has clearly invaded the territory that belongs exclusively to Jesus Christ the Lord of the church. But government has its responsibility, too. It must preserve law and order, and safety, and a minimum of education for its citizenry.

Sometimes we find the line between these two areas difficult to trace. A government cannot forbid worship, but it has the right to forbid people to meet in an unsafe building. A hostile government, of course, could readily interfere with a Christian group's right to worship by, for instance, trumping up false charges of building code violations. Still, the church must recognize government's proper sphere. By unnecessary and unwise confrontation we bring the cause of the gospel into disrepute with thoughtful people.

In addition, we harm all people by unnecessarily undercutting respect for both government and law and order. Especially in an undisciplined age such as ours, Christians should do all they can to strengthen law and public obedience to it, for these are the foundations of justice. Therefore, when we flout government unnecessarily, and for the wrong reasons, we do severe damage both to the church of Christ and to the community we live in.

No doubt, too, Christians in a democratic society should urge their government not to tempt people of conviction. In a pluralistic society, we should insist that laws permit as much freedom as possible—freedom for churches, and freedom for all people of good will. And always we should look upon disobedience as a last recourse, being careful to render to Caesar what is properly his.

Also, we should be slow to confront, taking care in our study of the Scripture and wisely applying it. But above all we must stand courageously for God's truth, and we must obey whatever he commands, at whatever cost.

Kenneth S. Kantzer and Paul Fromer, "When Should Christians Stand Against the Law?" *Christianity Today* 27, No. 5 (March 4, 1983): 10–11.

★ *July 10, 1987* ★

THE WALL THAT NEVER WAS

Separating church and state does not require
separating religion and politics.

TERRY MUCK

*Congress shall make no law respecting an establishment of
religion, or prohibiting the free exercise thereof; or abridg-
ing the freedom of speech, or of the press; or the right
of the people peaceably to assemble, and to petition the
Government for a redress of grievances.*

———————

T he First Amendment to the Constitution of the United
    States, ratified in 1791, protects five freedoms. Few of us
feel threatened with the loss of free speech, press, assembly, or
petition. Although each is periodically reexamined in the light
of new cultural or political realities, all have been regularly reaffirmed—indeed made even stronger—because of the challenges.

But this is not so of our freedom of religion. Few of us feel
secure with the current interpretations of the First Amendment's
religion clauses. Far from feeling that recent challenges have

strengthened it, some feel the lifeblood of our religious freedom is slowly being sucked from our constitutionally protected veins.

Many reasons are given for this anemic state of affairs: secularization, privatization, or trivialization of religion are the ones most often mentioned. Yet one crucial misunderstanding threatens our ability to address them. We have failed to distinguish between questions of church and state on the one hand, and questions of religion and politics on the other. We treat them as if they are the same, and in so doing put ourselves in an impossible position. Christians must affirm the separation of church and state as institutions, but not the separation of the more loosely defined attitudes and values of religion and politics.

A DOUBLE FORTIFICATION

Failure to make this distinction is all the more unfortunate because the language of the First Amendment religion clauses requires such an understanding. Unlike the other First Amendment freedoms, the religion clauses form a double fortification, protecting the government and its citizens against oppression by church institutions, and protecting both institutional and personal religion against government interference. Religion was— and is—such a potent force that it merited this special attention that speech, press, assembly, and petition did not.

The first clause, against "an establishment of religion," calls for church-state separation. The question is one of liberty, of freedom from governmental regulation, and from church domination and the power plays of bishops and other hierarchies. It is a hands-off policy that says the less interaction between government and church institutions the better.

The second clause, directing against "prohibiting the free exercise of religion," is a religion-politics clause. Its intent is to make sure individuals (even groups) can express themselves and their faith freely. And that includes injecting personal religious values into the political process. It does not necessarily advocate interaction between man as religious and man as politician, but it does defend the right for that to occur. The question is one of equality, of individual freedom ensured by law, if necessary.

There is real genius in the way the Constitution protects against large religious groups ganging up on everyone else, without forfeiting the benefits of foundational religious values seasoning the political process through individually active Christians. Unfortunately, there has been a notable lack of genius in applying the constitutional mandates to the real world of law. Courts and Christian activist groups regularly behave as if the beneficial tension between the two clauses does not exist.

Courts have been singularly uncreative in trying to interpret this tension. Take the matter of school prayer, for example. Laws that would allow prayer (a practice so universal that it satisfies the separation concerns of the first clause), yet do not specify the content of prayer (thus allowing individual religious differences), have consistently been disallowed. In cases like these, the courts treat every case as if it is a church-state separation problem, ignoring the constitutional window of opportunity that allows for the seasoning of public life with spiritual values.

Similarly, some religious activist groups behave as if the second clause gives the institutional church the freedom to take over the political process altogether. They have come dangerously close to advocating that church institutions be used to force sectarian beliefs on the whole country. Instead of looking at creative ways of educating individual Christians on how the values of our faith should impact the world at large (and trusting that such wholesale awareness will inevitably have the desired effect on public life), they have succumbed to the temptation to reduce the church to political party status. When religious groups ignore the constitutional mandate for a democracy that is culturally and religiously pluralistic, they forfeit their spiritual stature. Even though the moral and social agendas of Christian activist groups may appear attractive, the church must be wary of being drawn into a strictly political posture. Throughout history, whenever the church has functioned primarily as a political force, the gospel has been compromised.

Only by recognizing the important tension between church-state and religion-politics can we efficiently attack the other threats to modern religious life.

THE SECULARIZATION OF THE SPIRITUAL

Part of that recognition is to avoid being too idealistic about what constitutes spiritual issues. Religion and politics overlap in their spheres of interest. Both are concerned with values that determine how we live our lives. For example, both governmental and religious institutions have a strong interest in family issues— the education of children, the nutrition of pregnant women, the protection of battered wives, the regulation of divorce, and the collection of child-support payments. Both have methods and organizations that deal with these issues. It would be wrong to merge the efforts of church and state; it would be equally foolish, though, to think that they deal with totally different spheres.

But we must also recognize—and strongly reaffirm—the unique role of the church as the identifier of where "good" values come from. Recently, an organization called the Institute for Cultural Conservation announced a campaign to make "a case for cultural conservatism ... in wholly secular terms." We applaud such a movement insofar as it promotes values compatible with the Christian vision.

However, we reject the notion that the values themselves can be secularized. Values must be rooted in authority, or like all rootless plants they either wither and die, or else are blown about by the first strong gusts that spring up.

Lasting, true values have a transcendent source. They can be endorsed by a constitutionally based government because they "work"; but they work, and we believe in them, because the Bible tells us it is so.

The genius of our Constitution, rightly interpreted, is that it has been prophetically pragmatic, while at the same time it has defended our right to live by the values we hold dear.

Terry Muck, "The Wall That Never Was," *Christianity Today* 31, No. 10 (July 10, 1987): 16–17.

TOO MUCH DEMOCRACY

CHARLES COLSON

F irst a disclaimer: I've often expressed my conviction that pastors or heads of Christian organizations should not make partisan endorsements. (And besides, I'm out of politics, having done my time, both figuratively and literally.) So my reflections here should not be interpreted as passing judgment on a candidate—even if he is only a former candidate. But I must comment on one issue that Ross Perot's short-lived but remarkable campaign has brought to the fore. The application of electronic technology to politics raises profound questions about the very character of American government.

To understand, we must go back a few years. The computer age triggered an unprecedented information explosion—and in turn, a paradigm shift in how business is done. We now have the ability to provide instant information and analysis from, say, the production line to the manager's office. Computers are replacing the intermediaries who laboriously used to process, evaluate, and report data to their superiors. Because of such computerized efficiency, GM, IBM, and businesses across the country are laying off thousands of midlevel executives. Today's unemployment lines are filled with white-collar workers.

This streamlining is good for business—good for everyone, in fact, except those who are losing their jobs.

It is this techno-efficiency that Perot and others are proposing to carry over into the political system.

COUCH-POTATO DEMOCRACY

We should not be surprised that Perot would promote such an idea; after all, the company he founded, EDS, was one of the pioneers in the communications revolution. Perot argues that we can streamline our national management just like business has done: by bypassing the middle layers and going straight to the people. He says, "With interactive television, every other week we could take one major issue to the American people [at a time] ... have them respond, and show by congressional district what the people want."

Clearly this idea has hit a nerve. The American people have had it with politics as usual. They are fed up with Washington's gridlock—all those self-serving congressmen and bloated bureaucracies. When someone says, let's clear out the middle man, the public loves it.

It sounds straightforward enough. Say the issue of the day is health care. The president presents the alternatives on national television: Option one is curtailing Medicare and Medicaid; option two is a tax increase and universal coverage; option three includes private plans, and so forth. Management experts explain the intricacies of the issue within 30 minutes. (That's the sitcom generation's attention span.)

Then comes the vote. All across America, there is a huge, simultaneous click as millions of couch potatoes press their remote-control devices.

Computers tot up the numbers. Presto! National policy is made. Never mind all those meddlesome and frustrating intermediaries. We'll get action fast, straight from the people.

It sounds like the old New England town halls, nineties style. So efficient. So democratic.

But that is precisely the problem.

Shocking though it might sound to some, pure democracy is what some of our Founders feared most. To them, the tyranny of the masses was no less a danger than the tyranny of the monarch. They knew that people are swayed by fads and fashion, or by demagogues playing on the passions of the moment.

That is why John Adams wrote that unbridled democracy would lead to "everlasting fluctuations, revolts and horrors," finally requiring police action to impose order.

Adams and his fellow Founders explicitly created a republic. Only one part of government was intended to be directly representative: the House of Representatives, kept responsive to the people by its two-year terms.

The Senate, with its six-year terms, was meant to be more protected from the fluctuating moods of the masses so that senators could vote on the basis of principle, not popularity. (Senators, remember, were at first appointed by the states and thus all the more insulated.) And the Supreme Court, with its life terms, was intended to be immune to public opinion.

TAMING PUBLIC PASSIONS

Not incidentally, the republican form of government best reflects the Judeo-Christian world view. It recognizes human sinfulness and the need for checks and balances to power. It is based on the belief that law is objectively rooted and thus binding on the present, that tradition is to be respected, that citizenship demands civic responsibility and, often, delayed gratification. And most important, a republic is consistent with the belief that government is God's ordained instrument, not simply a mouthpiece for the masses.

A republic is not the most efficient system. All of those cumbersome checks and balances and covenants with the past slow things down. But that's precisely what they are supposed to do.

An electronic democracy would bypass this careful system. Laws would be made the same way television ratings are determined. The nation would be run like one vast talk show, with the president as host.

What is ironic about all this is that while it sounds like it would fix the system, in reality, it would only make it worse. Our problem today is not too little democracy. It is that our leaders cannot stand against the public passions that demand more spending and more programs. And so the black hole of the deficit grows bigger and bigger. Tele-democracy would simply increase these pressures.

There is no way to know what the political landscape will look like when you read this, but then, that's not really the point. My concern is about the public's enthusiastic response to techno-politics. No matter who is elected, emerging technology will intensify the pressure for instant democracy.

But we need to remember we are a republic, not a democracy. And a republic is a fragile thing. We used to worry about it being destroyed by a Soviet finger on the nuclear trigger. But now the greater threat could well come from within—from millions of fingers poised on remote-control buttons in living rooms across our nation.

Charles Colson, "Too Much Democracy," *Christianity Today* 36, No. 9 (August 17, 1992): 64.

★ *January 9, 1995* ★

THE SCHOOL PRAYER TEMPTATION

Americans now have a rare opportunity
to preserve all student religious speech.

STEVEN T. MCFARLAND

Rep. Newt Gingrich's call for a constitutional amendment to allow prayer in public school has rekindled the smoldering debate over this issue. The resulting conflagration on Capitol Hill will burn up much time, money, and political capital as religious and nonreligious constituents vent their passions in letters, lobbying, and legal analyses.

Unless evangelicals unite, the process leading to a vote promises to divide believers. The end product needs to be worth the investment and the risk. A clarification of students' rights to all forms of religious expression would be worth the fight; an amendment simply permitting audible prayer in the classroom would not.

Revising the Bill of Rights sets a potentially dangerous precedent. Because too many school officials persist in their disrespect for, and outright denial of, student religious expression, such a drastic measure is not unreasonable. Too many teachers, administrators, and lawyers adhere to the insidious notion that the First Amendment's prohibition on establishment of religion requires them to keep their schools "religion-free." In many schools, that means no singing of religious songs at choir concerts (there go most of the classics), no sharing of religious literature on campus, and no wearing of T-shirts with a religious message. All too frequently, principals and school boards deny student Bible clubs' request for meeting space, despite the ten-year-old federal statute that expressly guarantees equal access to campus facilities. The time has come for an amendment to stop this foolishness.

PROTECT ALL STUDENT RELIGIOUS EXPRESSION

So what should a constitutional solution look like? It should primarily be a restoration (rather than a modification) of First Amendment law. The Free Speech and Free Exercise of Religion clauses, as currently interpreted, already provide some protection for student religious expression in public schools. Yet school officials sometimes conclude that the Establishment Clause "trumps" those other freedoms and legitimizes suppression of religious speech. Any proposal should address this bankrupt analysis and educate school officials about what the Establishment Clause actually permits and protects.

Give credit to Rep. Ernest Istook (R-Okla.) for focusing much-needed national scrutiny on student religious speech, an overlitigated, underexercised civil liberty on today's campuses. However, the proposal (lifted from a 1982 Reagan initiative) goes both too far and not far enough. It should clarify that student prayer (at least outside compulsory classroom time) is a constitutional right. By stating that "[n]othing in this [federal] Constitution shall be construed to prohibit individual or group prayer in public schools," the proposal does not prevent courts from concluding that state constitutions do prohibit prayer in schools. Even the most resolute advocate of states' rights would concede that free speech is not a privilege that should be at the mercy of state or local law.

The current proposal is also underinclusive; it should protect all student religious expression, not just "individual and group prayer." Thankfully, because he is interested in crafting a useful tool, Rep. Istook is open to considering broader language. If we are going to take the serious step of amending the Constitution, we ought to include other areas where students have been silenced (prayers at graduation, sharing their faith with other students, religious content in their homework assignments, and the like).

These issues have tied up Christians in courtrooms nationwide for decades, and a constitutional amendment not limited to the "prayer issue" could put most of them to rest. America's schools could redirect taxpayers' dollars from legal fees to education. And future generations would start learning firsthand the correct civics lesson: that religious expression by students is protected (not prohibited) speech, in and outside the classroom.

Finally, there is the difficult question of audible student prayer during class, which the current OK proposal would allow. From the vantage point of the Golden Rule, it is undesirable. A lone Baptist student in a mostly Mormon classroom in Salt Lake City would quickly come to empathize with the Jewish pupil surrounded by Southern Baptists in Tennessee. True, both would learn more about the majority faith (at least how they pray). But do we want elementary school children getting the message that their faith is unacceptable and foreign to their classmates? The fact that a student could walk out of class will neither deflect the stigma nor ameliorate the coercive, indoctrinating nature of this exercise. The student of the minority faith—which increasingly could be your child—will have three choices: insult her classmates and teacher (and embarrass herself) by leaving the room, plug her ears and try to pray her own prayer, or else listen to others' prayers each day.

If the teacher were permitted to "organize" the prayer time (Protestant prayers on Monday, Jewish prayers on Tuesday, New Age or Hindu mantras on Wednesday, etc.), then the government would be fostering the myth that all paths lead to the same Place or Deity, and students would see their constitutional right evaporate into a once-a-week window. Official, daily, audible prayer in the classroom should not be part of any amendment to the Constitution.

The incoming House leadership floated the current proposal with little prior input from evangelical Christians. If such input had been solicited, most individuals and organizations concerned about religion in the public schools would have targeted all the barriers to robust student expression of their faith and witness. There is still time to think carefully and cooperatively. A sober respect for the foundational document they propose to amend requires no less.

Steven T. McFarland, "The School Prayer Temptation," *Christianity Today* 39, No. 1 (January 9, 1995): 18–19.

★ *January 8, 2001* ★

PANDER POLITICS

Poll-driven elections turn voters
into self-seeking consumers.

CHARLES COLSON

One should not have been surprised that last year's presidential campaign, in which both candidates made similar promises to give voters what pollsters said they wanted, would end up in a litigious deadlock. Campaign rhetoric scrupulously avoided great issues, and the candidates' increasing reliance on polls and focus groups so stifled genuine debate that neither candidate surged and rallied voters with a commanding mandate. But the deeper concern is that such poll-driven elections threaten to change the nature of government from deliberative republicanism to passive consumerism.

Campaign promises are a venerable American tradition, but this time they were the campaign. Vice President Gore and Texas Gov. Bush argued over who could better micromanage education, how to make taxpayers pay for other people's prescription drugs, what kind of accounting fiction can best guard Social Security, and whose tax plan would benefit whom. Grave issues like missile defense, international trade, questions of human life, the role of the courts, human rights, and "civil unions" were addressed only in passing.

How did political discourse get so dumbed down? One expla-nation is the end of world wars, hot and cold. These times are not like those when Franklin Roosevelt, through extraordinary ora-tory, summoned Americans to defend freedom; or when John F. Kennedy challenged citizens to ask not what their country could do for them; or when Ronald Reagan raised spirits to defeat the Evil Empire. The lifting of international threats allows campaigns to treat voters more like consumers than citizens. Computer technology profiles swing voters in battleground states so that campaign messages are precisely targeted. Focus groups found the term *vouchers* out of favor, for example, so the word never crossed Bush's lips. Gore carried the technique to its extreme, bringing his own handpicked focus group to debate preparations.

One might think poll-driven campaigning the purest form of democracy, but it is the system the Founders feared most. They chose a representative system—a republic, not a democracy. They envisioned a majority rule that is tempered by a deliberative pro-cess. Such a system assumes representatives will have the charac-ter to rise above public passions and do right. For example, when Abraham Lincoln and Stephen Douglas held their great debates, they weren't trolling for votes among the rank-and-file. The two were debating because the issues needed airing, and people flocked to hear them. U.S. Senators were chosen by state legisla-tures until 1913, when the 17th Amendment made them electable directly by the people, thus turning them into representatives with longer terms and bigger egos. A victory for popular democ-racy? Maybe. But one wonders if it is a coincidence that the fed-eral government began to expand dramatically at the expense of the states after 1913.

Christians since the Reformation have believed that a deliber-ative republic best meets biblical standards. John Calvin rejected monarchy and the "divine right" theory because of human depravity. He rejected pure democracy because individual members are no less depraved than kings. Instead, Calvin and other Reformed theologians advocated a republican system in which the people would be represented by leaders fortified against the passions of the herd and pledged to the higher law, serving the commonweal. The idea of limited government and the rule of law were contributions the Reformation made to the Western political understanding.

But if last year's campaign is a harbinger of things to come, our biblical-republican roots are withering. A generation ago, I sat at a president's side trying to end an unpopular war honorably. For four years, he had to go against the polls. What hope is there that today's politicians will do that? What mandate can the incoming president have? More benefits? Better test scores? How does a poll-driven president summon the electorate to the routine burdens of citizenship, let alone heroic efforts?

We have chosen a president-elect, not because he was persuasive on great issues, but because he promised wealth transfers to key constituencies and posed little threat to the comfort of everyone else. This brings to mind the scene in Dostoyevsky's *The Brothers Karamazov* of the "Grand Inquisitor." The Inquisitor, the devil incarnate, tells the returning Christ to go away because the people do not want what he is offering. They want bread, the satisfaction of their lower appetites. If the political debate is to be elevated in America, Christians will have to insist that bread alone does not satisfy the natural man, much less the spiritual man.

Charles Colson, "Pander Politics," *Christianity Today* 45, No. 1 (January 8, 2001): 104.

RALLY ROUND THE FLAG

America may not be God's chosen nation, but it
does have a mission that churches can support.

THE EDITORS

It may be time to put the American flag back in American
churches. Though we say this metaphorically, the statement
will still make many nervous. And for good reason. Since the
attack of September 11, most Christians have been thankful that
the nation turned so readily to prayer and national worship services. We recognize the moral justness of the war on terrorism
and have lent our support to it. On the other hand, we hesitate.
Many fear that patriotic fervor will turn into nationalistic hate.
Some balk at singing patriotic hymns, especially in church. And
don't even think about putting the flag back in the sanctuary. No
one wants a return to God-and-country Christianity, a civil religion whose John 3:16 is "My country, right or wrong!"

But is this fear justified?

Perhaps. *The Dallas Morning News* recently noted that "the
American flag has replaced the cross as the most visible symbol in
many churches across the country." As an attempt on one Sunday
to signal sympathy with terrorist victims and loyalty to country,
all well and good. Anything more is idolatry.

Fortunately, at the highest levels of the nation's life, civil religion is not currently a threat. In his September 20 speech to the nation, President Bush set out the issues in decidedly nonreligious terms. What is under attack, he said, was "democratically elected government" and freedom: "our freedom of religion, our freedom of speech, our freedom to vote and assemble and disagree with each other."

Given the occasion, Bush ended in a curiously humble way: "In all that lies before us, may God grant us wisdom and may he watch over the United States of America." This is hardly the stuff of which a jingoistic religious nationalism is made. No official in this administration has even implied that America is God's chosen nation. But many have sought God's wisdom, protection, and favor. We hope that government officials would always do that.

Still, as a result of September 11, church and state are dancing, trying to figure out the new relation of religion and society. In the meantime, we think the church has an important role to play in national affairs.

After Vietnam and Watergate, churches joined the culture and fled from patriotism. That's when the flag was removed from sanctuaries, literally and figuratively. This was largely good. We reminded ourselves that the church is not the servant of the state, that our calling transcends that of the nation.

At the same time, though, many churches became sentimental—that is, they practiced justice as a mere sentiment or wish. They imagined they could pursue justice by merely criticizing national and international injustice from the safety of the pulpit (or with the scathing editorial).

This will no longer do. We've been reminded that real justice in the real world means one must commit to supporting real, fallible, human institutions that pursue justice. The apostle Paul says government is instituted by God and "is the servant of God to execute wrath on the wrongdoer" (Rom. 13:4).[1] As such, the nation-state is God's most powerful instrument of social justice.

Furthermore, the United States is one among many nations that hold justice at the center. G. K. Chesterton's analysis of our Declaration of Independence gets it right: "It enunciates that all men are equal in their claim to justice, and that governments exist to give them justice, and that their authority is for that reason just."

In brief: We believe it is time for churches to recommit themselves to our nation and to its highest purpose. We are indeed a "nation conceived in liberty and dedicated to the proposition that all men are created equal," a people committed to "the great task," as Abraham Lincoln put it, "that government of the people, by the people, for the people, shall not perish from the earth." Thus, to evangelism, relief work, Christian education, and foreign missions must be added a particular form of social justice—engagement with the American experiment.

That means, for one, that American churches should not hesitate to celebrate our fundamental political values. We should prepare the occasional sermon and Sunday-school class that shows the connection between theological and political liberty. We should sing the occasional hymn asking God's blessing on our nation. We should honor members of the armed services, and recognize members who work in the judicial system, politics, or law enforcement—callings that attempt to pursue real justice in the real world.

But this also means that churches should continue to hold the nation accountable to its highest ideals. Speaking of church and state as the City of God and the City of Man, Richard Neuhaus says, "At the deepest level the two cities are in conflict, but, along

---

1. NRSV.

the way toward history's end, they can be mutually helpful. The [city] constituted by faith delineates the horizon, the possibilities and the limits, of the temporal [city]. The first city keeps the second in its place, warning it against reaching for the possibilities that do not belong to it. At the same time, it elevates the second city, calling it to the virtue and justice that it is prone to neglect."

No, we're not talking about literally putting the American flag in sanctuaries, though some congregations may well choose to, or continue to, do that. We're simply suggesting that the era of cynicism and despair regarding the American experiment is over. We should once again plant "the flag"—the national pursuit of liberty and justice for all—in the midst of our churches' life and mission.

The Editors, "Rally Round the Flag," *Christianity Today* 45, No. 14 (November 12, 2001): 36–37.

CONTRACT KILLER

Why ministries were concerned about Obama's
executive order—though few were directly affected.

RUTH MOON

When the White House announced plans to bar federal contractors from considering sexual orientation or gender
identity when hiring, Christian leaders mobilized.

Dozens of leaders at colleges, relief and development organizations, publishing houses (including *CT*'s parent company), and
megachurches signed letters urging President Obama to include
explicit protections for religious organizations. Without such
exemptions, one letter warned, the move—intended to circumvent Congress's long-standing impasse over the Employment
Non-Discrimination Act (ENDA)—"will come at an unreasonable
cost to the common good, national unity, and religious freedom."
The letters made national news, with signer Michael Lindsay,
president of Gordon College, becoming a focus for criticism in
Massachusetts and Washington, D.C.

Obama signed the executive order in late July, and it included
no such exemptions. (The U.S. Senate passed an ENDA bill that
explicitly exempts religious organizations, but it languished in
the House.)

But Obama's order also didn't directly affect most organizations whose leaders signed the letters.

Many Christian organizations that work with the government—such as World Vision and World Relief—do so not through contracts but through grants, in a process that is much less regulated. Meanwhile, the president left untouched a 2007 Bush administration memo allowing World Vision (and, implicitly, other religious organizations that partner with the government) to hire and fire on the basis of religious belief.

So was the order actually a quiet win for religious groups? Leaders say no. They believe that, even though few ministries contract with the government, lobbying for an exemption was important.

"Our main concern is its implication ... down the line, where future executive orders could also include not just federal contractors but grantees as well," said Jenny Yang, vice president of advocacy and policy for World Relief. "It's a slippery slope, and we feel the need to speak up whenever we feel like religious freedom is threatened."

Experts say government departments such as the U.S. Agency for International Development (USAID) are pursuing fewer grants and more contracts. A few large religious organizations currently work through contracts. Catholic Charities recently completed a five-year $1 million federal contract to aid in U.S. disaster relief. And the Salvation Army operates federal contract facilities for some prison ministries and social services. (The Salvation Army, which has hundreds of millions of dollars in federal contracts, declined to comment to *CT*, except to note that it has a "deep commitment to nondiscrimination in hiring practices and service.")

The Department of Labor is still working out how to implement the executive order. But Carl Esbeck, law professor at the

University of Missouri, says the order opens the door to lawsuits challenging the "World Vision" memo and other Bush-era provisions that form the current patchwork of legal protection. A Christian organization is likely okay with hiring a gay Christian who affirms its beliefs on sexual ethics. But is asking about that belief a religious question or a sexual orientation question?

For small organizations thinking about contracting with the government, "you might very well just say it was marginal anyway because of the administrative costs, and now with this new burden it's just not worth it," Esbeck said. "Only if you're big can you say, 'Well, we can do some risk planning and adjust to the new environment' and soldier on."

Because so few religious organizations are currently federal contractors, it seems Obama passed up a chance to make an easy but important statement on religious freedom, said Galen Carey, vice president for government relations of the National Association of Evangelicals. "It's a lost opportunity for the government to create a more tolerant space for a very divisive issue," said Carey. "That's what we're particularly concerned about. If religious freedom is not clearly protected here, it's less likely to be protected elsewhere."

Ruth Moon, "Contract Killer," *Christianity Today* 58, No. 7 (September 2014): 24.

SUBJECT INDEX